Performing the American Frontier, 1870–1906

Performing the American Frontier, 1870–1906 examines how the American frontier was presented in theatrical productions during the critical period from the end of the Civil War to the beginning of cinema. In chronological fashion, the book explores the post-Civil War resurgence of interest in drama about the frontier, which led to a host of action-packed melodramas. From famous personages such as Mark Twain and "Buffalo Bill" Cody to lesser-known individuals such as Native American playwright and actress Gowongo Mohawk, Hall examines the plays, the players, and the playwrights who helped to define the American westward migration in theatrical terms and covers the complete dramatic experience including scenery, performance, and staging. The book demonstrates the extraordinary variety of subject matter and theatrical styles used to dramatize the frontier, and places frontier drama within the context of its society by framing the productions with the contemporary debates on national policies.

ROGER A. HALL is Professor of Theatre at James Madison University, Harrisonburg, Virginia. He has written extensively in the field of American theatre and has published in a number of journals including *Theatre Journal, Journal of American Culture, Theatre Survey, Nineteenth-Century Theatre,* and *The Journal of American Drama and Theatre.* He contributed to the *Cambridge Guide to American Theatre* (1993) and the *American National Biography* (1999).

CAMBRIDGE STUDIES IN AMERICAN THEATRE AND DRAMA

General editor
Don B. Wilmeth, *Brown University*

Advisory board
C. W. E. Bigsby, *University of East Anglia*
Errol Hill, *Dartmouth College*
C. Lee Jenner, *Independent critic and dramaturge*
Bruce A. McConachie, *University of Pittsburgh*
Brenda Murphy, *University of Connecticut*
Laurence Senelick, *Tufts University*

The American theatre and its literature are attracting, after long neglect, the crucial attention of historians, theoreticians and critics of the arts. Long a field for isolated research yet too frequently marginalized in the academy, the American theatre has always been a sensitive gauge of social pressures and public issues. Investigations into its myriad of shapes and manifestations are relevant to students of drama, theatre, literature, cultural experience and political development.

The primary intent of this series is to set up a forum of important and original scholarship in and criticism of American theatre and drama in a cultural and social context. Inclusive by design, the series accommodates leading work in areas ranging from the study of drama as literature to theatre histories, theoretical explorations, production histories and readings of more popular or para-theatrical forms. While maintaining a specific emphasis on theatre in the United States, the series welcomes work grounded broadly in cultural studies and narratives with interdisciplinary reach. Cambridge Studies in American Theatre and Drama thus provides a crossroads where historical, theoretical, literary and biographical approaches meet and combine, promoting imaginative research in theatre and drama from a variety of new perspectives.

BOOKS IN THE SERIES

1. Samuel Hay, *African American Theatre*
2. Marc Robinson, *The Other American Drama*
3. Amy Green, *The Revisionist Stage: American Directors Re-Invent the Classics*
4. Jared Brown, *The Theatre in America during the Revolution*
5. Susan Harris Smith, *American Drama: The Bastard Art*
6. Mark Fearnow, *The American Stage and the Great Depression*
7. Rosemarie K. Bank, *Theatre Culture in America, 1825–1860*
8. Dale Cockrell, *Demons of Disorder: Early Blackface Minstrels and Their World*
9. Stephen J. Bottoms, *The Theatre of Sam Shepard*
10. Michael A. Morrison, *John Barrymore, Shakespearean Actor*
11. Brenda Murphy, *Congressional Theatre: Dramatizing McCarthyism on Stage, Film, and Television*
12. Jorge Huerta, *Chicano Drama: Performance, Society and Myth*
13. Roger A. Hall, *Performing the American Frontier, 1870–1906*

Performing the American Frontier, 1870–1906

ROGER A. HALL

James Madison University, Harrisonburg, Virginia

CAMBRIDGE
UNIVERSITY PRESS

PUBLISHED BY THE PRESS SYNDICATE OF THE UNIVERSITY OF CAMBRIDGE
The Pitt Building, Trumpington Street, Cambridge, United Kingdom

CAMBRIDGE UNIVERSITY PRESS
The Edinburgh Building, Cambridge CB2 2RU, UK
40 West 20th Street, New York, NY 10011–4211, USA
10 Stamford Road, Oakleigh, VIC 3166, Australia
Ruiz de Alarcón 13, 28014 Madrid, Spain
Dock House, The Waterfront, Cape Town 8001, South Africa

http://www.cambridge.org

© Roger A. Hall 2001

First published 2001

Printed in the United Kingdom at the University Press, Cambridge

Typeface Adobe Caslon 10.5/13pt   *System* QuarkXPress™   [SE]

A catalogue record for this book is available from the British Library

Library of Congress Cataloguing in Publication data

Hall, Roger A.
Performing the American frontier, 1870–1906 / Roger A. Hall.
p.   cm. – (Cambridge studies in American theatre and drama)
Includes bibliographical references and index.
ISBN 0 521 79320 3
1. American drama – 19th century – History and criticism.   2. Frontier and pioneer life in
literature.   3. American drama – 20th century – History and criticism.   4. American
drama – West (U.S.) – History and criticism.   5. West (U.S.) – In literature.   6. Pioneers in
literature.   I. Title.   II. Series.

PS338.F76 H35 2001   812'.409355 – DC21   00-065138

ISBN 0 521 79320 3 hardback

For Lynn, Cassie, Bryce, and Morgan

Contents

Illustrations

Acknowledgments

One name appears as the author of a book, but I have long believed that books, like productions of plays, should have a program to identify all the backstage personnel who have contributed to the work. Lacking that, I would like to steal this opportunity to repay with these acknowledgments the help so many people have graciously given me in preparing this book.

I especially want to convey my thanks to Debra Ryman, Anna Lee Newman, and Susan Huffman of the Interlibrary Loan Department at the Carrier Library at James Madison University. Many were the times I asked them if they could find a dusty, nineteenth-century script, an out-of-print book, or a microfilm of a newspaper that had long since ceased publication, and usually, often to my surprise, they were able to come up with the goods. In that same vein, I want to thank those many institutions who participated in the Interlibrary Loan process by lending materials without which I could not have undertaken this project.

In the course of my research I encountered an array of helpful people. The copyrighted scripts in the Rare Book and Special Collections Division at the Library of Congress constitute a wonderful and underutilized resource, and I am indebted to Charles Kelly and Clark Evans, who assisted my work with that collection. I also appreciated the aid of Paul Fees, the incredibly busy but always helpful Curator at the Buffalo Bill Historical Center in Cody, Wyoming.

For the illustrations in the book, I am indebted to Laurence Senelick, Don B. Wilmeth, and Michael Gnat for making their collections available to me. I also benefited from the help of Elizabeth Holmes at the Buffalo Bill Historical Center; Jeremy Megraw at the Billy Rose Theatre Collection of the New York Public Library for the Performing Arts; the staff at the Theatrical Poster Collection of the Library of Congress; and photographer Darren Setlow.

Several scholars read earlier versions of this manuscript. One of them was Douglas McDermott, Professor of Drama at California State University, Stanislaus, and his insights were invaluable. Because of the strictures of the review process I do not know the names of other readers, but I am deeply appreciative of their detailed comments and suggestions. Their praise was encouraging and their criticisms just. This is a better book for their anonymous input.

I am thankful for the support of my colleagues in the School of Theatre and Dance at James Madison University. I have been fortunate indeed to be surrounded by such bright, caring, and industrious friends and co-workers.

I also owe a thank you to the James Madison University sponsored research program, which supported my efforts by awarding me educational research grants in 1988 and 1995, and a variety of summer research grants in 1976, 1977, 1979, 1982, and 1991.

My students have always proved a source of amazement to me, and I want to thank them for constantly reinvigorating me. At various times students in my American theatre course and other friends assisted my research. Two who deserve particular mention are Libby Gardner for her help at the Library of Congress and Clay Daniel for his assistance at the Harvard Theatre Collection.

At Cambridge University Press I was fortunate to have Vicki Cooper and Laura Hemming overseeing the production of this book, guiding me through the process, and advising me along the way, and Laura Davey was an excellent copy editor.

Along with the thanks, I want to make an appeal for the conservation of America's theatrical history. While I have been working on this project I have seen theatre collections close for lack of funds, and I have seen materials deteriorate virtually before my eyes. My plea goes out for redoubled efforts to preserve and document America's theatrical heritage, and my appreciation goes out to those who are laboring to bring that about.

Finally, I want to say a special word of thanks to Don B. Wilmeth, the editor of the Cambridge Studies in American Theatre and Drama series. Don has been personally supportive of my writing over the years. He worked with me in minute detail through several drafts of this manuscript, and I know that without his encouragement and determination this volume would not exist. In a larger sense, Don has been a source of inspiration not only for me, but to many of us working in the field of American theatre, and for his enlightened leadership, his tireless enthusiasm, and his unflagging promotion of American theatre, I have the deepest respect.

Introduction: conditions and contradictions

Perhaps, after all, these Bowery playhouses were the "cradles of the American drama," though the hands that rocked them were very crude.
George C. D. Odell, commenting on *Silver Knife; or, The Hunters of the Rocky Mountains* at the Bowery Theatre in New York in September 1859.

CELLULOID PRESERVES THE IMAGES OF THE EARLY MOVIE cowboy heroes. Even in the twenty-first century, students of cinema know William S. Hart, "Bronco Billy" Anderson, Tom Mix, and Hoot Gibson through their film exploits. They are lionized as the pioneers of a new industry and a new art form, and the products they created are still visible. Later cowboy heroes such as Gene Autry and Roy Rogers parlayed their movie and television success into enormous wealth, emerging as virtual icons of twentieth-century society – one as an owner of a baseball team, and the other with his name in restaurant lights from coast to coast.

The full-blown frontier images that these actors depicted, however, did not spring magically onto movie-house screens. Those images developed throughout the nineteenth century, with pockets of border drama in the 1830s and 1850s, and, from 1870 on, a constant stream of frontier plays. Artists such as Frederic Remington and Albert Bierstadt provided visual images of the frontier. Writers and poets including Mark Twain, Bret Harte, and Joaquin Miller celebrated the people of the plains, the mining towns, and the west coast. Pulp writers Prentiss Ingraham and Ned Buntline translated western events into the popular literature of the dime novel, and Theodore Roosevelt and Owen Wister supplied later upscale literary depiction. Still, words and pictures were not the only means of transmitting a vision of the American frontier. There was also action: the action of the stage.

I

In the winter of 1872, William F. "Buffalo Bill" Cody arranged a hunting trip for the Grand Duke Alexis, the third son of Czar Alexander II. The previous year he had hosted a similar outing for an illustrious group of Americans that included James Gordon Bennett, editor of the *New York Herald*; Charles L. Wilson, editor of the *Chicago Evening Journal*; and other notables. These outings provided a variety of frontier experiences for the visitors. They met Indians and watched the natives hunt and dance. They themselves hunted elk and buffalo. They interacted with scouts and military heroes. They witnessed and participated in horse races and stagecoach runs. They viewed authentic western outfits and experimented with a variety of frontier firearms. They encountered first-hand the majestic western landscape. Through their activities and the trophies and memorabilia they brought home with them, these famous gentlemen purchased and assumed ownership of a piece of the West.

Ever since early New York settlers purchased Manhattan, the advancement of the frontier involved ownership and possession. Hunters and trappers wanted to capture skins, trophies, and pelts. Settlers wanted to own land. Miners wanted to acquire gold and silver. Those who moved into the frontier wanted to possess it, to own it in some way. Meanwhile, those who remained behind in the cities of the East could hardly assert ownership in the same way. They had no claim to the minerals, to the pelts, or to the soil.

There were, of course, other means. Not everyone could go west to be a scout, a soldier, or a miner. Not everyone could afford to hire guides to teach them the intricacies of the frontier. But in the late nineteenth century various opportunities existed for those who were not wealthy businessmen or foreign nobles and who wanted to buy a piece of the frontier. Anyone could own a vicarious parcel of western life through the writings of Harte or Twain. Young people could purchase a slice of border adventure through a dime novel. But reading, no matter how entertaining, had its limitations. For one, it was a solitary activity, without the intrinsic comradeship and interaction exhibited by an Indian tribe, a company of soldiers, or a wagon train. Furthermore, it lacked the primal sounds of horses' hooves, guns firing, and war-like yelps. It lacked the raw scents of gunsmoke and animals. Except for the occasional drawing, it lacked the visual exhilaration of scenic vistas and distinctive apparel. It lacked the reality of actual human beings engaged in live action. Theatre provided those sensory elements in a distinctive phenomenological experience, and the citizens of the East could stake their claim to a portion of the frontier simply by purchasing a ticket.

Readers of the *New York Herald*, for example, could follow the progress of the Modoc War in 1873 and thus participate in the campaign as a solitary reader, but they were not physically engaged with the troop of soldiers who seized possession of the lava beds at Tule Lake. However, when those same patrons bought tickets to cheer Donald MacKay and the Warm Springs Indians reenacting the capture of Captain Jack and his band, they became actual group participants in the victory. Through the production, they claimed ownership of the territory; together with Donald MacKay they celebrated the seizure of the land. Frontier drama became, in essence, a contract between the playwrights and performers, as vendors, to sell to the audience, as buyers, a segment of the frontier experience.

But what kind of experience did that audience purchase? Here the waters become rather murky, for the late nineteenth century produced an outpouring of drama about the American West that provided an enormously wide range of possible experiences, from the chauvinistic to the sublime, and from the martial to the romantic. The plays placed on stage vivid pictures of the western landscape, sometimes quite realistically presented, and they adorned those pictures with the garments and the paraphernalia of the region. Within those pictures, they brought to life the cowboys, outlaws, natives, horses, and gunfire of the border lands.

With the immediacy that only live theatre can offer, these productions not only told stories of the border, but also showed them taking place. Here was Jesse James' horse escaping through the window of a house – the actual sights, sounds, and smells. Here – live on stage – was a frontier marksman shooting through the rope of an innocent man about to be hanged. Here were a horse and rider plunging from a bridge as it collapsed twenty feet above the stage floor. The jolting crack of rifles and revolvers and the authentic smell of gunsmoke permeated the theatres. For that reason, this study is not limited to textual analysis. It seeks to examine the whole dramatic experience, including elements of scenery, performance, and staging, as well as the written words.

The drama of the frontier as it was presented to eastern audiences in the late nineteenth century was certainly fictional, even when it sprang from actual events. It both perpetuated myths and provided realistic images. Theatrical presentations reinforced popular but misleading images of white settlers as victims of native populations, responding with violence only when provoked by savage atrocities. What is more, the theatre offered its images in a particularly compelling manner in that the elements it employed were so tangible – genuine heroes, horses, guns, and natives.

This study has several goals. A primary objective is to demonstrate the great variety of subject matter and style represented by frontier drama, as well as the contradictory sets of meanings the frontier expressed. The American frontier was an area where the encroaching European culture confronted native populations and natural elements. This meeting of European culture with unfamiliar circumstances produced numerous conflicts, and not only that of whites versus native tribes. European settlers encountered earlier European settlers – especially the Spanish of the Southwest and the west coast – and their differences generated animosity. The encroaching culture also faced natural hazards in the vast and barren landscapes and severe weather conditions, as well as psychological and emotional factors including fear, anxiety, and loneliness spawned by those conditions. Most frontier plays, at least in the late nineteenth century, were set in the West, but since the frontier broke like a wave from the east coast to the west, authors set frontier or border plays – the terms were used interchangeably – in Virginia, New York, Tennessee, and anywhere else in the United States where a frontier had once existed.

Stuart Hyde, in his research into the representation of the West in drama, cites twelve hundred frontier plays written between 1849 and 1917, including Indian plays, mining plays, and cattle plays.[1] The works contained an extraordinarily broad cast of characters: not only cowboys and Indians peopled the landscape, but also soldiers, gunfighters, trappers, traders, scouts, guides, homesteaders, ranchers, lumberjacks, Mormons, miners, Chinese, gamblers, outlaws, Mexicans, dudes, law officers, wagon masters, stage drivers, and numerous individuals just looking for an opportunity or a second chance. The list included those bringing elements of eastern civilization to the border areas, especially teachers, shop owners, and preachers – representatives of the onrushing society set among the wilds of the frontier.

Although a few of the frontier plays were comedies, and some even satirized the conventions of other frontier plays, melodramas constituted the majority of the works. The primary characters in traditional melodrama included the hero, the heroine, the villain, and the comic. Naturally those leading lights had their supporters – the sidekick to the hero, the henchmen of the villain, and the confidante of the heroine, for example. The comic elements, sometimes connected to the main story but just as often staunchly extraneous, provided contrast and entertainment. While the stories of melodrama regularly and dynamically interlocked the hero, heroine, and villain, emphasis on the three was not necessarily equal, which led to vast differences in the tone of the plays. Some frontier melodramas placed primary emphasis on the battles between the hero and the villain, while others focused on the burgeoning affection between the hero and the heroine.

Perhaps the most common image of a frontier play involves a hero brandishing a firearm and shooting menacing villains, usually natives. Those plays did exist, and, in fact, they formed one of the main threads of the genre. The category ranged from jingoistic plays featuring victory over native tribes to exhibitions of shooting stunts and the development of Wild West shows. While not all such plays included Native Americans, they all featured frenetic action, appeals to patriotism, and powerful displays of artillery. Many employed "red fire" – an impressive display of red-tinted gas flames used at climactic moments to represent a burning prairie or the torching of a settler's cabin. These "red-fire" plays seldom addressed the problems that the westward movement created, and they gave scant attention to the role of social institutions or of women, save as hostages. Rather, through vigorous and violent action, they signified victory over perceived threats to outposts of white society, and they confirmed the rightness of America's westward momentum and the dominance of white European male culture. Most such plays contained demonstrations of frontier skills including trick shooting or roping, and many incorporated animal stunts. In those plays that included Indian characters, white renegades frequently incited the indigenous peoples, or the "Indians" turned out to be whites in disguise. The natives almost always attacked whites and just as invariably came to a bad end. They constituted, for the most part, objects to be shot at like moving targets in a shooting gallery or, even worse, caricatures to be laughed at.

In most frontier plays, however, the main characters had little or no contact with native populations, and numerous frontier dramas employed gunfire sparingly, if at all. Such plays focused instead on a romantic and sentimental story between hero and heroine, which happened to be set on the frontier, and those plays constituted the second major thread in the development of frontier drama. The heroes were usually simple, rough, goodhearted men. The heroines were typically better educated and more refined. Heroes and heroines alike existed as morally outstanding individuals beset by compulsively evil villains. As the genre developed, some of the main characters exhibited flaws, including drinking, swearing, lying, and fornicating. Their basic moral strength, however, remained firm. Likewise, a few of the villains acquired redeeming traits – a sense of honor among thieves or a willingness to change their sinful ways. A few daring dramas pushed the edges of convention and produced endings where a bad man reformed and got the girl; a fallen woman married and attained a happily-ever-after future; or a white married a Native American or Hispanic.

The romantic melodramas regularly addressed significant problems of ethnicity and race-consciousness, but they invariably found ways to avoid the implications of the issues or to sugarcoat the solutions. While they raised social questions, they ultimately confirmed white, European models just as the more flagrantly chauvinistic thrillers did.

The first type of melodrama, featuring sensational action, dominated the stages of the 1870s and early 1880s. Through the 1880s, however, romance and sentiment emerged as the more influential strain in theatres while action-packed frontier displays transferred to outdoor arenas. At the turn of the century, the most complete and sophisticated of the frontier plays successfully combined martial and romantic threads, suggesting in the process that the violence and social unconventionality inherent to the frontier are not only justifiable but necessary tactics for consummating the romance of the hero and heroine. Through this steely amalgamation of violence, rebellion, and romance, the hero and heroine achieve success and ensure the transmission of European culture.

The frontier landscape, while it did not influence every play, supplied a recurring motif for border dramas with its suggestion of beauty and majesty on a divine plane; it also suggested natural and psychological dangers.[2] In the less artistic romances, the dramas simply employed conventional melodramatic devices and placed the plot and characters in a border locale that had little apparent impact on the characters. In more complex romances the frontier setting meshed intrinsically with the characters and their actions and suggested that the freedom of the western setting generated anomalous situations that were reasonable even though they violated accepted social conventions. Occasionally the physical environment even engendered a thematic cleansing of past wrongs, serving as a purgatory from which characters emerged, their sins burned away in the fire of difficult circumstances. Although some touring productions used only what scenery was available at the theatres where they performed, many of the productions featured carefully designed sets that provided the audience with graphic visions of frontier locales. In addition, characters painted landscape pictures with words, referring almost hypnotically to the grandeur of the terrain.

The main characters of frontier drama were Americans of northern European descent. While the red-fire and revolver plays were predominantly male, in the romance category love affairs provided the central interest, and females regularly played major roles. The productions treated non-whites and foreigners in extremely conventional – that is to say, highly negative – ways. Many plays contained a Chinese man – never a Chinese woman – who usually washed laundry and appeared primarily to generate laughter. Although fodder for comedy, the Chinese were generally depicted as hard-working and honest, and occasionally they played a significant role in resolving the plot. Blacks – again, generally male and, of course, played by whites in black makeup – were also employed for comic effect or for musical interludes. They were usually portrayed as slow-witted and afraid of the dangers of their western surroundings. The Irish – males and females – were played for comedy, and the Irish males almost always drank excessively. The English were typically portrayed as effete, snobbish, and cowardly objects of comedy and ridicule, or, occasionally, as conniving villains.

Indians were dramatized more frequently than any other minority group in the plays, and they displayed a range of attitudes. Most commonly they were the attackers, often abducting white women, which allowed for rescues later in the plays. Frontier dramas utilized the capture–pursuit–rescue scenario over and over – often several times within the same play. The scripts usually furnished the natives with some rationale for their attacks, most often a general statement of defending their lands. In numerous instances, however, a white man pretended to be a friend of a tribe and incited actions for his own ends. A few plays depicted the Native Americans as genuinely aggrieved parties. In those cases Indian characters were trapped between contending forces such as sympathetic and antagonistic settlers or belligerent and peaceful tribe members. Occasional plays showed natives who lived among whites. In early plays such characters were usually drunk and pitiable, as though their animal natures could not rise to the challenge of existing within the more elevated white society, or, conversely, as though whatever primitive nobility they once possessed had been contaminated by contact with sin-infested whites. Later works at the turn of the century, however, examined with some degree of complexity the limbo of a person floating between two cultures. Indian women were confined to a narrow range. Just as Pocahontas and Sacagawea provided historical icons representing a female native helping whites, so, too, frontier dramas created numerous young Indian maidens who loved and assisted whites, and that became their conventional role.

Of all the ethnic groups depicted in frontier plays, Mexicans were the most vilely caricatured. Mexicans were almost always portrayed as dirty, villainous, and deceitful, much like the then current stereotype for southern or

Mediterranean Europeans. Mexicans were seen as racial degenerates, mixed between Spanish and Indians, and hence worse than either.[3] Whereas Native Americans were at least understood to be defending their lands, Mexicans were given little rationale for their base behavior. They seemed rather a dramatic version of evil incarnate. The Spanish of the Southwest and California fared somewhat better. Authors provided them with a more regal, aristocratic bearing, and, like the Native Americans, they were usually portrayed as unfortunate victims of the westward march of history known as "manifest destiny."

There are so many frontier dramas – the genre became such a mainstay of American entertainment – that only by oversimplification can they be given one definitive reading. As this book examines the whole range of plays, it will also demonstrate the complexity of meanings that reverberate through them. In his incisive *Melodrama and the Myth of America*, Jeffrey Mason asserts, "Melodrama of the West is doomed to fail" because "[it] enforces a stability that runs counter to the restlessness and transience . . . characteristic of the postbellum West." Mason continues: "Indeed, the paradox of the westward movement . . . is that the 'happy ending' . . . required that the immigrants rob the West of the wilderness that supposedly drew them out in the first place."[4] By attempting to read the message of frontier melodrama in one particular way, Mason sees paradox as failure, rather than reading paradox itself as the message. This review of frontier drama will show that it is exactly the unresolved tension, which to Mason "dooms" western melodrama, that in fact kept melodrama of the West continuously alive on stage for thirty-five years, and vibrant through various media for over a hundred consecutive years.

Forrest Robinson postulates a similar ambiguity in certain classic western stories where authors recognize painful social problems and then retreat from their significance through a process he calls "having things both ways."[5] Most frontier plays lacked such complexity, pressing instead an agenda of having it *one* way only. Some of the later plays, however, evolved the "simultaneous acknowledgement and denial, seeing and not seeing," that Robinson refers to, especially as they addressed significant questions and then found ways to dodge the implications of those questions. Still, the border plays were so numerous that they approached the subjects and issues of the frontier from a variety of perspectives, which led to inevitable contradictions and paradoxes.

Rosemarie K. Bank, in her *Theatre Culture in America*, notes that two familiar and contradictory narratives – the supportive, nurturing hand of

Pocahontas and the unexplained disappearance of the Roanoke colony – provide the foundation for frontier literature. Thus, the frontier, from its beginnings, offered polarity, contradiction, and paradox. Bank expresses "the futility of defining [the frontier] in terms either of heroic images or national sins, since such binary readings deny the complexity of the ideological content depictions of the frontier contain."[6] Similarly, Richard Slotkin, writing of the defeat of George Custer at the Little Bighorn River, calls attention to the culture's "contradictory impulses of ambition and nostalgia, racialism and sympathy for the victims of injustice."[7] Such sets of contradictions are given theatrical shape in frontier drama.

One contradiction involves violence. Gary A. Richardson is right when he asserts in his study of American drama that violence in frontier plays is presented as "a normal element in the life of the characters" rather than as "a cultural anomaly, a momentary aberration" as in other melodrama. Even in the more pacific, "romantic" strain of frontier drama, violence remained a significant component. The guns, knives, and rifles typically carried by the characters furnished a fundamental aspect of their bearing and provided a measure of what set them apart from city dwellers. Photographs of actors in their costumes and illustrations of the plays usually show a gun or rifle prominently displayed, and virtually every play included theft, murder, or lynching.[8] Hence, violence employed to confront violence becomes one of the paradoxes evident in frontier melodrama from the plays of the nineteenth century to the movies of Sergio Leone a hundred years later.

Americans perceived the West as a cornucopia of economic opportunity offering a seemingly endless bounty of land, water, and timber. Moreover, it rendered up gold and silver free for the taking by those industrious enough to claim it. In Richardson's words, "The well-known pattern of western development made the linkage of western lands to individual labor and wealth readily apparent to the audience."[9] Possession of the land and its resources figures prominently in the plots of many border plays: settlers battle native tribes over control of the land; whites threaten and kill one another over ranches and gold mines.

The frontier provided moral as well as economic opportunity. It was an unspoiled Eden – a place for second chances. After Michel de Montaigne met three Brazilian natives in 1562, he formulated the idea that the indigenous peoples of the "New World" possessed a natural sense of culture, dignity, and beauty superior to their European conquerors, whom he regarded as barbarians. That notion of natural goodness passed through John Locke's sense of people born with inherent rights to Jean-Jacques

Rousseau's assertion that human beings in a primitive state were naturally good until corrupted by societal greed and aggression. Those ideas undergirded the concept of the American frontier as a second Eden. Yet, as numerous writers have pointed out, that paradise was paradoxical. As settlers moved in, the West became an archetypal symbol both for civilization and for savagery. It offered, in Bank's words, "equal potential for salvation or for damnation – in material terms, success or failure." It was equal parts "civilized" and "savage," what the author called "simultaneously 'in here' and 'out there.'"[10] Another paradox. Just as a detective cannot investigate a crime without altering the crime scene, so settlers could not move to the promised land without affecting it in the process. And, as the settlers themselves inadvertently carried corruption into the Garden, violence and greed became the snakes of their temptations.

Yet again, paradoxically, all is not lost, for, as Bank writes elsewhere of the western society, "those who possess the gifts of civilization – education, culture, know-how – are the best equipped to lead that society toward an affirmation of good and away from evil." Moreover, "Combining the evils of the 'civilized' frontier environment with the positive value given to 'civilized' heroes and heroines yields a somewhat schizophrenic portrait of the frontier in melodrama in the last decades of the nineteenth century and the early years of the twentieth."[11] In other words, the western Eden – Rousseau's primitive state – is destroyed by the encroachment of settlers, but, evil having once entered, the sin is best exorcized by the other, positive forces of civilization – Thomas Hobbes' Eden of social responsibility. In the plays, this new utopia involves a more personal, internalized state of grace, a sense of individuals reconnecting with primal life forces and establishing their own identities within that landscape, especially in such works as David Belasco's *The Girl of the Golden West*, William Vaughn Moody's *The Great Divide*, and Rachel Crothers' *The Three of Us*.[12] Schizophrenic? Indeed. And illustrative of the paradoxical elements that tumble through the frontier melodramas.

Yet another contradiction involves the person who is often one of the chief perpetrators of violence: the frontier hero. If the West is an Eden, then the western heroes usurp the place of Montaigne's naturally superior natives. Experts in the elemental skills of the wilderness, they are in touch with the world around them. Nature speaks to them. Richard Nelson writes that "there is something unique to the American character that allows profound innocence and cold ruthlessness to inhabit the same being."[13] That combination applies directly to border heroes and heroines. In them, child-like innocence and naivete combine with a relentless drive to succeed, and, once crossed, with a ruthless desire for what could be described – again paradoxically – as justice or vengeance. The heroes and heroines of frontier drama establish their own moral codes, often violating society's normal conventions in the process. Yet they retain an essential goodness and an unerring sense of which rules and rights are most important.

The hero and heroine in frontier plays were especially important in late-nineteenth-century American society, for they were, in effect, defining postbellum approaches to masculine and feminine behavior. The male role during the Civil War was easy to gauge, but after that conflict, with the pace of industrialization accelerating, ideals of masculinity underwent stark reevaluation.

Several currents buffeted the concept of masculinity, and not all of them were congruent. One set of values that materialized in the second half of the nineteenth century identified men with their primitive animal instincts in a positive, almost social-Darwinian manner. The ideals of impetuosity and primitivism extolled by the Romantic poets further contributed to this view. Self-assertiveness and a competitive spirit were judged valuable commodities in the business world as well as in the emerging sphere of individual and team sports. Strength and a physically fit body suddenly became important concerns. Perhaps as a holdover from the war, the idea of male bonding in teams, clubs, and associations took on great significance. The mastery of skills – especially outdoor skills – gained new prominence, and cleverness became a worthwhile attribute. This notion of animal spirits included an appreciation of boyish charm, which could be translated into jokes and pranks, but it also extended to a tolerant view of aggression, even of violence.[14]

As with aggression and violence, however, many of these qualities needed correctives, and another set of values supported by a traditional moral framework retained prominence. These included such standbys as thrift, industry, bravery, and duty. They championed a disciplined control of the animal nature and preached quiet humility mixed with stoic endurance. Patriotism retained a powerful appeal, as did the idea of self-sacrifice, especially the notion that men should shield and protect women, who were regarded as weak and dependent creatures.

Over all these ideas of maleness reigned the concept of freedom, and as city dwellers turned into wage earners and lost the autonomy of farms and small businesses, the ideal of freedom of movement and action became even more important. And where better for a young man to identify with a paragon of masculine freedom than in a frontier drama?

Although there were not as many frontier heroines, their role as models at a time when women were beginning to demand equal rights was significant, and they, like their male counterparts, exhibited almost a split personality. Within the frontier landscape women enjoyed opportunities for independence, and plays reflected that. Female characters operated bars, ran hotels, and owned gold mines. Although moral sanctions still applied, the frontier provided women with less rigid sexual restraints, which the plays dramatized. In addition, female frontier performers demonstrated physical skills such as riding and shooting. Although nineteenth-century society still viewed education for women with suspicion, many of the female frontier characters were educated. While the degree of their erudition was sometimes inversely proportional to their ability to handle the challenges of the frontier, their education nevertheless stood as an outward signal of their independence and self-sufficiency. In several theatrical situations women disguised themselves as men and performed masculine tasks, and in several other productions actresses assumed male parts, declaring, in effect, that women could perform male "roles" both on stage and in life. Still, these same female characters and performers maintained or were forced to maintain typical feminine patterns. Within the plays, female characters ultimately wanted or needed a man, and actresses who displayed masculine skills on stage emphasized feminine talents off stage.

In the late nineteenth century, approximately five to ten percent of all the touring productions in the United States were plays about the frontier. Many of those plays gained enormous popularity, packing theatres in all the major cities, and some toured for as many as ten, twenty, or even thirty seasons. Despite their undeniable popular appeal, critical examination of frontier dramas, of their productions, of their audiences, and of the ways in which they fit into their society has been meager both in their own time and since.[15]

Another objective of this study, therefore, is to examine the critical response to border plays. The modern perspective toward popular culture is vastly different from the attitude that existed in the nineteenth century. Critics today are inclusive when it comes to art. Almost anything from a conception to a life-style is "art" to someone, and writers scrutinize the most popular forms of expression from television programs to tabloids not only as products, but as statements about the society that produces them. Such examinations of popular art within the context of its society had no place in the nineteenth century.

In the 1800s, art was a pinnacle to be achieved. In theatre, Shakespeare's plays, certain other classics, and a few new but worthy pieces from Europe represented that pinnacle. Anything that was not at the pinnacle was necessarily a lower, inferior work, which perhaps did not even attain the stature of art at all. Critics treated American plays as an afterthought in comparison to their European counterparts, and they relegated frontier plays to the lowest level of that secondary rank. Those who practiced in such lower depths were, naturally, lesser artists, or perhaps not even artists at all. And if those performers did not at least *aspire* to Shakespeare and the other classics, then they represented a direct threat to the collective cultural judgment, personified most conspicuously by newspaper critics. Moreover, if the lower-level dramatic work happened also to be immensely popular, then that work posed a particular threat because the approbation of the general populace undermined the accepted cultural norm as well as the very status and authority of the critics themselves. Hence, it is no wonder that reviewers reacted to popular performances of frontier drama like police controlling street riots: at first they patronized, and then they turned vicious. "Rot," "trash," and "heart-sickening" are merely three of the pejoratives critics flung at popular frontier plays in their attempt to suppress what they considered the "unworthy." As Lawrence Levine demonstrates in his book on the emergence of cultural hierarchy, the critics' placement of themselves as guardians of the cultural mantle led to "denigration of popular audiences and [a] propensity to blame them for the low state of the drama."[16]

The critics' sense of superiority does not mean that they never said anything good about the frontier plays. Critics, too, enjoyed their contradictions. Some reviewers genuinely wanted to promote home-grown drama – so long as it conformed to the proper European rules and did not threaten accepted standards. Several border plays were labeled "the best American play" by one or another writer. In almost all of the reviews, however, qualifications abounded. If a reviewer liked a play or a production, the writer reminded the readers that "it's the best *of its kind*," or added some similar phrase relegating the play to a lower artistic plateau. In addition, critics often praised individual performers while criticizing the material they performed. Those reviews followed a pattern: "Such and such an actor or actress is a remarkable performer. It's too bad his/her efforts aren't being put to use in material more worthy of his/her abilities." Gerald Bordman in his book on nineteenth-century American drama points out that truly native drama – "American plays on American themes" – really developed at the theatres that the critics usually ignored. That so few American plays were performed at more highly regarded theatres, he notes, could be a function of "the pretensions of more affluent, knowing playgoers or the works' inherent weaknesses."[17] Or, he might have added, "the pretensions of all-knowing critics."

In his *Melodramatic Formations*, Bruce McConachie identified the "republican revolution of the people against aristocratic oppression" as one of the characteristics of what he called "apocalyptic drama."[18] Frontier drama contains little sense of a political order exerting force on the community or an aristocracy oppressing the settlers. Indeed, people journeyed to the frontiers to avoid such forces. Most of the evils in border melodramas arise from individuals within the frontier communities, and most of the decisions are made by individuals, small groups, or the entire community meeting together. The strongest impression of regulation by outside forces in frontier plays is that affecting the native populations, whose lives are circumscribed by settlers, Indian agents, and the army.

The eastern theatres, however, were another matter. There the aristocracy of the critics derided the citizenry for turning out to see their beloved frontier melodramas. As Susan Harris Smith observes regarding the critical reception of America drama, "any deviation from the approved model would be excluded, castigated, or, at best, marginalized and positioned as an anomaly by the dominant critical voices."[19] Critics conveniently marginalized audiences at frontier plays by labeling them "ignorant," "ingenuous," and "unwashed." Drawing the conflict in those terms, frontier drama represents not the *theatrical* revolt of the oppressed against their aristocratic oppressors, but the *actual* revolt of the "ignorant" audiences against the strictures of the elite critics. Through the frontier drama, the marginalized public seized control of their own entertainment. They went to what pleased them until, finally, frontier drama resulted in the ultimate conquest of the "lowbrow" over the "highbrow." Frontier drama, therefore, represents the victory of the wilderness over the city, of the unlearned over the educated, of the popular masses over the critical establishment, and of the democracy of the "unwashed" over the aristocracy of the well-dressed. By the end of the century the lowbrow triumphed so convincingly that they dragged the highbrow – virtually kicking and screaming – along with them until the highbrow legitimated the frontier subject matter by adopting it for their own.

Unquestionably, later frontier plays demonstrate advances in playwriting skills and thematic depth. Such plays as *The Great Divide*, *The Three of Us*, and *The Girl of the Golden West* confirm the emergence of sophisticated thematic motifs, and this study documents how playwrights adapted the local-color detailing of Bret Harte and other writers to the stage to create a cast of vivid frontier personalities. However, in many ways turn-of-the-century border drama exhibited simply a more elaborately produced version of older forms. Certainly the moral contrivance of a play like *The Squaw Man* was little different from similarly concocted moral dilemmas in a raft of earlier border fare.

What really changed near the turn of the century was the social acceptability of frontier drama, and, with that, the reception accorded by the critical establishment. At that time, prominent producers and writers including Charles Frohman, Augustus Thomas, and David Belasco began to mount frontier plays. Writers who were products of elite eastern society, such as William Vaughn Moody, Owen Wister, and Henry C. DeMille, composed frontier scripts. Commentators lavished extensive coverage on their productions and hailed them as vast improvements on the efforts that preceded them.

If critics regarded the frontier plays with a contempt born of superiority, they treated the performers in those plays with nearly equal disdain. Usually the performers were patronized. Often they were castigated. Reviewers regularly reminded them that their skills were slight and their products worthless.

Whether the performances were good or not, whether the frontier plays were valuable or not, one thing is certain: the productions, being a part of the ephemeral world of theatre, are gone. Except for a few scripts, the drama that brought the frontier to life for late-nineteenth-century audiences has vanished. Unlike the early movie cowboys, the actors and actresses who labored in border dramas in theatres throughout the country are, with the two exceptions of Frank Mayo and William F. "Buffalo Bill" Cody, forgotten. Oliver Doud Byron. McKee Rankin. Louis Aldrich. Annie Pixley. Frank Frayne. James H. Wallick. Fanny Herring. All of them were famous stars – the John Wayne, Clint Eastwood, Roy Rogers, and Dale Evans of their time – yet not one of them would earn more than a passing reference in any general history or encyclopedia of American theatre. They did not exactly labor in obscurity. All were enormously popular. Several acquired great wealth. But the characters and the dramas they created have long since disappeared. No celluloid documents their achievements. Only a few scripts remain, and those are painfully deceptive, for the words on a page are but one ingredient of frontier drama, and not always the most prominent ingredient at that.

"Buffalo Bill" Cody is one of the two exceptions of the forgotten band.

Cody's genuinely adventurous life, his stage career in plays, and his extraordinary success with his Wild West show have been well documented. Similarly, Frank Mayo, who played Davy Crockett for more than three thousand performances over twenty-two years, has received fair credit, and the play in which he starred, *Davy Crockett; or, Be Sure You're Right, Then Go Ahead*, is generally regarded as a highlight of the genre.

The rest of the men and women of nineteenth-century frontier drama have achieved only occasional notice. Several of them were related to well-known artists – the sister, granddaughter, or father-in-law of this or that noted star – but their work is virtually unknown. Their performances were critically discredited in their own times, their products have disappeared, their significance to other developments has been ignored, and, if they achieved any wealth at all, many of them saw it vanish like their productions.

One objective of this book is to offer those performers a small mead of remembrance and to grant them a grain of the serious consideration they seldom received. After all, in live theatre, performers *mean* just as scripts do. Patrons buy not only the text of a play, but also the text of the performer. In musical theatre in the late twentieth century, purchasing a ticket for *The King and I* purchased a ticket for Yul Brynner, the prototype Siamese king and also the actor fighting cancer. In the realm of frontier drama, one could hardly separate Louis Aldrich from *My Partner*, Frank Chanfrau from *The Arkansas Traveller*, Annie Pixley from *M'liss*, or numerous other stars from the vehicles in which they appeared. A patron buying a ticket to Frank Mayo's *Davy Crockett* after it established its reputation was purchasing a ticket to see a frontier icon AND a theatrical icon. They were buying a piece of American mythos AND a theatrical experience – rather like seeing venerable Jimmy Stewart in *The Man Who Shot Liberty Valance* or watching James Arness age over the years in *Gunsmoke*. The meaning the performer carried could, of course, change with time, just as it did with Brynner. Anyone buying a ticket to see McKee Rankin in *The Danites* in its early days bought a dashing romantic figure within a well-received play based on stories of Mormon outrages. Later, a patron of the same play bought an overweight, scandal-plagued miscreant. In that context, this book will examine the texts of performers as well as texts of scripts and productions.

This study of the drama of the frontier on American stages begins in 1870, with the emergence of three popular productions that ushered in a wave of border plays. There had, of course, been other plays set on the frontier, including a spate of such dramas in the 1830s and several more in the 1850s. But when *Across the Continent* opened in 1870, twelve years had elapsed since *Nick Whiffles* and a trio of plays about the Mormon conflicts – the last previous notable border dramas – had played in New York. From the debut of *Across the Continent* on, however, a virtually unbroken line of frontier plays regaled audiences across America into the twentieth century. Several factors contributed to that surge of frontier drama, and as this study explores the breadth of frontier melodrama and the contradictions inherent in the material, it also seeks to locate the plays in the context of their time. A theatrical production is, after all, a function of numerous factors including economic realities, politics, social structures, prevailing aesthetic criteria, and contemporary discourse, and several of those ingredients contributed to an increase in popular entertainment in general and to a surge of frontier drama in particular in the last third of the nineteenth century.

A population explosion that nearly doubled the number of Americans from 1870 to 1900 meant more people to buy tickets. Furthermore, the population was moving to the cities, where theatres abounded.[20] Advances in communication provided a second factor crucial to the swell of popular entertainment. The first transcontinental telegraph line, completed in 1861, drew the east and west coasts together. The telegraph dramatically increased the speed of news reporting, and other newspaper innovations including faster and larger presses contributed to the popularity and significance of newspapers. Advertising, reviews, and news reports publicized the theatre while theatrical trade journals disseminated professional information and promoted business transactions.

The importance of the railroad to late-nineteenth-century troupers can hardly be overemphasized. The driving of the golden stake at Promontory, Utah, completing the transcontinental railroad signaled not the culmination, but an acceleration of railroad construction. Railroad mileage, which consisted of just over 30,000 miles of track in 1860, crisscrossed the land with 192,000 miles by the end of the century. Furthermore, the railroad was not simply a mechanical device, for it represented a force of nature and of God, extending civilization into the wilderness.[21]

As major advances in transportation and communication made theatre more accessible, the post-war economic boom, which put discretionary money into the pockets of prospective patrons, allowed them to take advantage of the diverse opportunities. Even with the financial panic of 1873 and the depression that followed, the national wealth doubled between 1865 and 1880, and, despite another panic in 1893, it doubled again by 1900.[22]

Another factor that contributed to the flowering of popular entertainment was a rapidly changing moral climate. America's post-war attitude accepted entertainment as a valid and worthwhile pursuit, a distinct change from the Puritanical, pre-war moral code, and that attitude prompted audiences to go to see what they *wanted* to see rather than what critics or preachers told them they *should* see.[23]

The expansion of opportunities in popular entertainment coincided with an explosion of interest in the American frontier generated by the lure of riches, frequent warfare, and enhanced travel and communication – factors that particularly aided the development of frontier plays. The California gold rush of 1849 attracted rapt public attention to the western territories, followed a decade later by the rush to Pike's Peak, but that interest was interrupted by the Civil War. After the war, additional gold and silver discoveries in the Northwest and the Black Hills of Dakota reignited the public's imagination.

As riveting as the lure of gold, a string of conflicts focused attention on the struggles of western Indians to retain hunting grounds and freedom of movement. A series of battles with the Sioux in the central plains culminated in the epic events of Custer's Last Stand in 1876 and the Ghost Dance and the Massacre at Wounded Knee in 1890. In the Southwest, Kit Carson destroyed the livelihood of the Navajo in the 1860s, and battles with the fierce Apache Indians, which lasted until 1900, made the names Geronimo and Cochise famous. Smaller but widely publicized skirmishes included the Black Hawk War in Utah in 1865–68, the Modoc War in northern California in 1872–73, and the Nez Perce flight in 1877.

Other contemporary border events such as the deeds and misdeeds of the James brothers furnished additional dramatic material. Many plays featured as performers individuals who had participated in notable or notorious frontier episodes, including "Wild Bill" Hickok and "Texas Jack" Omohundro. Even when the plays were not directly connected to newspaper articles, current events often fashioned the background. As frontier plays featuring Indian and Chinese characters entertained audiences, for example, legislators debated laws to move indigenous populations and restrict immigration.

The same communication and transportation advances that brought theatre to audiences promoted frontier drama by spreading the word about events in the West. Before the transcontinental railroad, a stage coach took three weeks to travel from St. Louis to San Francisco. A wagon train from Nebraska to the coast lasted four months. With the completion of the western railroad, however, the Union Pacific could advertise a seemingly miraculous travel time of less than four days for the seventeen-hundred-mile trek from Omaha to San Francisco. With Chicago just five days from the west coast and New York seven, the western frontier was closer than ever before.[24]

The telegraph, with its almost instantaneous transmission of news, also reduced the distance between East and West. Newspapers used the telegraph to record western exploits with day-to-day regularity, even sending reporters out with army troops. The roll of men who died with George Custer at the Little Bighorn, for instance, included reporter Mark Kellogg.

The public showed an almost insatiable interest not only in accounts of actual events of the West but also in lectures and fictional writings about the region, and numerous plays lifted characters and episodes from current literature. Bret Harte's first collection of stories, *"The Luck of Roaring Camp"* *and Other Sketches*, was published in 1870. Incorporating pieces that had appeared in *Overland Monthly* in 1868 and 1869, it catapulted Harte and his idiosyncratic western characters into national prominence. Mark Twain's *Roughing It*, based on his western experiences in the 1860s, appeared in 1872. Meanwhile, Twain presented his "Roughing It" lecture and Harte his "The Argonauts of '49" speech hundreds of times in major eastern cities from 1869 through the mid 1870s. Joaquin Miller's *Songs of the Sierras* came out in 1871, and his *Life Amongst the Modocs* followed in 1873. Ned Buntline's first "Buffalo Bill" story ran in serial form in *New York Weekly* in 1869. Hordes of imitations and dime novels followed.

The theatre proved an exceptionally able distributor of border tales, for, as Richard Slotkin notes in writing of the mythos of the frontier, "elements that tend to maximize conflict, suspense, irony, and moral resonance may be highlighted at the expense of other no-less-factual elements that do not so palpably serve the tale."[25] What better vehicle to highlight conflict, suspense, irony, and moral resonance than dramatic presentation?

The theatre supplied a popular outlet for the public's fascination with border events, and, in 1871, the success of three plays on New York stages established frontier drama as a powerful and enduring influence in American life. The plays overlapped in their New York appearances between March and June and initiated an outburst of drama about the frontier. Significantly, the plays displayed the influence of the railroad, border warfare, and Bret Harte's stories. The first of the three produced in the metropolitan area was *Across the Continent*, by James J. McCloskey, which opened at the Park Theatre in Brooklyn in November 1870, starring Oliver Doud Byron, and played there again in March 1871, before appearing for a run of six weeks, from March 13 to April 22, at Wood's Museum and Theatre in New York. It featured the transcontinental railroad and a battle with Indians. The second production to appear in New York was *Horizon*, by Augustin Daly, based in part on a Bret Harte story and influenced by news reports of Indian conflicts. It ran for nearly eight weeks from March 21 to May 13, 1871, at New York's Olympic Theatre. The last of the three to play New York, *Kit, the Arkansas Traveller*, by Edward Spencer, T. B. DeWalden, and Clifton W. Tayleure, was actually the earliest of the three, first opening with Francis S. Chanfrau as Kit in February 1869, in Buffalo. *Kit* commenced its four-week New York city premiere at Niblo's Garden Theatre on May 9, 1871. Those three plays ignited an explosion of frontier productions, and, from the time they began their long runs in the spring of 1871 through a variety of touring plays, movies, radio programs, and television series, frontier drama of one form or another was continuously before the American public for the next one hundred years.

Although the western territories had their own flourishing dramatic traditions with professional theatres in New Orleans, the Ohio River valley, and on the west coast, this examination of frontier dramatizations concentrates on plays performed in New York because that city was the theatrical center for the nation. Managers from throughout the country descended on the city to book attractions, and theatre companies hired New York booking agents to schedule their routes. Productions that played New York garnered publicity not only from daily metropolitan newspapers, but from weekly trade publications as well. As a result, major touring combinations with the best-known performers and the most popular dramas routinely scheduled a season in New York to promote their reputations. Moreover, this study seeks to examine the dramatic frontier mythology purchased by those who were not themselves a physical part of the frontier.

This survey could have several end points – 1890, when the Census Bureau declared the frontier officially closed; 1898, when the country fought the Spanish-American War and attention turned from the western borders; 1903, when the movie *The Great Train Robbery* moved frontier drama into a new medium; 1912, when the admission of New Mexico and Arizona as states completed the western territory; or 1917, when America entered the First World War and "Buffalo Bill" Cody, a living symbol of the West, died. The year 1906 has been selected because, in 1905 and 1906, several frontier dramas emerged that marked a culmination of the staging of the frontier. In addition, almost all of those plays were quickly adapted to cinema, and that transition of frontier drama to the new medium of film also constituted an obvious moment of passage.

One could, in summarizing this period, compile a remarkable anthology of dramatic scripts on American frontier themes: *Across the Continent, Horizon, Davy Crockett, The Danites, M'liss, My Partner, The Girl I Left Behind Me, Arizona, The Squaw Man, The Girl of the Golden West, The Great Divide, The Three of Us,* and more. But such an anthology would exclude a multitude of plays that were not primarily literary vehicles. It would exclude the Wild West exhibitions, the shooting stunts, and the leaping horses. It would also fail to express adequately, even in the plays listed, the frontier drama as a production experience. The contributions of the scenery, the lighting, the music, and most especially the performers would all be diminished. Frontier drama did more than simply generate a body of dramatic literature. It created dramatic experiences that enthralled the senses while intrinsically expressing a series of paradoxes and contradictions. When patrons bought tickets to a frontier play, they were buying more than the words of the script. They were also purchasing the trick shooting, the animal stunts, and the scenic embellishments. They were acquiring proximity to actual participants in the westward movement and access to representations of historic personages and events, as well as to the sounds and the smells of galloping horses, exploding gun shots, and blazing red fire. It is that overall dramatic experience that led to a revolt by the popular audiences against the critical establishment and that eventually transferred to even wider audiences for film, radio, and television.

I

Reemergence: 1870–1872

All of these plays are bad in an intellectual sense, and some of them are bad
in a moral sense. They no more come within the sphere of true dramatic art
than the picture of a pound cake on the door of a Broadway stage comes
within the sphere of the art of painting.

The *New York Herald* on frontier plays, especially those starring Oliver Doud
Byron, January 1874

IN THE EARLY DAYS OF 1871, A REVOLUTION IN AMERICAN
theatre began. Within a period of two months, three plays debuted in New
York and established the frontier as the single most productive source of
dramatic material in America. From 1871, when *Across the Continent* opened
in New York, until 1973, when the television program *Bonanza* aired its last
original episode, frontier drama continuously entertained the American
public. On the stages of theatres, on movie screens, across radio airwaves,
and eventually through the tubes, transistors, and microchips of television,
the frontier reigned as the dominant subject of drama in America for over
one hundred years.

Across the Continent

The revolution began innocently enough when Oliver Doud Byron brought
his new play, *Across the Continent*, to Sarah Crocker Conway's Park Theatre
in Brooklyn at Thanksgiving in 1870. The play was a melodrama in five boisterous scenes by Brooklyn author James J. McCloskey. Despite some clever
devices and an appealing star, for most of its two and a half hours the production remained an entirely unremarkable melodrama, for, although *Across
the Continent* would initiate a flood of plays about the frontier, eighty
percent of the drama was set in New York.

The first act (or prologue) opens to a street in Five Points, a notoriously seedy pocket of the city, where George Constant dies of alcohol abuse encouraged by an evil bar owner.[1] His destitute wife also perishes, leaving their two young children to a passing good Samaritan, the merchant Thomas Goodwin. Act II resumes twenty years later as Joe Ferris, an outcast gambler, pursues John Adderly, the son of the wicked saloon keeper, through whose perjury Ferris was unjustly imprisoned. Ferris has become friends with Tom Goodwin, the adopted son of the merchant from the first scene. When Ferris visits Tom, he discovers that Adderly is trying to marry Louisa, the elder Goodwin's adopted daughter and Tom's sister, and Ferris exposes Adderly's nefarious scheme.

Up to this point in the play, *Across the Continent* offered nothing more than conventional melodramatic fare. It demonstrated the evil of alcohol. It visited fathers' sins on their sons. Young children were orphaned. Good characters cared for them. Evil characters oppressed them. The villain tried to entrap frail victims and force his romantic desires on the heroine. The performance was equally conventional in its comic elements. The Irishman, Johnnie O'Dwyer, provided an almost vaudevillian series of jokes and gags. Goodwin's servant, Caesar Augustus, presented black-face comic turns by incorporating dramatic quotations into his conversations, and Louisa's aunt Susannah enacted a comically flirtatious old maid. The play had not even moved out of New York, much less "across the continent."

In the final act, however, the play moves west, where Ferris is in charge of Station 47 of the Pacific Railroad two years after the previous act. A train stops and discharges the Goodwin family – Thomas, Tom, Louisa, Caesar Augustus, Aunt Susannah, and Goodwin's natural daughter, Clara – seeking a new home in the West after financial setbacks. The comedy in this act comes from Caesar Augustus, petrified at the threat of Indians, and from a Chinese who drinks Aunt Susannah's bottle. The bottle obviously contains something stronger than water, which leads this first in a lineage of comic Chinese characters in frontier plays to declare "Me makee mashee" as he ludicrously romances Susannah.

Nearby, a mysterious man urges a band of Piegan Indians to murder the men at the station and capture the women. The instigator is, of course, Adderly in disguise. The natives cut the telegraph line as they prepare their attack, but Ferris detects the severed wire and immediately recognizes the danger. He reattaches the telegraph equipment to the downed line and signals the next station to send troops. After a suspenseful silence, the instrument clicks back a response. The Indians attack, and Adderly gets the upper hand, but the groggy Ferris hears the approaching train through the tracks and springs into action just as the troops arrive, bringing the curtain down on a tableau of victory over the attacking band.

The play created a sensation. The *Brooklyn Eagle* (November 30) wrote of the theatre filled to overflowing and crowds turned away. By early December, Billy Rice and his minstrel troupe were already performing a comic burlesque of the piece at Hooley's Opera House – a sure testament to its popularity. In March, *Across the Continent* returned to the Brooklyn Park Theatre, and on March 13, 1871, the production opened for the first time in New York proper at Wood's Theatre. It maintained its enormous success and played six weeks until April 22. Three months later the production played at Niblo's Garden Theatre, where it continued almost another month in the heat of the summer.

Initially the production received favorable comments. The *Eagle* (December 12, 1870) called it "[t]he most thrilling and natural representation of American life ever played before the American public." The weekly theatrical trade newspaper the *New York Clipper* (March 25, 1871) declared the play well-mounted and well-acted and singled out the lead actor: "Byron acts the character of Joe Ferris with much effect. He has a clear musical voice, a well-proportioned figure, and a frank, manly appearance." The lead character epitomized a new masculine emphasis on physical qualities and animal spirits, not only through his nickname, "The Ferret," but also in his action-oriented motto: "I always act on first impulse." Naturally he also displayed fighting skills, and it did not hurt his reception that Byron was a handsome specimen.

The final stirring frontier scene emerged as the main attraction, with advertisements for the play featuring the oncoming locomotive.[2] As the train arrived at the beginning of the last act, it carried more than just the Goodwin family. It transported the public toward a reemergent form of American melodrama. The frontier was nothing new to American life in the 1870s. A frontier – in fact, several frontiers – had existed since the first European settlers arrived in America, and the invisible line of frontier had moved like a westward wave across the continent, from the Alleghenies to the Ohio River valley and on to the Mississippi.

Until the mid 1800s, the American frontier moved consistently westward from one contiguous area to another. The lure of gold on the west coast changed that pattern. Suddenly the frontier jumped two thousand miles, from the Mississippi River to the Pacific Ocean. From then on the American frontier had two fronts: an eastward push emanating from

California and Oregon over the great divide and a western edge moving out from the Mississippi and Missouri River valleys. The character of the frontier as well as the location changed in the mid 1800s. East of the Mississippi, the frontier had consisted of backwoods. Settlers traveled primarily along forest-lined rivers, and, when they settled, they established farming communities. The heroes were Daniel Boone and Davy Crockett. The natives represented a mixture of help and threat typified by Pocahontas and King Philip.

California was not populated by farmers, but by miners. The settlements were not farming communities; they were mining towns. As the western plains filled in, the ranch, rather than the farm, became the defining unit. Minerals, cattle, and horses gained prominence over game and crops. The vastness of the western plains, the majesty and danger of the Rockies, the barrenness of the desert, and the grandeur of canyons, mesas, giant trees, and towering peaks replaced the woods and rivers of the eastern frontier. A new cast of frontier characters emerged, featuring miners, ranchers, and cowboys. Even the natives of the western frontier were different. They lived in tepees and adobe villages rather than wooden huts, and the adoption of the horse provided them with great mobility.

Just as the frontier was a constant reality of American life, so, too, plays about the frontier had been a recurring feature of American theatre. Productions that included aboriginal peoples were particularly prevalent. Don Wilmeth listed over two hundred and thirty plays written or produced between 1606 and 1860 that featured Indians as major characters, but only a handful of those plays were performed with any frequency.[3]

Ponteach; or, The Savages of America, written by Major Robert Rogers in 1766, was not produced at all, and yet it stands as a revealing harbinger of border drama and one of the first serious plays on an American subject.[4] As with many of the most popular frontier plays that would follow, Rogers' play adapted historical material – in this case incidents from the French and Indian War. Rogers based his drama on his experiences with the great leader, Pontiac, in the early 1760s. Writing in iambic pentameter, Rogers focuses on Ponteach, a chief in the vicinity of Detroit whose tribe suffers injustices at the hands of English settlers and traders. The English use false weights to buy furs, they water the rum, and they maliciously shoot and scalp innocent natives. Administrators sent to deal fairly with the tribe confiscate goods intended for the natives, and steal tribal gifts intended for the king. Enraged, Ponteach makes war on the deceitful English, but personal disputes between his two sons undermine his plans.

A striking aspect of the play, besides the insidious actions of the English and the moral justification of the natives, lies in its powerful anti-clerical bias. The Catholic priest, who supports the French, uses religious hocus-pocus to trick the tribe into rebellion. He is the first in a long line of white antagonists who incite Indians to war for their own ends. Later, the priest attempts to rape an Indian woman, which he justifies as a purification ritual.

In 1808 James Nelson Barker's *The Indian Princess; or, La Belle Sauvage,* which adapted the Pocahontas story, was produced with music in Philadelphia, Baltimore, New York, and other cities.[5] Captain John Smith is separated from his recently landed colleagues, and warriors bring Smith to Powhatan's village, where Pocahontas, the chief's daughter, is expected to marry Miami, from the influential Susquehannock tribe. However, when a rescue party arrives at the village, John Rolfe and Pocahontas immediately fall in love. Rolfe and Pocahontas are united after Pocahontas saves the English from an ambush led by the embittered Miami. Featuring numerous musical numbers and lighthearted subplots involving the romantic inclinations of the settlers, Barker's iambic pentameter verses furnished an entertaining, simplistic treatment of one of the oldest frontier sagas.

George Washington Parke Custis' *Pocahontas; or, The Settlers of Virginia,* another of the many treatments of the Pocahontas story, was staged in 1830 in Philadelphia.[6] Like Barker and most of the other retellers of the Pocahontas legend, Custis invented a love triangle. In this version, Pocahontas is to marry Matacoran, who persuades Powhatan to attack the English. Pocahontas' warning prepares them for the charge, and, when the natives capture Smith, Pocahontas saves him. As in Barker's play, Powhatan ends as an ally of the British, and Pocahontas and Rolfe pledge their love. Both plays thus reinforced the supposed unity of the settlers and the native tribes.

Mordecai M. Noah's *She Would Be a Soldier; or, The Plains of Chippewa,* which opened at New York's Anthony Street Theatre in June 1819, used the western front of the War of 1812 as a backdrop.[7] In the process, Noah combined a frontier setting with a sharpshooting and sharp-tongued female in a breeches role. In Noah's play, Christine, the daughter of Jasper, a Frenchman who fought with Lafayette in the Revolutionary War and then settled near the Great Lakes, rebels when her father insists she marry a wealthy local boor. Christine disguises herself as a male and follows her love, Lieutenant Lennox, to the front. Christine misinterprets Lennox's attentions to the general's daughter, and, distraught, she enlists in the army after proving her shooting skill. When the jealous Christine tries to break into the general's tent, she is imprisoned and sentenced to death. In the end, however, Lennox leads the Americans to victory and rescues Christine.

Noah peopled his story with an assortment of finely drawn characters. The comics, including Pendragon, a foppish, fashion-conscious British captain, and LaRole, his valet, who speaks with an excruciating French accent, are hardly frontier caricatures, but Noah also created a command-ing chief with a keen sense of justice, and, in the character of Christine, Noah devised a courageous, well-educated, and forthright woman, skilled in the frontier arts, who also exhibits a romantic streak. Her adoption of men's clothing, her skill with a rifle, and her defiance of convention to pursue her own desires established a model frequently copied by later authors of frontier women.

Metamora; or, The Last of the Wampanoags by John Augustus Stone, first performed in New York in 1829, became the most famous play featuring a native character in the early American theatre.[8] Edwin Forrest, America's most prominent actor before Edwin Booth, initiated a contest to encourage American authors to write plays on American themes, and *Metamora* won the Forrest Prize. Forrest's energetic style suited the story of the heroic chief just as, a few years earlier, it had served effectively when he played the noble chief in Noah's drama. In Stone's drama, the great Chief Metamora – known as King Philip to the whites – tries to help Oceana, a young white girl he has sworn to protect, marry her beloved Walter instead of the influential villain, Lord Fitzarnold. In the course of the complicated plot Metamora is tricked by the whites and betrayed by his adopted son, Annawandah. He rescues his wife Nahmeokee from the whites and escapes from prison. When the English attack the Wampanoags, Metamora retreats to his stronghold with Nahmeokee and his child. After the attack-ers slay his son, he kills his wife so she will not be captured, and he defiantly denounces the British before he is shot.

Stone used the historical reality of King Philip's war as the doorway to his imaginative recreation. In it he employed several devices that became staples of frontier plays. One was the division among the Indians, used in almost every border play with native characters, and represented here by the discord between Metamora and his turncoat son. Another is the cycle of capture, pursuit, and rescue that played so great a part in frontier melo-drama. Ironically, in *Metamora*, it is the whites who hold Nahmeokee captive and who imprison Metamora. Finally, Stone utilizes one of the strongest melodramatic devices – killing a woman to spare her from degra-dation by the enemy. Here, however, the whites represent the degrading enemy. Forrest retained the gallant chief in his repertory until his death in 1872, and other actors occasionally revived the play after that. Metamora epitomized the romantic "noble savage" while also representing a second sentimental image, that of the "last" of his tribe.

In 1831, the first backwoodsman appeared in a drama. His name was Nimrod Wildfire, and he was the main character in James Kirke Paulding's *The Lion of the West*.[9] Like *Metamora*, Paulding's play won a contest, this one sponsored by James H. Hackett for a comedy with an American as the central character. Interestingly, Paulding's play is not set on the frontier but in New York as the man from the backwoods – "half horse, half alligator, and a touch of the airthquake" – rescues his relatives from the evils of the city. Paulding modeled the character in part on Davy Crockett, who served in Washington as a Congressman from Tennessee. Paulding's play – eventually revised by John Augustus Stone and completely rewritten by William Bayle Bernard and retitled *The Kentuckian; or, A Trip to New York* – reinforced a thematic dichotomy that reappeared again and again in frontier plays. The eastern city represented greed, corruption, weakness, and moral laxity while the border symbolized unselfishness, honesty, strength, and honor.

In addition to *Metamora* and *The Lion of the West*, a spate of other successful frontier plays focusing primarily on Indians debuted in the 1830s. Debate over the removal of the eastern tribes to land west of the Mississippi, which began with the passage of Andrew Jackson's Indian Removal Bill in 1830, aroused public interest. The subject remained current throughout the decade as the government forced one tribe after another to leave traditional lands for resettlement in the West. Forrest's ongoing success with *Metamora* spurred imitations, and the literary success of James Fenimore Cooper's *The Leatherstocking Tales* provided additional inspiration. The clever backwoodsman Natty Bumppo first appeared in novels in the 1820s, and those novels were dramatized in the 1830s. The most popular drama based on a Cooper novel, however, was *The Wept of Wish-Ton-Wish*, published in 1829 and dramatized a year later. In the isolated valley of Wish-Ton-Wish in Connecticut, Conanchet, the chief of the Narragansetts, raids a white village in revenge for the murder of his father. When he recognizes a family of whites who befriended him, he spares them and returns their daughter, Ruth, who has lived as his wife, Naramattah, since she was stolen years earlier. The whites eventually capture Conanchet and turn him over to his enemies for execution. Meanwhile, Ruth, who cannot readjust to life among the whites, dies, and the villagers bury her beside her beloved Conanchet.

The play was sometimes called *Naramattah* or *Miantonimoh*, the name of Conanchet's father and the name by which many of the whites knew the son. William Bayle Bernard's 1835 dramatization proved the most stageworthy, and companies performed it occasionally through the rest of the nineteenth century. As in *Metamora*, *The Wept of Wish-Ton-Wish* employed one of the most powerful and frequently used devices in frontier drama – a white woman abducted by a native tribe – although in this case Ruth/Naramattah adopted native ways, came to love her captor, and was returned to white society despite her protests.

Another durable success of the 1830s was the stage adaptation of Robert M. Bird's *Nick of the Woods*. Bird's 1837 novel – an unusually bleak characterization – depicted renegade natives as uniformly villainous, and dramatists in the last third of the century frequently adopted a similar portrayal. At least three dramatizations of Bird's novel followed by 1839, the most lasting version being that of Louisa H. Medina[10] Medina, one of the most successful playwrights of the time, turned out over thirty plays, including several featuring native Americans, primarily within a five-year period before her premature death in her mid thirties. Her *Nick of the Woods*, written the year she died in 1838, adhered to Bird's negative portrayal of natives and was, like *The Wept of Wish-Ton-Wish*, produced sporadically through the rest of the century.

Bird set the action in 1782 in Kentucky, but Medina's dramatization is less precise.[11] The central character is Reginald Ashburn. Bent on revenge against Indians for the massacre of his family, he adopts the name of Nathan Slaughter to cloak a double life. By day he appears an eccentric loner, known to the villagers by the ironic moniker "Bloody Nathan" because he shuns violence. But at night he becomes the "Nick [i.e. devil] of the Woods" known to the natives as the "Jibbenainosay, the spirit who walks," because they thought him dead. Bird's novel emphasizes Slaughter's internal moral tension at having been raised a pacifist Quaker, but Medina eliminates all reference to that. In the course of the drama, Slaughter protects a small band of travellers, who include Captain Roland Forrester and his cousin, Edith. Indians incited by Dick Braxley, a white man who wants to marry Edith and claim her uncle's estate, and led by the heartless Wenonga, who murdered Slaughter's family, attack the party. Slaughter thwarts their plans with help from Roaring Ralph Stackpole, a braggart horse thief and precursor of the brawling Mike Fink type. Secondary characters include Abel Doe, a white man who has joined the renegades, and his ward, Telie Doe. In the climactic scene – often illustrated in advertisements for the play – a flaming canoe rode over a waterfall.[12] The denouement reveals Telie Doe as the uncle's long-lost heir, but she dies before she can claim her inheritance. Joseph Proctor played the lead role in the 1839 Bowery production, and revived his portrayal periodically up to as late as 1882, a span of over forty years.

Even more centrally than *Ponteach*, *Nick of the Woods* used a white man to incite native misdeeds. *Nick of the Woods* also employed two other dramatic complications that became fixtures in border plays: an inheritance as motivation for the villain, and a character – in this case Telie Doe – unaware of her parentage. Both the inheritance and the long-lost relative were typical conventions in melodramas of all stripes, but they worked especially well in frontier plays. Since many people went to the frontier to start over or to cover up past misdeeds, a disarming uncertainty surrounded names and identities. Moreover, the lack of effective communication in isolated frontier outposts provided dramatic plausibility for ignorance of births, deaths, or happenings beyond a character's immediate vicinity.

Despite the success of plays about Native Americans and adapted frontier novels in the 1830s, the trend did not continue.[13] In the 1850s, however, a second boomlet of frontier plays emerged. In 1847, John Brougham had satirized Forrest and his noble chief with *Metamora; or, The Last of the Pollywogs*. In 1855 he turned his comic attention to the Pocahontas story with his spoof, *Po-ca-hon-tas; or, The Gentle Savage*.[14] Brougham's piece, written in rhymed couplets and crammed with puns, was subtitled "An original aboriginal erratic operatic semi-civilized and demi-savage extravaganza." In the first scene, Captain Smith baldly declares that his men have come to ravage the land and steal gold. Such satiric bluntness encouraged the dominant audience to laugh at and thereby minimize their own real transgressions. The play continues in an ironic vein as Smith invades the Tuscarora Finishing School of Emancipated Maidens, where he falls in love with Pocahontas. In the last scene, in which a set showing a tribal village is combined with one showing New York's Union Square, Smith and John Rolfe play cards to determine who gets to marry Pocahontas. At opposite extremes of seriousness and comedy, both Stone's *Metamora* and Brougham's *Po-ca-hon-tas* allowed white viewers to acknowledge their faults and, in essence, forgive themselves. Brougham's satire, though not usually a full evening's entertainment, remained a popular afterpiece for thirty years, and it represents part of a thin but durable line of satires that mocked the normal conventions of frontier plays. Tony Pastor, Joe Weber and Lew Fields, and Charles Hoyt would later produce parodies on frontier theatrics in the fashion of *Po-ca-hon-tas*.

John Hovey Robinson's *Nick Whiffles*, which was based on a *New York Weekly* story and premiered in 1858, emerged as the most widely performed frontier melodrama of the pre-Civil War era. The most striking aspect of the play is the title character. Rather than a young, virile hero, Nick Whiffles is an aging, fatherly frontier leader, and his loveable loquaciousness is more comic than heroic. The villain is "squaw man" Lot Halliday – a white man living with a native woman – who captures the heroine, Blanche, and tries to seduce her. Halliday's jealous wife, Molly Molasses, provides comedy, and helps Blanche escape. The employment of ignorant natives for comic caricature and the use of a setting west of the Mississippi River both anticipate later frontier plays.

The 1850s also saw the production of several topical plays about the Mormons. In 1830, Joseph Smith published the *Book of Mormon*, an account of early history and religion in America, which Smith claimed he received as golden plates through the divine intervention of the angel Moroni. In the same year, Smith and a group of believers founded the Mormon church. The following year Smith relocated the church from New York to Kirtland, Ohio, and in 1838 Smith and his followers moved again to join Mormons already in Missouri. Controversy dogged Smith and his new church wherever they settled, the Mormon practice of polygamy arousing the loudest protests. Mormons claimed they were persecuted for their beliefs, while non-Mormons accused Mormons of violent acts. Within the year, authorities jailed Smith and ordered the Mormons to leave Missouri.

They moved to Illinois and established the city of Nauvoo, which quickly grew to be the second largest city in the state. Smith escaped from jail in Missouri and joined the faithful there, but in 1844 Smith and his brother, Hyrum, were blamed for an attack on a newspaper critical of the group, and, while they awaited trial, a mob stormed the jail and killed the pair.

Continuing troubles prompted Brigham Young in 1846–48 to lead the faithful across the wilderness to Utah, where they developed a community near the Great Salt Lake. The population multiplied, and they applied for statehood as the "State of Deseret." In 1850 Congress established the Territory of Utah with Brigham Young as governor. Antagonism between Mormons and non-Mormons, however, forced President James Buchanan to replace Young with a non-Mormon, and in 1857–58 the federal government sent troops to the territory to maintain order. Those conflicts, known as the Utah War or the Mormon War, plus other violent incidents that the public associated with the Mormons, quickly found their way into dramatic form. Three plays about the Mormons were performed within two months at three different New York theatres in 1858. Burton's Theatre presented *The Mormons; or, Life at Salt Lake City* from mid March to early April. *Life of the Mormons at Salt Lake* followed later in April at the National Theatre, and *Deseret Deserted; or, The Last Days of Brigham Young* played in May and June at Wallack's Theatre.

To a predominantly white, Christian audience, the plight of the Mormons provided ideal melodramatic material. Polygamy threatened the moral order with its implications of unbridled sex, and stories of Mormon violence perfectly satisfied melodrama's need for rapacious, conspiratorial villains. Although none of the three Mormon plays performed in 1858 became standard fare, they served as a precursor for one that did. *The Danites*, another play based on Mormon conflicts, premiered nearly twenty years later in 1877 and emerged as one of the most famous of all the frontier dramas. Several less prominent works, such as Jack Crawford's *Fonda; or, The Trapper's Dream*, also mined the grisly tales of alleged Mormon atrocities.

Despite a run of frontier plays in the 1850s, the genre once again failed to establish a continuous foothold in American drama. The Civil War disrupted normal theatrical activity as the public relegated all entertainment, including theatre, to an afterthought by comparison with the drama of the great conflict of 1861–65. Despite the introduction of the backwoods hero, various plays about noble and ignoble Indians, and items of topical interest such as the Utah War, frontier drama prior to the premiere of *Across the Continent* continued to appear only sporadically.

The train that arrived in the final scene of *Across the Continent* carried with it the baggage of those earlier frontier plays. Like *Nick Whiffles*, it moved the action into the trans-Mississippi West. Like *Ponteach* and *Nick of the Woods*, it featured a white man inciting native marauders. Those natives, however, were no noble aboriginals. As in *Nick of the Woods*, the Indians were little more than objects designed to elicit fear and be eliminated. While *Across the Continent* mirrored some of the previous border dramas, it also established new ground. It was the first time, but certainly not the last, that a train appeared in a frontier play. It was appropriate that the railroad assumed a pivotal place in the drama of the frontier, for the railroad was not only a tangible symbol of the industrial revolution, it was also the primary means by which the vast distances and difficult terrain of the West were ultimately measured. The site of the last act, "Station 47 of the Pacific Railroad," reflected the intense public interest in the transcontinental railroad. Byron's first performances for *Across the Continent* in the spring of 1870 came less than a year after the May 1869 completion of the line.

With Joe Ferris, Byron did not adopt an established western hero. Instead he created a man of the East who travels to the West and *becomes* a western hero. That transformation was reinforced as Ferris changed from business suits to "the typical garments of the sturdy mountaineer"(*New York Dramatic Mirror*, September 17, 1881). *Across the Continent* established the device of soldiers arriving at the last moment to defeat the natives and rescue the innocents from the East. The play was also the first border drama to employ the telegraph – like the railroad a testament to the approaching civilization – in a crucial plot development. Actor and playwright William Gillette, who played in *Across the Continent* in New Orleans in 1875, created a similar heart-stopping telegraph scene twenty years later in his compelling Civil War melodrama *Secret Service*.

In only a short time, however, the reviews for *Across the Continent* began to change. The *Brooklyn Eagle* (March 14, 1871) qualified its earlier endorsement by noting that the production was geared to less sophisticated viewers. The New York *Spirit of the Times* (March 1, 1871) said the play was "gratuitously disfigured by the introduction of improbabilities." After Byron had been playing *Across the Continent* for over a decade, the *New York Dramatic Mirror* (September 17, 1881) wrote, "It is one of those pieces that caters to impulse and excites the passions of the unlettered admirer of worldly bravado and a mock sentimentality, while the *morale* [sic] – a little bit of truth, with a few flecks of romantic honor – peeps through the interstices of a vapory plot." The writer concluded, "The evident object of *Across the Continent* is to make money, which it probably does."

Indeed it did. Byron parlayed his dramatic hit into financial security. Born in 1842 in Fredericksburg, Maryland, Byron began his career at fourteen at the Holliday Street Theatre in Baltimore. He developed as any young actor of that time, playing roles in various stock companies, including Richmond, Virginia, where he worked with John Wilkes Booth. He played Shakespearean roles in *Romeo and Juliet*, *Macbeth*, and *Richard III*, and enacted Antony to Edwin Booth's Brutus in *Julius Caesar*.[15] Byron progressed to leading men's roles in Pittsburgh and New Orleans before moving to Wallack's Theatre in New York.

In 1869 Byron married Kate Crehan, a rising actress whose stage name was Kate O'Neil, and their marriage created a formidable acting team. Kate's younger sister was Ada Rehan, who started her career working in *Across the Continent* and eventually became a prominent New York actress, more famous than either her sister or brother-in-law.[16]

Figure 1. Advertising card for Kate Byron and Oliver Doud Byron, the stars of *Across the Continent*.

The newly wed Byrons cast about for an acting vehicle, and they discovered an unremarkable play by James McCloskey. McCloskey, born in Montreal on August 10, 1825, had pursued dreams of gold to California in 1849, where he began his theatrical career. He returned to the East to manage the Park Theatre in Brooklyn, a position he held when he wrote a play entitled *New York in 1837; or, The Overland Route*. He tried it out, but it was so unsuccessful that he sold it outright to Byron in 1870. That spring Byron tested the play in Toronto, Montreal, and Quebec. Then he reworked the piece and opened the revised version at the Trimble Opera House in Albany on September 12, 1870, before taking it to Brooklyn for its fateful Thanksgiving engagement.

With the production an established hit, the Byrons' financial future was secure. They bought a house at Long Branch, New Jersey, a popular seaside resort for summering theatre celebrities, and there Byron displayed souvenirs of his travels, including cowboy gear and Native American art.

Popularity and financial security, however, did not sway critics. In fact, the more popular Byron became, the more disparagingly commentators wrote of him. Byron realized that the frontier setting of the last act accounted for the spectacular success of *Across the Continent*. Consequently, he produced several other plays with a western milieu, all of which emphasized attacks and artillery. In 1873 he brought to New York *Ben McCullough; or, The Wanderer's Return* in which Kate Byron played Maude McCullough, whose honest California trapper husband is sent to jail on perjured testimony. The guilty party is Percy Burton, who abducts Maude while Ben is in jail. Maude escapes and arrives home to meet her weary husband, while Percy is apprehended for his crimes.[17] The plot is that of a typical melodrama, with little apparent reason for its being set in California.

The *New York Sun* (September 18, 1873) described the spectacular elements of the production:

> At the end of each of the five lurid acts the curtain goes down over a scene of destruction. The talented young tragedian snuffs out the human candle with neat and vociferous dispatch. The only limit to his homicide being the range of his battery and the celerity of the ordnance officer in bringing up the ammunition train. This is above all a play of gore and roar.

The *New York Herald* reviewer (January 13, 1874) proved even less kind, and the harsh language confirms Levine's distinction between "highbrow" and "lowbrow" art. To begin, the critic distinguished between high art and low art, allowing, "There must be a Bowery as well as a Booth's, and we have no inclination to sneer at the thousands of orderly and decent people who can find an evening's entertainment outside of Shakespeare and the legitimate." That sop of respect for what the reviewer obviously regarded as lower-class taste quickly evaporated. In the spirit of disseminating truth to protect "honest feeling and correct taste," the writer lambasted Byron's new piece. The writer, clearly exasperated with the playgoing public, noted that unnamed reviewers – no doubt including the writer of the review – became discouraged because they kept telling people not to attend and yet the stirring melodrama continued to attract huge audiences. In other words, he blamed the public for supporting the unworthy. Still, the wearied critic trudged on with his reviewer's duty because "when a bad thing is popular it is always well that there should be a habitual public protest against it." Or at least, apparently, a critical protest.

Then the reviewer arrived at the heart of the attack, taking Byron to task first:

> Mr. Byron is a bad actor, so bad that we do not believe he could obtain a permanent situation in any first class New York theatre. And *Ben McCullough* is a bad play, so bad that it could not possibly be enjoyed by an audience capable of appreciating a fine dramatic effort.

The class consciousness and the prescriptive circularity of the reasoning are both evident: if you appreciate good drama, you should not enjoy *Ben McCullough*.

Finally, throwing aside all attempts at control, the reviewer allowed all his anger and venom to cascade forth, castigating the play and ridiculing both the performers who acted it and the audience who supported it:

> *Ben McCullough* is bad, less because of any directly immoral element possessed by it, than because the intellect which constructed it . . . was not capable of imitating the coherence of life and nature, and because sentiments and actions, meant to be heroic, are described in language that is pinchbeck from end to end. We prefer treating the theme seriously to dismissing it with the shrug and the raised eyebrow to which the Buffalo Bill drama is usually treated when it comes up for critical mention.
>
> There is a large class of people who are amused by this kind of play. They come in family groups and hang with breathless interest upon the adventures of hero and heroine . . . But it is well that the true place of actor and play should be recognized and pointed out. Mr. Byron is a young man with an excellent set of teeth and a bad set of plays.
>
> All of these plays are bad in an intellectual sense, and some of them are bad in a moral sense. They no more come within the sphere of true dramatic art than the picture of a pound cake on the door of a Broadway stage comes within the sphere of the art of painting.
>
> We are sorry that a young man who time and patience might make a useful stock actor should be thought by so many people to be a great performer; but it is pleasant to reflect that the people who think him so are not those who leave a lasting influence upon the age or mould the opinions of a generation to come.

Thus the reviewer indicted the play, the performer, and the audience, finally retiring with the notion that critical opinion would be more influential and lasting than the despised frontier plays themselves.

Just a week later, in reviewing *Across the Continent*, the *Herald* critic took up the cudgels again (January 20, 1874):

> What crime have Mr. O. D. Byron and the ladies and gentlemen who at Wood's Museum assist him committed? Probably none. We do not for a moment believe that they are aware of the intellectual enormities they are committing in appearing night after night in plays which do not approach a truthful representation of anything in real life and which are mixed up with so much trash, buncomb, spread-eagleism, morbidity, mock-heroics and coarseness that none but a strong and uneducated palate could relish the compound . . .
>
> [T]he people who admire Mr. Byron as an actor are not remarkable for intellectual culture or fineness of sensibility . . . We should not spend so much time as we have done over Mr. Byron and his plays were it not

for the fact that so large a quantity of ignorant youths and ingenuous country cousins have been fascinated by them and receive them as truthful interpretations of moral heroism and border life.

What was it that so nettled this critic? Was it that Byron was a bad actor? If read carefully, even these poisoned denunciations hardly criticize the power of his performance. Was it that the play was "trash" and "buncomb," full of chauvinistic "mock-heroics" with "all probability outraged and coherency despised"? Surely if Byron's productions had *failed* the writer would not have lavished so much ink on them. The source of this reviewer's anger can be found in a comment from the *New York Clipper* (December 31, 1870), which reported that the crowds for *Across the Continent* in Philadelphia were so large they reduced the attendance for Edwin Booth, who was playing in the city at the same time. The phrases "a large class of people," and "so large a quantity" jump out from the *Herald* reviews. What rankles this critic is that "so many people" loved the frontier plays at the expense of the worthy drama. Furthermore, despite the slurs on Byron's audience as non-intellectual and unrefined, if the *Clipper* comment is accurate then Byron's "ignorant" fans were exactly the same patrons who would otherwise have been boosting the attendance at Booth's Shakespearean productions. Instead, despite insults, they voted with their feet for the frontier drama.

Byron's productions could hardly be labeled complex or contradictory. They were straightforward, flag-waving testaments to the westward movement with even the title, *Across the Continent*, preaching the dominance and the rightness of "manifest destiny." For his part, Byron ignored the critics. He played *Across the Continent* mixed with other works for thirty years. The play even achieved some success in England, which proved to be fertile ground for this and other frontier melodramas. While Byron was performing the play that first summer in 1871 at Niblo's, a production starring child actress Kate Logan as Delores opened at the Royal Alfred Theatre in London on July 8. The play also appeared in London in 1875, 1876, and 1882.

O. D. and Kate Byron eventually retired not because of any decline in interest in their frontier melodramas, but rather because Byron tired of fighting the Syndicate, which controlled touring theatre in the late 1800s. He died on October 22, 1920, and Kate followed him two months later, leaving behind a son, Arthur, who starred as a leading man with Maude Adams and Ethel Barrymore, and succeeded in achieving the critical respect that had eluded his father.

As for McCloskey, he wrote several additional plays, from temperance drama to border heroics, before his death in 1913. In 1881, he wrote a second extremely popular frontier melodrama, *Jesse James, the Bandit King*, which James H. Wallick toured for over ten years. Other frontier plays included *The Far West; or, The Bounding Fawn* (1870), *Poverty Flat; or, California in '49* (1873), *Over the Plains* (1874), and *Across the Rockies* (1903), none of which rivaled the success of the play he sold to Byron.

Horizon

At exactly the same time that galleries were cheering *Across the Continent*, another frontier play opened to stir the emotions of its audience. *Horizon* was written by Augustin Daly, who became one of the most influential practitioners in American theatre, authoring plays, managing theatres, and producing major dramatic works. *Horizon* was a much more sophisticated presentation than *Across the Continent*, with a complex, Bret Harte-inspired hero, distinctive scenic elaboration, and nuggets of clever satire and social comment. Nevertheless, critics dismissed the basic subject matter of the West as beneath the concern of refined audiences.

Daly was born in North Carolina on July 20, 1838, but he moved to New York with his mother and grew up around the theatres of the city. By 1871 Daly was a rising star. As a playwright he had enjoyed instant success four years earlier, in 1867, with the spectacular melodrama *Under the Gaslight*. That play contained the classic scene in which the heroine rescued a man tied to railroad tracks just as a huge locomotive was about to dissect him. A year later, in *A Flash of Lightning* (1868), Daly arranged for a ship to explode and burn on stage, and the same year in *The Red Scarf* he created another classic moment when his hero was stranded at a sawmill bound to a log about to be sawn in half. These striking actions typify Daly's interest in spectacularly realistic scenic effects.

In *Horizon* Daly put his abilities to work in the area of frontier drama, and the result was another successful step in his young career. In composing *Horizon* Daly was influenced by recurrent reports of warfare in the West. Kit Carson and his soldiers had overwhelmed Navajo resistance in the Southwest, the 1865–68 Black Hawk War with the Utes had just concluded, and there were ongoing tensions with the Sioux in the North. As a result, Daly copyrighted his script as "a play of contemporaneous events upon the borders of civilization."

Daly may also have been influenced by Lotta Crabtree and her production of Edmund Falconer's *Heartsease*, in which Lotta appeared as May Wylderose. Lotta, who grew up in California in the 1850s, won the hearts of audiences with her spirited dancing, singing, and banjo plucking. Constance Rourke identifies similarities between Lotta's early difficult life in California and that of Med, Daly's heroine in *Horizon*, as well as between Daly's play and the plot of *Heartsease*.[18] In Falconer's melodrama, May, a genteel English girl transplanted to the West by an unstable father, proves her mettle by operating a camp store and foiling the villains' plans to steal a miner's gold. Lotta first performed *Heartsease* in Boston in May 1870, and she followed with a six-week New York run at Niblo's Garden and two years of touring.

Although Daly managed New York's Fifth Avenue Theatre, he opened *Horizon* at the Olympic Theatre, whose manager, John Duff, was his father-in-law. *Horizon* debuted March 21, 1871, and its opening exemplifies differences between nineteenth- and twentieth-century theatre practice. The performance began at eight-thirty, half an hour late. Complications with the scenery led to four lengthy intermissions, and the first night did not end until a quarter to one.

Like *Across the Continent*, *Horizon* begins in the East and then moves west.[19] Act I takes place in the New York drawing room of Mrs. Van Dorp, whose husband abandoned her fourteen years earlier, taking their only daughter with him to the West. Now Mrs. Van Dorp's adopted son, Allyn, is about to depart for army service on the frontier. Leaving with him is Sundown Rowse, a talkative lobbyist who wants to inspect land grants he has acquired for railroad development. Accompanying Sundown is his daughter, Columbia, and Mr. Smithe, an English fop. In Act II the audience is introduced to Rogue's Rest, a small western town on the Missouri River, where the vigilance committee is expelling five undesirable inhabitants, a situation that echoes the beginning of Harte's "The Outcasts of Poker Flat."[20] The five miscreants include John Loder, a gambler; the Indian Wannamucka; a Chinese; and Wolf Van Dorp and his daughter Med. Van Dorp, half-crazed with liquor, defies the vigilantes and is killed, consigning the care of his beautiful daughter, Med, to Loder.

Everyone adores the lovely and virtuous Med. Wannamucka has deserted his tribe in his infatuation for her, and Loder, too, loves her as more than a guardian. When the visitors from the East arrive, Allyn Van Dorp also immediately falls under Med's spell without realizing she is his mother's natural daughter. Sundown Rowse, meanwhile, tries unsuccessfully to explain to the citizens that he owns their town, while they, guns in hand, escort him out of it. Act III consists of three scenes, the first of which is set on the bank of a river near the fort as a flatboat prepares to head toward new settlements. Loder wants to take Med back to New York, but Meddie wants to stay with him in the West. Loder is torn. Although he loves her, he knows that she would be better off with Allyn than with a man of his vices. The second and third scenes disclose a dense wood and a dark night, with the army patrolling along the river while a band of Indians led by Wannamucka attack the boat, forcing the travelers to escape to the safety of the fort. In Act IV, two days later, while the soldiers are out looking for the renegades, Wannamucka's band attacks and captures the women. The final act reveals Wannamucka's camp, where, at the climax, Loder arrives, shoots Wannamucka, revives Med, and then gives her hand to Allyn Van Dorp.

In addition to the obvious melodrama, Daly's writing also contained its share of wit. Columbia Rowse, for instance, makes a comment on "prominent men" that seems as appropriate to the twenty-first century as it was to the nineteenth: "Prominent men are not at all pleasant. You think they are great things 'til you know them. When you find them out, there's nothing particular about them, except that they are prominent."[21]

Daly also provided mild social commentary when it suited his comic purposes. The vigilance committee expels Loder because he gambles and the Chinese laborer because he works for half pay, provoking Mr. Smithe to comment on the irony: "You condemn one fellow because he don't work, and another because he does."[22]

With Loder, Daly took advantage of the roughness of the West to create a definitive frontier character similar to Harte's John Oakhurst. Loder, like the frontier drama itself, presents a maze of contradictions. As with many of Harte's creations, Loder is both romantic and anti-romantic, both good and bad. Frontier writers quickly learned that a hero could have rough edges and still be decent, and Daly discovered with Loder that western characters could lack social graces, could gamble or drink or swear or worse, and could still possess at their core a firm and noble foundation. Thus, Loder, a bum and a gambler with a heart of gold, presents a romantic version of the doctor in John Ford's epic film *Stagecoach* or the sanitized Maverick brothers from a television series and movie made a hundred years after Daly's play. Like many frontier heroes to follow, from Palladin to the Man With No Name, Loder is a loner, moving relentlessly from place to place. He defines himself as a traveler, rhapsodizing almost philosophically: "My business is to leave. I'm an outpost of progress! I open up the great West to the march of the mind. When things get settled about me, I go on!"[23] In *Horizon* the complex Loder is the staunch western hero, but the girl goes conventionally to the cultivated gentleman.

Combining a central love story with sensational attacks, *Horizon* located a midpoint between action and sentiment. Daly invented both positive and negative romantic situations. Burl Donald Grose in his study of the portrayal of Native Americans on stage identifies Wannamucka as "the first fully-developed stage Indian with an overpowering lust for a White Woman."[24] Daly could, however, just as easily mock romantic, "child of nature" notions. Sundown, played by noted comedian George L. Fox, takes cheap jewelry to the West intending to trade it for valuable furs, but Wannamucka, wise to the white man's world, pulls out a deck of cards and suggests they play poker for them instead.

Still, the success of the play lay in its melodramatic action and its scenic elaboration, which forced the opening-night delays. The Act I drawing room received its share of praise, but as with *Across the Continent*, *Horizon* only became special when the action moved west and, in the words of the *New York Sun* (March 22, 1871), introduced the "graphic frontier scenes, the hurly-burly of the vigilance committee, the pistols that hang in every man's girdle and are thrust into every man's face, the glimpses of wild Indian life and character, the flatboat scene on the Missouri, and the night surprise of a fort by the redskins." The Act II set for Rogue's Rest presented a hotel with a portico and a usable second story. Across the stage stood a building that housed the newspaper, "The Clarion of the West," on the top floor, and the Pacific Express office below. Loder's shanty occupied a corner of the set.

The Act III scene along the river particularly impressed audiences. As the flatboat departed, a moving diorama exposed western scenery passing by as the fort slipped into the distance. Reviewers also praised the Act V encampment, which exhibited Daly's scenic inventiveness. The Indian encampment sat in a ravine, tucked against a hillside as soldiers patrolled and searched above and behind, a juxtaposition that increased dramatic tension.

Noted theatrical manager Albert M. Palmer declared *Horizon* the best American drama he had ever seen.[25] *Horizon* played for nearly eight weeks until mid May, but even Daly's name as the author could not squelch critics' opinions that such western plays had nothing of importance to say to sophisticated playgoers. The *New York Clipper* (April 1, 1871), anticipating the *New York Dramatic Mirror*'s comments on the pecuniary objectives of *Across the Continent*, stated, "The play has evidently been constructed with the sole view of benefiting the treasury." That statement contains unconscious irony since managers at the best theatres resisted plays on American subjects or by American authors because they viewed them as financially risky propositions. The review concluded: "[The production] has nothing to do with art, and should it succeed in attracting numerous audiences who care to be amused for the hour it will achieve the end intended." The high-brow–lowbrow mentality was once again in evidence as the critic claimed that the mere presentation of the coarse events and settings of the West was unsuitable for the genteel public. The implication was clear that the lower elements who wanted that sort of thing should go to the cheap melodramas, and, by extension, frontier melodramas should confine themselves to the inconspicuous, second-rate theatres and not contaminate the more prestigious houses.

Between them, *Across the Continent* and *Horizon* included every characteristic that contributes to a frontier play.

- *Distinctive lead characters* exhibit a combination of naivete and bravery with a good heart and a streak of independence that causes them to violate social norms. Many, like Loder, mix positive and negative traits.
- *Characters represent different ethnic backgrounds* from those found in eastern settings. Indians, Chinese, Spanish, and Mexicans people the landscape, but often with comic or highly negative caricatures.
- *Characters dress in frontier attire* displaying long hair, coonskin or ten-gallon hats, fringed jackets, high boots, miners' red shirts, or native influences such as feathers, bead work, or moccasins. As Ferris discards his eastern suits for mountain garb, he pictorially transforms himself into a western man.
- *Characters brandish frontier weaponry* including Buntline Specials, six-shooters, and Bowie knives. Indians often use bows and arrows or lances. Byron's frontier plays relied on firepower, and *Horizon* featured ubiquitous pistols.
- *Characters represent frontier occupations* such as hunting, trapping, lumbering, ranching, trading, or stagecoach driving. Loder is an archetypal frontier gambler. Gamblers, of course, could be found anywhere, but since civilization tried to drive them away – as the vigilance committee does in *Horizon* – the roving gambler like Loder became a staple on the frontier fringes of society. Ferris' position is equally complex. A stationmaster, as in *Across the Continent*, is not a specifically western job, but isolated surroundings provide a western feel.
- *Characters use idiomatic border language.* Daly approaches a distinctive dialect with Loder, and later authors follow the leads of Harte and Twain to create idiosyncratic dialogue. Chinese and native characters speak in stereotypical broken patterns.

- *Plays evoke primal elements* ranging from natural elements such as wild animals, difficult terrain, or extreme weather to factors of otherness represented by Native Americans.
- *Plays include rudimentary social institutions* including vigilance committees, as in *Horizon*, town meetings, and trials. Settings often depict a lonely outpost such as the train station in *Across the Continent* or the fort in *Horizon* connected tenuously to the eastern civilization. Other early signs of social organization are a teacher, a newspaper office (like "The Clarion" in *Horizon*), or a telegraph, as in *Across the Continent*.
- *Plays utilize special modes of transportation* such as the stagecoach or the wagon train. Although horses and trains were common in the East as well as the West, the centrality of the horse to western travel and the importance of the railroad in covering vast distances give them unique significance. *Across the Continent*, of course, employed a train, while *Horizon* used a primitive keelboat. As a corollary to the type of transportation, frontier characters often exhibit a restlessness and freedom of movement that propels them from place to place. Like Loder, they are travelers.
- *Plays emphasize the importance of the land*, which might be accomplished through descriptive language from the characters or scenically, as Daly did with the moving panorama and the levels of staging.
- *Plays redefine traditional melodramatic devices with characteristic frontier twists*. Both *Across the Continent* and *Horizon* use the capture–pursuit–rescue cycle. The fact that the captors are western aboriginals – savages to the audience's mind – augments the danger and leads to climactic resolutions. The relative isolation of western outposts enhances the plausibility of disguises and long-lost relatives common to many of the plays.

Kit, the Arkansas Traveller

Just as *Horizon* opened at New York's Olympic Theatre while *Across the Continent* was still playing at Wood's Theatre, so, even before *Horizon* had run its course, another frontier drama emerged as a major hit despite the fact that it contained few of the characteristics associated with the genre. This one, *Kit, the Arkansas Traveller*, featured Francis S. Chanfrau, an actor who was already prominent. In February 1848, at Mitchell's Olympic Theatre, Chanfrau befriended a colleague by acting in a benefit performance for prompter Ben A. Baker, who wrote a little sketch for the occasion.[26] The piece, entitled *A Glance at New York*, featured Mose the Bowery B'hoy, a tough Bowery fireman who became an instantaneous success, and over the next few years Chanfrau acted in a dozen different plays featuring Mose.[27] Although modeled on an actual firefighter, Mose took on the epic proportions of a folk hero, a Paul Bunyan of the cities who could fight fires, tell jokes, sing songs, and love girls – all with an endearing swagger.[28] Along with the Indian, the backwoodsman, and the northeastern Yankee character, Mose represents one of the first distinctive American dramatic types.

Over twenty years later Chanfrau created yet another distinctive American character in the persona of Kit Redding. Chanfrau first performed Kit on April 20, 1869, in Buffalo, New York. As with many plays of the time, the precise authorship of the piece was unclear, but apparently Edward Spencer wrote the play for Chanfrau in 1868 and sold it to him for $300 under the title *Down the Mississippi*.[29] Chanfrau hired Thomas B. DeWalden to alter the script, and the play opened in Buffalo as *Kit, the Arkansas Traveller*, a title Chanfrau himself selected.[30] It was not a success, so Chanfrau asked Clifton W. Tayleure, a friend, a theatrical manager, and the author of the sentimental hit *East Lynne*, to revise the play once more, emphasizing its humor. At its New York debut both DeWalden and Spencer were credited, and subsequently Spencer or Spencer and Tayleure usually received authorship credit.[31]

The revised version proved a hit, and in May 1871, Chanfrau brought the play to Niblo's Garden Theatre in New York. The play begins with a prologue set in 1858, in which the scoundrel Manuel Bond kidnaps the wife and daughter of Kit Redding, an Arkansas farmer.[32] Act I takes place twelve years later in the barroom of a St. Louis hotel. Kit has amassed a fortune even though he drinks to excess to forget the loss of his wife and child. He enters the barroom intoxicated and encounters Bond, now known as Hastings, and both men book passage down river on the steamer *Medora*. Act II switches to the saloon of the steamship where Kit sees his daughter, Alice, now a beautiful young woman of twenty, who, as Netty Ashton, accompanies Bond. Although it seems obvious, Kit does not recognize his daughter. In the highlight of the act, Bond tries to cheat Kit at poker by taking a card under the table from an accomplice, but Kit intercepts the card and passes on one of his own, a trick that elicited extravagant praise. It was, said one *Clipper* reviewer (June 10, 1871), "one of the most effective and ingenious devices that we have ever witnessed. It is nightly received with lavish applause." Thus the card game became a significant part of border drama, and several important frontier plays exploited clever card games for dramatic effect. Act III moves to the deck of the *Medora*, and, in the sentimental climax of the play, Kit's daughter recognizes him. Just as their happiness seems assured, Hastings sets fire to the steamship and it explodes. The final act features a chase along the river bank, where, after a vicious Bowie knife struggle, Kit kills Bond, and father and daughter are joyfully reunited.

Figure 2. Francis S. Chanfrau in the title role of *Kit, the Arkansas Traveller.*

Like *Across the Continent* and *Horizon*, *Kit* found enormous success, playing almost five weeks at Niblo's in its initial New York season. Critics recognized Chanfrau's portrayal of Kit Redding as an extraordinary characterization, as exemplified in the *New York Clipper* (May 20, 1871):

> Mr. Chanfrau's impersonation of Kit is a great piece of acting . . . The drunken scenes were naturally acted, and not overdrawn or exaggerated as is too often the case in stage representations.

The reviewer had particular praise for the recognition scene on the deck of the ship:

> In the touching scene upon the hurricane deck of the *Medora*, where he enters into conversation with his daughter, he displayed a depth of tender feeling and true pathos in describing scenes which occurred in his childhood which visibly affected the audience. And when the cloud was raised from the child's mind and she recognized her father and was folded in his arms there burst forth from the audience a torrent of applause which was long continued.

Not everyone, however, loved Chanfrau in his new role. The critic for the *New York Sun* (May 10, 1871) cast a dissenting vote:

> The character of Kit is utterly unfitted to Mr. Chanfrau's school of acting. The characters in which he reigns predominant are of the school of light comedy and Kit is anything but a comedy character . . . Mr. Chanfrau acts it precisely as a schoolboy recites a lesson which has been beaten into him. His business is all correct, painfully so at times, but if we except the Bowie knife fight at the conclusion, he seems to have no soul in the matter.

Chanfrau continued to tinker with the play even after it opened. *Clipper* accounts (May 3 and May 10, 1871) refer to changes in action and lines that streamlined the play and to the introduction of a free-for-all at the hotel.

Although Chanfrau as Kit Redding and the exciting and sentimental actions of the drama were the most prominent features of *The Arkansas Traveller*, the performance had other advantages as well. The excellent cast included, as the eight-year-old child kidnapped in the prologue, Minnie Maddern, who later, as Minnie Maddern Fiske, became one of the leading actresses of the American theatre; and Charles T. Parsloe, who eventually gained notoriety as the definitive comic stage Chinaman.

The scenic units designed by William Voegtlin provided another strength of the production. For most plays of the nineteenth century little remains of the set but a few passing references in reviews and perhaps a poster or advertising card. But when Chanfrau played New York's Booth's Theatre at the holiday season of 1873–74, a conscientious stagehand made meticulous notes and floor plans.[33] He noted the steamer working off at the end of Act I. He made a diagram of the complicated "Saloon" set of Act II and the hurricane deck of Act III with a moving panorama of the Mississippi River. He also sketched the final act with four water ground rows and a steamboat, which moved on stage as though floating through the water.

The attention to the scenery did not go unnoticed. The *Clipper* (May 20, 1871), while criticizing the depiction of the hotel, praised the scenes aboard the ship:

> The scenes representing steamboat life upon the Mississippi River were excellent . . . The explosion of the *Medora* was most effectively managed and was very realistic. The immense volumes of smoke and flame which burst from various parts of the stage was [sic] most artistically effected.

Within months, Chanfrau's performance of the Arkansas farmer became an established part of American theatrical tradition. A San Francisco critic, writing of a production at the California Theatre in October 1871, labeled it, "the best drama of American life on stage." In New York the following year the play drew "some of the largest audiences ever assembled in the auditorium at Wood's Theatre." That review praised the "super-excellence" of Chanfrau's "masterly and artistic" performance, especially its "manliness and brusqueness of address."[34]

Although Chanfrau and the play occasionally received criticism, the biting antagonism applied to Byron and his frontier plays was absent. The difference lay in the lead actor. While Byron had worked at Wallack's, he was regarded as an upstart, not an established New York actor. Chanfrau, on the other hand, was a native New Yorker, a popular local boy who had already established himself as a legend with his depiction of Mose. When patrons bought *Kit*, they also bought Chanfrau, the local hero and New York icon. He might be subject to criticism, but never to ridicule.

Chanfrau made from $450 to almost $1,000 per week performing *The Arkansas Traveller*. With that, he, like Byron, purchased a comfortable living, summering at Long Branch. Chanfrau was still playing Kit when he was stricken on October 1, 1884, at the Academy of Music in Jersey City, New Jersey. He died the next day at the age of sixty-three, and his good friend and neighbor O. D. Byron served as a pallbearer. Even after Chanfrau's death his name remained associated with the part of Kit

Redding, for Chanfrau's son Henry took over the part and continued performing *The Arkansas Traveller* into the mid 1890s.

In many respects *The Arkansas Traveller* fails to meet the requirements of a border play. Kit is hardly a frontiersman. He's a farmer in Arkansas and goes into meat-packing in Kentucky. The settings, in addition to his farm, are a hotel in St. Louis and a riverboat. Spencer's original title, after all, was *Down the Mississippi*. Still, critics and patrons clearly perceived *Kit* as a frontier play. One reviewer spoke of the scenes "of frontier life," and another remarked on the similarity of Kit to Bret Harte's characters. Yet another referred to Kit as "the South-westerner, the man of the Missouri and the Mississippi."[35] Only a few elements justify such a conclusion. Kit is certainly a rural man who exercises freedom of movement. Although flawed by his drinking, he is good-hearted and persistent in his pursuit of his wife and child. His foe is a gambler – a sort of evil John Loder – and Kit cleverly outgambles the gambler. Kit is also skilled with his rifle, and, at the climax, wields a Bowie knife to defeat his nemesis. Chanfrau also accentuated the border quality of the character by adapting a distinctive dialect. These qualities no doubt contributed to the "manliness" cited by the *Clipper* reviewer. Still, while *Across the Continent* and *Horizon* portray obvious western incidents, *Kit* resides near the border of border drama.

With *Across the Continent, Horizon,* and *Kit, the Arkansas Traveller* all achieving popular success in New York within the span of a few weeks, frontier drama received an extraordinary boost. But that was just the beginning. The next two theatrical seasons saw a dramatization based on the heroic Davy Crockett with a notable performance by Frank Mayo and numerous stage versions of the exploits of the contemporary hero William F. "Buffalo Bill" Cody played by several stage actors and, ultimately, by Cody himself.

2

Explosion: 1872–1876

Such a combination of incongruous drama, execrable acting, renowned performers, mixed audience, intolerable stench, scalping, blood and thunder, is
not likely to be vouchsafed to a city a second time, even Chicago.

The *Chicago Times* review of *The Scouts of the Prairie*, starring William F.
"Buffalo Bill" Cody, in December 1872

WITH THE DEBUTS OF *ACROSS THE CONTINENT*, *HORIZON*, AND
The Arkansas Traveller, frontier drama emerged in 1870–71 as a major force
in American theatre. The next five theatrical seasons saw a veritable explosion of the form as performers hopped aboard the train to the dramatic
frontier. The growth of frontier drama is especially remarkable because it
occurred even as the theatrical community and the country suffered through
the depression of 1873 and the terrible dislocations that followed. Other
events in the mid 1870s, however, promoted frontier drama. Warfare in the
Southwest, on the west coast, and in the northern plains filled the daily
papers and created instant border heroes. Buffalo Bill, George Custer,
Sitting Bull, and Wild Bill Hickok are among the better-known contemporary frontier figures who were central characters in plays during this
period. Other dramas reached back to historical heroes Davy Crockett and
Daniel Boone. Lesser-known dramatic subjects included the Modoc
warrior Captain Jack, United States Army scout Donald MacKay, and
scouts Charlie Emmett and "Texas Jack" Omohundro. Actors battled for
the rights to plays about these men and fought for parts in which they could
be identified with the heroes of the West.

Two men emerged in very different ways during this period as major
factors in American theatre. Frank Mayo developed through a conventional
dramatic apprenticeship until he burst forth as Davy Crockett in the part

that defined his theatrical career. The second individual was not really a man of the theatre at all. William F. "Buffalo Bill" Cody was an industrious and gregarious scout and guide who stood at the center of a fortuitous sequence of events, and, with his charismatic presence, took full advantage of being in the right place at the right time. The two men represent polar directions for frontier drama and different models for the masculine border hero. Cody's plays constructed a wild, action-packed present loaded with gunfire and hostile natives. Mayo's play, on the other hand, depicted a sentimental and romantic past laden with poetic overtones.

Buffalo Bill

The Buffalo Bill craze began inauspiciously as a serial story in *New York Weekly* in December 1869, entitled *Buffalo Bill, King of the Border Men*. The author, Edward Zane Carroll Judson, better known as Ned Buntline, had met "Buffalo Bill" Cody earlier that year. Cody had some legitimate claim to his representation as a rough-and-tumble hero. William Frederick Cody was born in Iowa in 1846, but the family soon moved to Kansas, where his father, Isaac Cody, served as a member of the Topeka legislature and worked to make the territory a free – that is, non-slavery – state.[1] Isaac died in 1857 while William was still a boy. After that, William drove an ox team, an occupation termed "bull-whacking," to earn money for the family. Eventually, he took a job as a rider, delivering messages for a telegraph office, then hired on as a driver on a wagon train. During his time with the train, Cody became friends with James B. "Wild Bill" Hickok, found himself in the middle of the so-called Mormon War in Utah, and fought in battles with Indians – all before he was much more than twelve years old.[2] Short stints as a trapper and an unsuccessful prospector followed, but when the Civil War erupted, Cody joined an unofficial militia whose anti-slavery activities, sometimes bordering on vigilante violence, were termed "jayhawking." After he turned eighteen in 1864, Cody enlisted in the Seventh Kansas Cavalry of the Union Army, and, in the next year and a half, he scouted and fought in Tennessee, Arkansas, Mississippi, Missouri, and Kansas.

With the war over, Cody married and tried his hand at running a hotel. When that failed, he signed on as a civilian scout for the army, at one time working with George Custer. Scouts not only performed reconnaissance but also carried messages and acted as guides. They could also of course, be involved in fighting. After the birth of his daughter, Arta, in 1866, Cody again tried to settle down, but in 1867, after his real estate speculation faltered, a railroad company hired him to provide meat for their construction teams. He was contracted to kill twelve buffalo a day, for which he received $500 a month, and his efficient killing of thousands of buffalo established his nickname.[3]

When the railroad work ended, Cody rejoined the army as a civilian scout, this time under Generals Philip H. Sheridan and Eugene A. Carr. Sheridan became one of Cody's most conspicuous boosters. The general placed Cody on the army payroll at a premium wage in 1868, and the next year Cody played an instrumental role in the Battle of Summit Springs, an army attack upon a group of natives accused of raiding settlements and stealing horses. During the raid, which was later featured in Cody's Wild West shows, a captive woman was rescued while a second died in the attack. Sheridan repaid Cody by arranging for him to guide hunting expeditions for prominent visitors to the West in 1871 and 1872.

Not long after Cody's heroics at Summit Springs he met Ned Buntline. Buntline had lived what might charitably be called a checkered life.[4] During the Seminole War in the late 1830s he served as a midshipman in the navy, resigning his commission in 1842. A literary journal he began in 1844 was bankrupt by 1845. A year later he was almost lynched after he killed a jealous husband in a duel. Altogether, in 1849 alone, Buntline was sued for divorce by his wife, Annie Bennett; for slander by the *New York Herald* owner, James Gordon Bennett; and for fraud by a man who had provisioned Buntline's yacht. At the same time, Buntline was sentenced to a year in jail for instigating the infamous Astor Place Riot in which supporters of American actor Edwin Forrest tried to prevent the performances of English actor William Charles Macready. After his release from Blackwell's Island, Buntline went to St. Louis, where, as an organizer for the American Party (or "Know-Nothing" party, as it was called), Buntline provoked violence against German immigrants before he was indicted for his activities and fled Missouri. Soon after, his next wife sued Buntline for bigamy, and authorities in Maine arrested him for the unprovoked shooting of a black man. During the Civil War Buntline enlisted as a member of a New York rifle unit, but was jailed for desertion before his discharge. As late as 1881 and 1884, Buntline was again accused of bigamy in cases involving three additional women.

Judson's "Buntline" pseudonym arose from his writing, which enjoyed some success. He started, ended, and restarted various magazine and dime novel publications before he finally established himself with his exaggerated accounts of derring-do in the West. And, of course, he invented the unique, long-barreled .45 caliber Colt six-guns, designed to function as a handgun and a short rifle, which were called "Buntline Specials."

Buntline published his serialized version of Cody's adventures in 1869, with little immediate result. Cody continued as an army scout and a guide for hunting parties. At that time, the American West was a huntsman's paradise, and wealthy eastern nabobs joined aristocratic English gentry for what amounted to nineteenth-century American safaris as they hunted bear, elk, and buffalo. These sporting huntsmen included such influential individuals as the future Earl of Dunraven, who became the British undersecretary for the colonies; James Gordon Bennett, owner and editor of the *New York Herald*; Charles L. Wilson, editor of the *Chicago Evening Journal*; and, most significantly, the Grand Duke Alexis, third son of Czar Alexander II. In 1871 and 1872 Cody served as guide and teacher for the visiting dignitaries and lined up entertainments such as races and native dances.

In theatrical terms, the Buffalo Bill craze began on February 19, 1872, at the Bowery Theatre in New York, when John B. Studley starred as Buffalo Bill in *Buffalo Bill, King of the Bordermen* by Fred G. Maeder based on the 1869 Buntline story. Studley, a popular actor, had appeared recently in two of Augustin Daly's productions, enacting the important role of Byke, a Bill Sykes clone, in *Under the Gaslight*, and playing Wolf Van Dorp, the drunken father, in Daly's *Horizon* the previous season. Now he originated the part of Buffalo Bill and played it for four weeks. The production created a sensation. A prior engagement forced Studley to leave the role after a month, but William H. Whalley continued it for another two weeks. Before that run had even closed, J. W. Carroll impersonated Buffalo Bill in the same Maeder play at the Park Theatre in Brooklyn, and Hooley's Opera House in Brooklyn presented a burlesque version called *Bill Buffalo, His Great Buffalo Bull*.

The loosely constructed play began in 1861 as the villain, Jake McKandlass, supported by other pro-slavery ranchers, shot Bill's father.[5] In the main action of some twenty years later, Bill sought revenge. The play provided ample opportunity for yelling, screaming, and gunfire. It also featured a Bowie knife fight – a nearly mandatory component of frontier plays – and a prairie fire. Each act ended with exciting action and "red fire," a nineteenth-century special effect that burned with a reddish glow.

Maeder's play demonstrates how a writer could employ actual frontier incidents as the germ for a play but then wrench those incidents into an unrecognizable conglomeration. Historically, David Colbert McCanles (often spelled McKandlas or McKandlass) and two other men were killed in a controversial gunfight at Rock Creek, Nebraska, July 12, 1861.[6] Widely distributed accounts claimed that ten or more ruffians were slain by a heroic frontiersman with just six bullets and a knife. But the man charged with murder in that incident and found to have acted in self-defense was not Buffalo Bill at all but Wild Bill Hickok. Buntline and Maeder had simply lifted a name from the Wild Bill legend and adapted it to Buffalo Bill instead.

Reviews praised Studley for his "bold, vigorous impersonation of Buffalo Bill," which the *New York Clipper* (March 2, 1872) found "powerful, yet natural."[7] Critics invariably commented on the popularity of the piece, with the *Clipper* noting that "every seat and all available standing room [was] occupied whilst numbers were turned from the doors." "The drama," the review concluded, "may be pronounced the hit of the season," and later an advertisement for the Bowery declared the play "the greatest hit in the Bowery since 1845," the year the structure in place at that time was erected.

The enthusiastic response to the Buffalo Bill material demonstrates how factors completely unrelated to the quality of the production influenced critics, for Buffalo Bill enjoyed unusual connections with the rich and famous. His associations with Bennett and the grand duke had received elaborate, timely coverage; Alexis' western hunt had taken place just a month before the play premiered. Furthermore, the premiere coincided with Buffalo Bill's first visit to New York, where he was received like a modern Hollywood celebrity at a Senate hearing. He attended the opening night of Studley's performance as a guest of honor and addressed the packed audience. Although the Bowery was generally regarded as a theatre for the lower classes, citizens of all stripes turned out for Buffalo Bill. Despite lucrative offers to portray himself on the stage, Cody returned to the frontier, leaving behind him an ardent following that included Bennett's upper-crust friends.

Meanwhile, Buntline latched on to the success of Buffalo Bill as promoted by Bennett. While Buntline is often credited with creating an idol of an obscure scout, the real credit for popularizing Cody should go to Bennett, whose *Herald* accounts lionized the handsome, long-haired westerner. Buntline did not follow up his 1869 story with another Buffalo Bill tale until more than two years later, in March 1872, one month *after* the theatrical success of Studley in Maeder's play and the heralded visit of Cody to New York. Buntline rushed this second Buffalo Bill saga into print in March and followed it with a third in July. By that time, Cody had been involved in another border skirmish, and, for his gallantry in that fight, he received the Congressional Medal of Honor in May 1872. The award, of course, augmented the exploding interest in Buffalo Bill.

Although Studley had originated the part, other performers would not let him have this choice role all to himself. By early April, 1872, theatrical trade newspapers carried numerous offers from actors to appear as Buffalo Bill, as Theodore Hamilton did at the Holliday Street Theatre in Baltimore, or from managers advertising the rights to Maeder's *Buffalo Bill*, as William Lannier did for six New England states.[8] While Studley was performing Buffalo Bill in late January and early February 1873 at the Bowery, J. M. Ward enacted Buffalo Bill at Wood's Theatre. Still, Studley was the first and most frequent impersonator of the western scout – until Cody himself entered the fray.

Studley's advantage evaporated in December 1872, when Cody made his stage debut in Chicago along with Buntline and a fellow scout, John B. "Texas Jack" Omohundro. Omohundro was born in Virginia in 1846 and fought in the Civil War. He made his way via Texas to the frontier, where he became an army scout and Cody's close friend. Their first appearance occurred in a Buntline drama entitled *The Scouts of the Prairie*. Cody insisted that Buntline wrote the play in four hours, which is not as improbable as it sounds.[9] Buntline had produced *Hazel Eye, the Girl Trapper; or, The Gold Hunters*, which played the Bowery in August 1872, and he had just finished writing a serial story entitled *Buffalo Bill's Last Victory; or, Dove Eye, the Lodge Queen*, which appeared in 1873. The female characters in *The Scouts of the Prairie*, plus the reappearance of Cale Durg from *Hazel Eye*, suggest that Buntline simply cobbled a scenario based on his already prepared stories and characters. For the title he chose *The Scouts of the Prairie; or, Red Deviltry As It Is*.

The Scouts of the Prairie included a Bowie knife fight, a prairie fire, marauding Indians, evil whites, and rescue from a tribal camp.[10] Buntline, enacting Cale Durg, a fictitious scout, served as a kind of master of ceremonies, narrating the story and delivering lengthy moral homilies. In Act I the lascivious Mormon Ben sends his native friends led by Wolf Slayer to capture Durg's ward, Hazel Eye, whom Ben intends to marry. When they return with both Durg and the girl, the villains prepare to burn Durg at the stake. Dove Eye, the ubiquitous friendly native maiden, unties Hazel Eye, who frees Durg. That action precipitates a fight in which Buffalo Bill and Texas Jack vanquish the villains.

Act II virtually repeated Act I as Mormon Ben's henchmen recaptured

Figure 3. Ned Buntline, "Buffalo Bill" Cody, and "Texas Jack" Omohundro, stars of
The Scouts of the Prairie.

both women, and, once again, seized Durg. This time, while bound to a
tree, Buntline unleashed a fiery temperance lecture. Eventually Buffalo Bill
and Texas Jack once more came to the rescue, shooting and roping the
Indians. Durg, however, was killed in the melee as the curtain descended.
The third and final act reprised the action of the first two, with Buffalo Bill
and Texas Jack seeking vengeance for their friend's death. Meanwhile,

Mormon Ben and his cohorts continued their scheming to snatch Hazel Eye, and Wolf Slayer fatally knifed Big Eagle, Dove Eye's father, who questioned his bloodthirsty leadership of the tribe. The climactic battle was fought against a raging prairie fire as the Indians attempted to burn out the whites. Naturally, Buffalo Bill, Texas Jack, and Hazel Eye dispatched the attackers, and Dove Eye avenged her father's death by shooting Wolf Slayer.

The message of the production was a bloody one. The Indians – whether played by white professional actors, hired extras, or actual Pawnees as was the case with a few of the performers later in the season – were the villains. Although they were prodded to their villainy by evil whites, they were, in the end, there to be shot, and shot they were – in the three large battles that ended the three acts. Since Buffalo Bill and Texas Jack epitomized western society, their complete victory over aboriginal people signified the conquest of all that was good over the forces of evil. Thus, in the words of one astute critic, "morality is advanced through bloodshed."[11]

In addition to Buntline and the two scouts, the cast included Giuseppina Morlacchi, an Italian danseuse of considerable skill, who played Dove Eye. William S. E. Coleman credits Morlacchi, who eventually married Texas Jack, with being the first in a long line of Latins to impersonate a Native American.[12]

After a week, the production moved to St. Louis, where Cody's wife lived while Buffalo Bill was off on campaigns. From there the troupe moved through Cincinnati, Indianapolis, Louisville, Cleveland, Rochester, Buffalo, and Boston before arriving in New York in March 1873. Cody could hardly have picked a better time for publicity, for newspapers were headlining conflicts in every corner of the West. In January and February the papers featured daily wire descriptions of the Modoc War in California, illustrated with detailed maps. In addition to accounts of the Modoc War, the *New York Herald* (February 1 and 25, 1873) ran stories about the opposition of the Sioux to a railroad in Minnesota, about the "civilization" of the Navajo in New Mexico, and about the Apache War in Arizona.

The reviews of Buntline's play and the comments of the participants provide an illuminating look at this unusual production. The performance, at least at its inception, was so rough and informal that accounts stagger the imagination. According to Cody he had such a bad case of stage fright that he was unable to speak a word. Finally, Buntline began asking him questions, which prompted Cody to launch into a series of entertaining anecdotes about a hunting expedition with a prominent Chicago businessman in the audience.[13] Cody's wife, Louisa, related that, when the show played St. Louis, Cody stopped after his first entrance, turned to her, and lamented, "Oh, Mamma! I'm a bad actor. Does this look as awful out there as it feels up here?"[14]

While Cody enjoyed the patronage of the New York aristocracy, in other cities his production felt the arrows of the critics, and a class-conscious snobbery dripped from their reviews. In Boston, the audience was "the great unwashed," which "it would seem that the slums had been drained to supply."[15] Chicago writers complained of "the pestilential atmosphere redolent of every well-defined stink from a Canal Street boarding stable to the Ainsworth glue factories" and the "presence of 2,200 bad breaths and twice as many unclean feet."[16]

Reviewers who evaluated the production on an aesthetic basis castigated it. The *New York Sun* – not insignificantly a New York rival of Bennett's *Herald* – called it "a nondescript dramatic piece miscalled a play" and went on to deride the "grotesque combination of absurd elements." The review of April 1, 1873, condemned the loose plot and Buntline's "utterly stupid lectures," concluding that it was "absolutely deficient in wit, vivacity, or sense." The *Chicago Times* (December 18, 1872) wrote, "Such a combination of incongruous drama, execrable acting, renowned performers, mixed audience, intolerable stench, scalping, blood and thunder, is not likely to be vouchsafed to a city a second time, even Chicago." In Boston the *Daily Globe* reviewer (March 5, 1873) called the play "brutal, commonplace, and disgraceful," and, like the writer's Chicago counterpart, hoped the show would never see a Boston stage again:

> So painful an exhibition as that of Monday night we trust we may be spared from seeing on the stage of the Boston Theatre. The whole affair . . . was inexpressibly heart-sickening, and was sadly discreditable to the reputation of the theatre, which is no place for so miserable and so brutalizing an exhibition.

The *Boston Daily Advertiser* (March 4, 1873) mocked the play as "worse than *Across the Continent*," and, commenting on Buntline's claim to have written the play in four hours, added, "we are surprised that it should have taken him so long."

By the time the play reached New York, Buntline was declaiming not only on the evils of liquor but also on government policy on Indian affairs, concluding that extermination was God's will and the only acceptable policy. So irritating were these tirades that the *Boston Daily Globe* opined, "[his] death at the end of the second act proved one of the few really agreeable incidents of the piece."[17]

Unlike many border dramas, which emphasized striking scenic elements, *The Scouts of the Prairie* carried no scenery of its own. Since the piece was written virtually at the last minute, the production employed whatever stock flats each theatre possessed. Of a performance in Brooklyn one *Clipper* reviewer (April 15, 1873) noted that the mountain setting had recently serviced Joseph Jefferson, and Buffalo Bill and Texas Jack made their entrance "over the heights constructed for Rip Van Winkle's goblins." The writer concluded, "The scenes are laid generally among the Rocky Mountains, that is, they are arranged for the convenience of scene painters, so that a lava bed, a Yellowstone canon, or a forest of 10,000-year-old California pine traces may with equal propriety be called into use."

As with *Across the Continent*, however, another constant in accounts of the production was the size of the audience. The *Chicago Evening Journal* (December 17, 1872) reported that "not less than 2,500 boys and young men crowded the amphitheatre to catch a glimpse of their heroes." The audience in Cincinnati, wrote the *Daily Star* (December 31, 1872), was "one swelling mass of humanity, packed into a compass hardly big enough to contain their numbers," and, according to the *New York Sun* (April 1, 1873), "an immense audience which filled the house from orchestra to loftiest gallery" greeted the production at Niblo's Garden Theatre in New York.

Critics frequently praised Buffalo Bill and Texas Jack. The scouts, and especially Cody, presented a model of manliness that combined patriotism, outdoor skills, and humility with a powerful and energetic physical presence. Their unpracticed theatrical style lent charm, naivete, and self-effacing humor. A few writers showed the perspicacity to analyze the performance not solely as a dramatic presentation, but within its cultural context – the merging of actual frontier elements that had captured the public's attention with the theatrical presentation of those elements. "They are no sham," the *Chicago Times* wrote on December 19, 1872. "There they stand before you in the habiliments and trappings to which they have been long accustomed . . .They are the real attraction." In Boston, the *Evening Transcript* (March 4, 1873) said the two scouts "lend an intensity to the piece that has never been witnessed in representations of the semi-savage drama here before." In New York, the *World* (April 1, 1873) concluded, "As drama it is very poor stuff. But as an exhibit of three remarkable men it is not without interest." Even the *Sun* (April 1, 1873), which vilified the production, praised Buffalo Bill and Texas Jack, saying they "play their simple parts with considerable ease and dash, especially in the matter of firing pistols in which many an actor would do well to take a lesson from Buffalo Bill."

Here then arose contradiction aplenty. The material was straightforwardly chauvinistic, even brutal in its treatment of Native Americans, and was clearly identified as such. Yet audiences responded enthusiastically to that and to the stars who brought to their mayhem a natural, unpracticed charisma. Furthermore, the joining of actual elements to theatrical presentation created a tension between fact and fiction, for while Buffalo Bill and Texas Jack lent authenticity in terms of what they had done, the way they dressed, and the way they talked, the incidents in Buntline's play were outrageously fictional.

Given the friendship that existed between Buffalo Bill and James Gordon Bennett, a complimentary review in the *New York Herald* might be expected. The paper commented (April 1, 1873) that "these were the genuine heroes" whose acting had a "piquancy and interest . . . seldom felt at the appearance of real actors." Bennett might have felt somewhat torn in his response to the play. Clearly he liked Buffalo Bill, but just as clearly he despised Buntline, a man he had sued for slander some years earlier.

The Scouts of the Prairie left New York after a two-week engagement and moved south through Philadelphia and Baltimore, and on to Washington, where President Ulysses S. Grant received Cody at the White House, a testament to the recognition Cody had already achieved. The show closed in June, and, although Cody was disappointed with his $6,000 share of the profits, he returned to the boards the following year.[18]

In 1873 Texas Jack rejoined Cody in the company. Buntline was gone, but an even more widely known frontier personality, Wild Bill Hickok, replaced him in the cast. Their play for the second season, *The Scouts of the Plains*, was written by Fred G. Maeder, and the script appears virtually identical to accounts of the Buffalo Bill version that Studley had performed.[19] Cody and his friends Wild Bill Hickok and Dave Tutt seek revenge on Jake McKandlass for killing Cody's father. Tutt, however, is a false friend who, with Raven Feather and his Oglala Sioux, kidnaps Cody's sister Lillie. As Cody and Hickok attempt to free Lillie, another band of villains – Alf Coyle and his southern-sympathizing bushwhackers – abduct Cody's mother, his other sister Lottie, and Kitty, the comic Irish housemaid. By the end of the second act, Cody and Hickok have routed the villains and rescued all the women.

The third act takes place six months later at the home of Cody's girlfriend, Louise LaValliere, and introduces a new set of adventures. Hickok eventually guns down Tutt, prompting Tutt's wife to vow revenge, which she almost achieves by stabbing Wild Bill in the back in the last act. Meanwhile, with a backdrop of a prairie fire, Buffalo Bill finds McKandlass and kills him in a knife fight. The fourth act returns to Mrs. Cody's house, where she and Lillie fear retribution from McKandlass' friends. Indeed, Lillie, Kitty, and Mrs. Cody are again carried off to the village of the Oglala Sioux. There Wa-no-tee Ma-no-tee, known as the Turtle Dove and Princess of the Oglala, taunts the captives, but Cody, Hickok, and their friends come to the rescue once more, defeating Alf Coyle and his Sioux henchmen.

As with the name "McKandlass," the inclusion of Dave Tutt recalled a frontier legend, for Hickok had killed Tutt in Springfield, Missouri, in 1865.[20] By some accounts Tutt, as in the play, betrayed Hickok, who shot him in a duel in the public square. Despite his connections to mythic events, Hickok turned into an acting liability. Jack Crawford, a former scout who gave vent to his literary impulses by writing a book of poetry, recalled that the first time Hickok was hit with a "calcium light," an early version of a powerful follow spotlight, Hickok froze completely and then fell off the bridge where he was standing.[21] Cody recounts that Hickok also had a disturbing habit of abusing the "supers," the low-paid extras who hung around theatres hoping for a bit of employment. They comprised the hordes of "Sioux warriors" for the show, and Hickok, "putting his pistol close to their legs, would fire at them and burn them with the powder . . . This would make them dance and jump, so that it was difficult to make them fall and die."[22] According to Cody, such shenanigans on and off the stage led to Hickok's quick departure.

Maeder's characters are cardboard and seldom rise above mechanical contrivance. As the evil princess, Wa-no-tee Ma-no-tee gains distinction by departing from the Pocohontas stereotype of maidens assisting the whites. The plot is anything but a model of unity, as characters and plot lines appear, disappear, and reappear with astonishing rapidity.

While the melodramatic action of the play is confused but relatively conventional, the comedy conceals a vicious message. Maeder's script contains numerous puns, ample wordplay, and occasionally some witty repartee, which provides a lighthearted backdrop as counterpoint to the violence of the action. Comic characters include two of Cody's buddies, an addled Old Vet and Snakeroot Sam, whose comic turns are integrated into the plot. In Act I Sam and his friends subject the Indian Fire-Water Tom to a mock trial and whip him for his misdeeds. In a memorable Act II scene the warriors set fire to a hollow log in which Cody is napping. He crawls out, leaving his gunpowder behind, and the ensuing explosion wreaks havoc among the Sioux and blows off Tom's arm – a cartoon-like comic action. At the climax of the play, the Old Vet uses his crutch to fight one of the tribe while Sam captures the crippled Fire-water Tom by offering him a bottle and then shooting and scalping him. The incidents themselves are dreadful, yet they are handled with a comedic air that makes the overall tone something like *Cat Ballou* without the irony. In this version of the West, natives do not even rise to the level of a genuine threat. Worse than that, they are marginalized to insignificance and treated as objects of scorn, derision, and laughter.

Like *The Scouts of the Prairie* the year before, however, and even in the face of the financial panic that was sweeping the country, the production enjoyed an enthusiastic reception. Cody, in particular, seemed to be finding his performance legs. The *New York Herald*, in another favorable report (June 30, 1874), wrote glowingly:

> [W]hile the ordinary border hero of the stage rants on every conceivable occasion, Buffalo Bill conducts himself on all occasions with that quiet, subdued manner which belongs to men who are truly brave in moments of danger . . . Buffalo Bill has a fine presence and moves about the stage with an ease and grace which at once wins the heart of the audience. He is remarkably sympathetic and possesses the power of electrifying his audiences as was visible in the hearty way in which the galleries received his points though delivered without any clap-trap appeals.

The reviewer was clearly aware that the appeal lay not so much in dramatic artistry, but in the linkage of real events with their fictional representation:

> It is not every day that one can see on the stage a real border scout fighting over again his battles. As we look on the actor and remember that it is no merely mimic performer, but a man who has passed through similar scenes, that we see filling the stage, the interest is doubled and the realism of the scene forcibly impresses itself on the spectator.

Thus the presence on stage of an actual participant in frontier events reinforced the vicarious and psychological connection of the audience to those events – even though, as we now recognize, the real events differed markedly from those depicted in the play.

Cody toured plays for nine more seasons. Texas Jack was not with him in 1874–75, but rejoined Cody in 1875–76. The following year Texas Jack and his wife Morlacchi toured their own vehicle, *Dashing Charlie*, which was based on an 1872 Buntline story, *Dashing Charlie, the Texas Whirlwind*.

Figure 4. "Texas Jack" Omohundro and Giuseppina Morlacchi, about 1875.

Photographs of the pair suggest that the play provided an unusual combination of artistic elements: the long-haired, mustachioed Texas Jack in his fringed frontier garb juxtaposed with the beautiful Morlacchi in her ballet tutu. The two played various productions including their own version of *The Scouts of the Prairie* in 1877–78 and *The Trapper's Daughter* in 1879 before the premature death of Texas Jack in 1880.

Cody continued his theatrical career with at least one new play every year between 1875 and 1882. Of those, three deserve particular attention: *Life on the Border*, by J. V. Arlington, which conveniently sidesteps the Native American issue; *The Red Right Hand; or, Buffalo Bill's First Scalp for Custer*, also by Arlington, with its echoes of historical incidents; and *Twenty Days*, by Charles Foster, which exists in tantalizing partial form and typifies a change for Cody to a still active but much less gory theatrical format.

To expand his offerings, Cody hired Arlington to compose the five-act melodrama, *Life on the Border*, which he played in New York in 1875. It was not an especially popular play for Cody, and, in the 1876–77 season, Cody seldom played the lead role because of the presence in the company of Jack Crawford. Irish-born John Wallace "Captain Jack" Crawford, who worked with Cody as an army scout, had gained some recognition as a writer, earning the sobriquet "The Poet Scout of the Black Hills," and, in the fall of 1876, he joined Cody's combination. Cody allowed "Captain Jack" to play the lead in *Life on the Border*, while Cody assumed a supporting role.

Act I is set in a rustic cabin where Emma lives with her mother, for their father, Jim Reynolds, has disappeared.[23] Johnston Huntley, a captain of the local vigilantes or "regulators," conspires to keep Jim his prisoner until he marries Emma. Buffalo Bill, meanwhile, vows to find Jim and marry Emma himself. At the end of Act I Huntley and a band of natives burn down the house, but Cody thwarts his plan to capture Emma. Acts II and III, which take place at a nearby fort, reveal that the "Indians" were actually whites in disguise carrying counterfeit money. Huntley tries to frame Bill for the crime, but Bill persuades the general of the fort to allow him to search for Jim and the counterfeiters. Bill trails the criminals in Act IV while his friends rig a fake grave to convince his enemies that Bill has been killed by a bear. In the final act Huntley offers to pay a $10,000 ransom for Jim's release if Emma will marry him. When she agrees, he whisks her off to the fort chaplain, but Bill interrupts, exposes Huntley, restores Jim to his family, and pairs off with Emma.

One of the most striking elements of Arlington's script is the ease with which the whites disguise themselves as natives. That play-acting underlines how contrived the use of natives as villains was in these "red-fire" melodramas. In almost any of the plays from *Across the Continent* to the Buffalo Bill pieces, the tribal warriors could just as easily be whites in disguise, as here, with virtually no effect on the plot. Only when actual Native Americans played the tribe members, as they did in some of Buffalo Bill's melodramas, did the plays achieve a kind of *performance* verisimilitude even though the *incidents* remained outlandish. And only much later, when the rationale for Indian frustration is more sympathetically elaborated in plays such as *The Girl I Left Behind Me*, does the reality of Native American resistance become a significant factor.

At the end of the season, Cody apparently gave the right to perform the play to Crawford, although Cody later asserted he still owned it. Crawford acted it occasionally, but Cody never performed it after the 1876–77 season. Julian Kent, who used a trained bear for the Act IV action, played the same piece – calling it *Wild Bill, King of the Border Men* – from 1875 to at least 1882.

This is the same play that surfaced in 1878 and 1879 under the title *The Trapper's Daughter* with Texas Jack Omohundro, Donald MacKay, and former scouts Dashing Charlie Emmett and Arizona John.

Crawford, meanwhile, resumed his career as a scout in New Mexico while he continued to write, composing hundreds of stories and poems and at least two other plays before his death in 1917, the year Buffalo Bill died. One of those plays, *Fonda; or, The Trapper's Dream*, also known as *California Through Death Valley*, combined anti-Mormon sentiment reminiscent of *The Danites* with original songs penned by Crawford. The plot concerns a wagon train led by Captain Jack Crawford encamped in the Salt Lake Valley on its way to California.[24] Fonda, a young girl who believes her father has been killed by the Mormons, joins the train. The Mormons, led by Elder Force, want the women and the supplies from the wagons, so, behind Captain Jack's back, they lead the train into the desert and attack it. Captain Jack returns to save most of his company and lead them to California, where Fonda and Captain Jack pair off. Surely one of the first musicals about the western frontier, the play, despite its anti-Mormon bias, featured specificity of place and action, reasonably defined characters, and decent comic subplots.

Between theatrical seasons Cody usually returned to the West either as a military scout or as a guide for hunting parties. After Cody closed the 1875–76 season, he headed to the Dakotas, where he assisted the army in their campaign against the Cheyenne and the Sioux. During that engagement, Cody killed and scalped a Cheyenne leader, Hay-o-wei, called Yellow Hand. That incident occurred only about three weeks after George Custer and his five companies were destroyed in the same campaign. Although Cody's fight was geographically separated from Custer's disaster by hundreds of miles and involved a Cheyenne warrior rather than a Sioux, it was quickly adopted as a symbolic retribution and reinforced Cody's already remarkable reputation as a genuine icon of the frontier. The incident also marked the blurring of Cody's army life and his stage life. Cody's performances had always emphasized the violent nature of the frontier – his early stage photographs show him carrying rifles and handguns – but during this campaign he brought the stage to the frontier. In the battle Cody wore a gaudy theatrical costume of black velvet trimmed with scarlet accents, silver buttons, and lace. Cody, for his part, did all he could to reinforce the symbolic connection between himself and Custer, and, a year later, used the incident as the basis for his production *The Red Right Hand; or, Buffalo Bill's First Scalp for Custer*, which was arranged for the stage for the 1877–78 season by Arlington after an earlier dime novel version.

Figure 5. William F. "Buffalo Bill" Cody in his melodrama days, about 1875.

Cody performed two other plays that season, *May Cody; or, Lost and Won* and *Viva Vance; or, Saved from the Sioux*. These were followed by two plays by Prentiss Ingraham, who became a prolific writer and publicist for Cody: *The Knight of the Plains; or, Buffalo Bill's Best Trail* and *Buffalo Bill at Bay; or, The Pearl of the Prairie*. Ingraham's plays represented a major shift for Cody, for instead of slaughter and mayhem they emphasized romance and senti- ment. Although the scripts themselves have not survived, reviews indicate that the productions virtually eliminated the use of evil natives and volleys of gunfire. The kidnapping and rescue of vulnerable women, however, remained a staple. In *Buffalo Bill at Bay*, Guy Woodbridge loves Buffalo Bill's sister, the Prairie Pearl. Captain Hart, the villain, also loves The Pearl and twice kidnaps her in his dual role as the renegade Red Reid – yet another white disguised as an Indian. Each time, of course, Buffalo Bill frustrates his evil machinations.[25]

Cody's trend toward romance continued in *The Prairie Waif*, a play by John A. Stevens, manager of New York's Windsor Theatre, where Cody frequently appeared, and *Twenty Days; or, Buffalo Bill's Pledge*, written by Charles Foster. The latter play is especially intriguing because a handwritten copy of Buffalo Bill's part still exists.[26] That document provides all of Cody's lines and actions and the last few words of lines by other characters that served as Cody's cues. Such compilations of one character's lines and actions, known as "sides," were especially common when scripts were written out by hand or individually typed. In *Twenty Days*, Buffalo Bill's actions are so restrained he does not even dispatch the villain. While on a twenty-day furlough from his scouting duties with the army, Buffalo Bill accidentally comes upon and rescues a man who claims to be Captain Merton Mortlake just as he is about to be lynched by the villainous Lariat Dan. While Bill is visiting his friend, Mr. Weldon, and his daughter, Grace, Weldon learns that his brother has died, leaving a fortune to Grace on condition she wed his adopted son, Captain Mortlake. Meanwhile, the ringleader of the bad guys, Montana Mike, is passing himself off as the Captain in order to kidnap Grace. Eventually Bill and the real Captain track the villain to his gambling hole near Denver, and, when they confront Montana Mike, he is accidentally slain by one of his own men.

Even though Cody's plays veered progressively toward romance and sentiment, critics continued to rail and Cody and his troupe continued to rake in audiences and money. The *New York Clipper* (April 26, 1879), commenting on Cody's remarkable gross of nearly $10,000 in one week at the California Theatre in San Francisco, summarized the situation neatly: "It seems, after all, that though we may despise the prairie drama with its Indians and gunpowder and indiscriminate shooting and scalping, the public hold it in higher estimation."

In the spring of 1883, Cody joined forces with sharpshooter William F. Carver to form a Wild West exhibition designed for outdoor arenas in the heat of the summer when regular theatrical companies ceased touring. That enterprise opened in May 1883, and eventually became a phenomenon of the entertainment business. Cody's last recorded New York area performance in a play occurred during the week of January 28, 1884, when he performed *The Prairie Waif* at the People's Theatre.

As for J. B. Studley, who originated Buffalo Bill as a dramatic role and impersonated Buffalo Bill successfully for three weeks in early 1873, once the real Buffalo Bill appeared in New York in March and April, Studley's attempts at the role proved futile. He tried playing the part again in June, but the production, according to a *Clipper* report (June 14), "failed to draw," and he was forced to substitute another play. After he lost the presentation of the character to the real Buffalo Bill, Studley returned to more traditional roles, especially villains and Shakespearean parts. Studley died in 1910 at the age of 78, a cynical recluse avoiding anything and anyone that reminded him of the theatre.[27]

Davy Crockett

Studley first presented the character of Buffalo Bill to the public on February 19, 1872. Almost exactly one year later and just five weeks prior to Buffalo Bill's initial foray onto Broadway the New York area received its first glimpse of another frontier hero in a very different play. This hero had also lived, but he was played by a professional actor. The play and the actor gained almost as much fame and popularity as Buffalo Bill and his plays. Certainly both the play and the actor received greater critical respect and acclaim, and the popularity of the subject matter proved so lasting that even eighty years later productions based on the life of this hero created a nationwide sensation.

The play was, of course, *Davy Crockett*, composed for the stage by Frank Murdoch and enacted by Frank Mayo. Its New York area debut occurred at the Park Theatre in Brooklyn on February 24, 1873. Given the impending economic chaos of that year, Mayo could hardly have picked a more inopportune moment to launch a new play, but he was a careful man, and his success was no fluke. Frank Mayo was, by all accounts, an excellent actor. His home was Boston, where he was born on April 18, 1839, but his first successes occurred in the West. In Virginia City, Nevada, he not only gained a popular following, but made the acquaintance of Mark Twain. His friendship with Twain later affected his portrayal of Davy Crockett and also led to a major success in the last years of his life when he starred in his own dramatization of Twain's *Pudd'nhead Wilson*. At Thomas Maguire's Opera House in San Francisco, where he worked in the mid 1860s, Mayo honed his talents and achieved youthful success.

In 1865, secure in his skills, Mayo headed east. He scored an immediate hit as Badger in *The Streets of New York* at Henry Jarrett's Boston Theatre, but Mayo yearned to become a touring star, so in the late 1860s and early 1870s he put together a traveling company and hired himself out as a guest star in midsized cities such as Buffalo, Albany, and Rochester. Charles T. Parsloe, who was later to create the definitive comic Chinese stage characterization, frequently filled comic roles in Mayo's productions. Mayo and Parsloe received encouraging notices for *The Streets of New York* and *The Three Guardsmen*, a dramatization of Alexandre Dumas's *The Three Musketeers*. They even took the two productions to New York in December 1871, but the reception was chilly and Mayo vowed not to return until he led a production he felt sure would succeed with the New York press.

The following season, 1872–73, Mayo managed the Rochester theatre. There, on September 23, he first performed *Davy Crockett*. *Davy Crockett* and the plays of Buffalo Bill, emerging at virtually the same time, represent two ends of the frontier drama spectrum. Cody's early plays were full of "blood and thunder" with lots of gunfire and dead bodies. Plots were a hodgepodge; dialogue was simultaneously overblown and insignificant. They did, however, feature a real and current hero, and they were set in the part of the country that was the frontier at that time. *Davy Crockett*, on the other hand, was constructed from its inception with romantic, poetic, and artistic aspirations, looking back to a hero whose time had already passed. Crockett had died in 1836. As a stage character, he had already been celebrated in 1831 as Nimrod Wildfire in James Kirke Paulding's *The Lion of the West*. By 1872, his frontier in Tennessee had been a state for seventy-six years, and "The Alamo" was a thirty-six-year-old story. To an America that was still a very young country, Crockett was practically nostalgic.

Author Frank Hitchcock Murdoch, nephew of Shakespearean actor James E. Murdoch, ignored the more storied aspects of Crockett's life – there is no Alamo in his drama – and instead centered his play on Davy Crockett falling in love.[28] Act I opens at the forest cottage of Davy's mother, who informs Davy that his old sweetheart, Eleanor Vaughn, has returned from her schooling to marry Neil Campton. When Davy meets Campton and Campton's uncle Oscar, Davy senses that the uncle has some peculiar hold over Eleanor's guardian, Major Royston, and he follows them, proclaiming his well-known motto for action: "Be sure you're right, then go ahead." In Act II Davy finds Eleanor lost in the woods and nearly frozen in a snowstorm and carries her to his cabin where he builds a fire to warm her and reads Sir Walter Scott's *Lochinvar*. At the end of the act, a pack of wolves attack the cabin, and, in one of the most dramatic moments of the play, Davy places his arm in the brackets to bar the door. The next morning, his arm swollen from his act of heroism, Davy proclaims his love for Eleanor and then hikes ten miles through snowdrifts to get help. At Major Royston's elaborate mansion in Act IV, the wedding preparations proceed, and Campton reveals that Royston arranged Neil's marriage to the wealthy Eleanor because of Royston's debts to Campton. After Eleanor confesses to Davy that she loves him but feels duty bound to marry Neil, Davy rides into the wedding and whisks away his beloved Eleanor. Act V returns to Davy's mother's cottage where Davy is about to marry Eleanor. When Neil, Royston, and Campton interrupt, Eleanor simply agrees to pay off Royston's debts, thereby freeing herself to marry Davy.

Davy Crockett is a frontier play primarily because of the presence of the title character. The settings of Dame Crockett's cottage and Davy's cabin suggest the frontier of an earlier time, with the twin dangers of wolves and snowstorms. Still, there are no Indians, and the scenes seem more pastoral than dangerous. The major's mansion certainly represents a developed society, and the villains have traditional melodramatic motives – to secure money and the girl – as appropriate for Boston or New York as for Tennessee.

The single strongest quality of the play lies in its sense of nostalgic romance. Scott's *Lochinvar* infuses the piece. It generates a poetic atmosphere and underscores the artistic intent of the drama. More importantly, it provides a structure as Davy replicates the feats of young Lochinvar. The most striking aspect of the plot is the manner in which it almost magically transforms Davy from a backwoods commoner into a dashing and romantic Scott-like action hero. Like Cody, Mayo presented through Crockett an image of a heroic male – the words "manly" and "manliness" appear frequently in reviews.[29] Davy shares innocence and humility with Buffalo Bill, and is his equal in demonstrating physical prowess. But Mayo's Davy is pastoral, romantic, and essentially non-violent. His seriousness of purpose outweighs his low-key humor, especially compared to the raucous laughter of Cody's first plays.

Davy's most daring moment – his rescue of Eleanor at the wedding – illustrates a significant melodramatic device. Rescues, of course, constitute a fundamental part of all melodrama, and in the frontier plays they take a variety of forms. In some plays, such as *Across the Continent*, a contingent of troops arrives at the last second to save an imperiled group. In the gunfire-filled dramas of Buffalo Bill, the hero often rides into a tribal encampment to free prisoners or rescue the heroine. In the more sentimental plays, the hero spares the heroine from a flood or, as in this case, a dreaded marriage.

While most of the incidents in the play are pure fiction, a convincing case can be made that Murdoch used an event from Davy Crockett's autobiography as a springboard for the play.[30] Crockett wrote that while on a wolf hunt he happened upon a girl whom he had once met at a party, and circumstances forced them to spend a night together in a cabin in the woods. Later, she became his wife. These incidents clearly parallel the events in Act III.

Davy Crockett became one of the most revered plays of the nineteenth-century American theatre. It was not, however, an immediate hit. Mayo recalled that when it opened the critics hated the play. "[A]lmost the first review I read ended with the words 'of the play little can be said; the chances are Mr. Mayo will never play it again.' Others let it down easy."[31] Murdoch, who was acting in Philadelphia when the piece first opened in Rochester, fell seriously ill and died on November 13, 1872, at the age of twenty-nine, without ever seeing a production of his new play.

After the February date at the Park Theatre in Brooklyn, Mayo went back on the road. He continued to rework the play until he was convinced it would succeed in New York. Finally, on June 2, 1873, he ventured into Manhattan and opened at Wood's Theatre for two weeks. The critics liked the play, and they liked Mayo in it. The *New York Clipper* (June 21, 1873) again praised the production, and it noted the changes in the play:

> The drama has undergone many changes since its first production, the dialogue having been curtailed, and it may now be pronounced one of the most effective of its class. The language is far above that of the average modern drama, and at time borders closely upon the poetical. The situations and incidents are effectively grouped, and the drama as a faithful picture of backwood life may be pronounced well nigh perfect. Its dramatis personae are free from the rough class of scouts, Indians, et cetera usually found in border drama.

Obviously this was a different kind of portrayal from those of Oliver Doud Byron and Buffalo Bill. Even that glowing notice, however, contains the telltale "of its class," announcing the qualification of the positive comments. A few months later in Chicago, the *Daily Tribune* (September 7, 1873) commented that the performance included "some little bits of quiet acting into which Mr. Mayo infuses all his power, and it is these which render the drama so attractive." A week later (September 14), the same paper summarized that Mayo "succeeded in elevating the sensational drama to his individual standard, without sacrificing his own reputation." Mayo played another week at Wood's Theatre in October 1873, and by the spring of 1874 when the production ran for six weeks at Niblo's the reputation of *Davy Crockett* was secure.

As a script, *Davy Crockett* has its share of problems and improbabilities. The snowstorm in Act II, for instance, contradicts the fine weather of Act I, and it is unlikely that such an experienced woodsman as Davy Crockett would have no firewood in his cabin. From a gender perspective, Eleanor spends four acts passively complying with her guardian's marriage wishes concerning her and allowing herself to be rescued by Davy. While it is rather satisfying that Eleanor in the end controls her own wealth and determines her destiny, that denouement seems incredibly simplistic. Although critics mentioned these problems, they were swept away by the romance of the play, by the power of the two interrupted wedding scenes, and by Mayo's remarkable acting. During its third season, when it played New York's Park Theatre for six weeks, the *Herald* (March 23, 1875) labeled *Davy Crockett*

> immeasurably the best of American dramas. In it the realities of life are so mingled with the poetic that our judgment and feeling become involved and we are carried along by the sweetness and beauty of the story past the snags of improbability that we see but heed not. Davy Crockett is one of the most charming creations of the modern stage; to see him is to love him; and we pity the man or woman who is not moved by his simple manliness and his unconscious heroism.

Even that critic acknowledged that travelers would not find such a backwoodsman in nature, but the writer argued that Davy was better than the actual article. "Davy Crockett is that thing which is better than nature which we are agreed to call art. He is the assemblage of the virtues found in many members of his tribe into one ideal creation, which we are called upon to admire." Later critics were equally enamored of the play. Laurence Hutton, in his *Curiosities of the American Stage*, wrote:

> It is almost the best American play ever written. A pure sylvan love-story, told in a healthful, dramatic way, it is a poem in four acts; not perfect in form, open to criticism, with faults of construction, failings of plot, slight improbabilities, sensational situations, and literary shortcomings, but so simple and so touching and so pure that it is worthy to rank with any of the creations of the modern stage in any language.[32]

Accolades for the actor who created the role continued. The *Herald* (March 10, 1874), which just two months earlier had crucified Byron for his representation of a frontiersman, lavished encomia on Mayo:

> Mr. Frank Mayo as Davy Crockett plays with care and a fidelity to sense that captivates. He allows nothing to tempt him into rant . . . His is the nearest approach to true American comedy acting that has been yet seen.

While Mayo's performance as Davy was obviously remarkable, reviewers had other reasons to praise the actor. Mayo was widely regarded as a decent and honorable man with many friends in the profession and few enemies. Buying Frank Mayo was like buying Jimmy Stewart – an investment in a rosy, earnest, rural vision of America. Most importantly to the critics, however, Mayo aspired to "better" things: he wanted to do Shakespeare. That desire confirmed the proper artistic order and the critics' place in it, which allowed them comfortably to heap qualified praise on his more common efforts.

Critiques of Mayo's acting read much like critiques of the performances of Joseph Jefferson. Both men were for years identified with one humble, rustic character, and both men received constant praise for their natural, understated technique. The New York *Spirit of the Times* (August 30, 1879) summarized Mayo's vocal and physical skills as well as his apparently effortless acting:

> With a splendid presence, a rich voice, variety almost endless of facial and vocal expression, as also of picturesque attitude, he gave us a fresh, breezy picture of a new life, and was by turns friendless and vigorous, humorous and tender, always truthful.

Mayo once indicated in an interview that he patterned his Davy Crockett after two men who, along with Mayo, formed a triumvirate of friends in Virginia City, Nevada – Joe Goodman and Mark Twain:

> [A]ll that is sweet, wholesome, and lovable – the happy, frank, open nature in the title role – is based upon my conception of the nature and character of Joe Goodman; and all that is quaint and humorous was taken from the other friend of the trio, Mark Twain. And during all the years of my playing *Davy Crockett*, there was not a night that those men were not present with me.[33]

One criticism of Mayo's acting that recurred regularly prior to his work in Murdoch's play was that his carefully executed performances failed to strike an emotional chord. The *Chicago Daily Tribune* (March 2, 1889) wrote precisely on that problem and on Mayo's overcoming it with *Davy Crockett*. Commenting on his more stately roles, the reviewer said that Mayo acted too much with his head instead of his heart – except when he was playing Davy Crockett.

Figure 6. Frank Mayo in the title role of *Davy Crockett*.

Mayo performed *Davy Crockett* almost exclusively through the 1870s, reaching his thousandth performance in Rochester, the place where he had started, at the Corinthian Hall on May 10, 1877. Two years later he took his play to England.

By then Mayo, concerned that he was completely identified with just two parts, Badger and Davy Crockett, was searching for new challenges.[34] Mayo had heard reports of the radical integrated staging by the troupe of the Duke of Saxe-Meiningen. Rather than a small touring group featuring individual stars, the German duke's troupe was a large company based on the idea of an ensemble. The performances of the Saxe-Meiningen company in London in 1881 and throughout the European continent redefined contemporary theatrical production.

Mayo wanted to be the Saxe-Meiningen of the United States, and in 1881 he initiated his most ambitious project, assembling a troupe of forty performers for a season of stately Shakespearean drama. Critical reception glowed as they visited the major cities of the East and the Midwest, but the costs of the huge company undid Mayo. Deeply in debt, he folded the attempt in the spring in Baltimore and spent the next two and a half years reprising Davy Crockett and repaying creditors. By then, he had performed the role more than three thousand times.

In the mid 1880s Mayo tried out *Nordeck*, a play about Polish nobility, and he resurrected his role as D'Artagnan in *The Royal Guard*, a revised version of *The Three Guardsmen*. Although Mayo insisted on extensive rehearsals and elaborate staging, the productions were only mildly successful, and by the end of the 1880s Mayo had returned to a schedule that featured *Davy Crockett*. Even that old standard did not attract audiences as it once had, and after the 1893–94 season, consumed with self-doubt, Mayo took ten months off to prepare a dramatization of Mark Twain's *Pudd'nhead Wilson*.[35] Despite his advancing age and recent setbacks, Mayo secured financial backing, and he opened *Pudd'nhead Wilson* in the spring of 1895 to immediate acclaim. The homespun, mentally precise title character perfectly fit Mayo's personality and acting skills. Finally Mayo had found a part other than Davy Crockett in which the public would accept him. He played *Pudd'nhead Wilson* over three hundred and fifty times in the next year before he died suddenly on June 8, 1896, at the age of fifty-seven. Mayo died as he had lived – on the road, returning on a train from an engagement in the West.

Mayo left behind a wife, who lived only four months past her husband, and three children: Edwin, who continued to perform the frontier role his father had made famous; Eleanor, who was born the year that *Davy Crockett* opened and who was named after the heroine of the play; and Deronda. Mayo also left behind the Crockett Lodge, his home in Canton, Pennsylvania, and a legion of friends and admirers. Finally, Mayo left behind the legacy of the romantic frontier hero.

Between them, Mayo and Cody defined the poles of sentiment and fierce action that influenced virtually every succeeding border drama. At one pole stood the reality of Buffalo Bill in the midst of cartoon-like improbabilities, while at the other end stood the created Davy Crockett, living in a romantic world of make-believe.

Herring, Wood, Winter, Frayne, and others

The popularity of *Davy Crockett* and the Buffalo Bill plays inspired a host of imitators. If the Mayo and Cody vehicles represented the extremes of frontier drama, most of their immediate successors followed Cody's action-packed lead. In the process they created a significant variety of work that ranged from the daring to the dangerous.

James J. McCloskey, one of the managers of the Park Theatre in Brooklyn, tried to duplicate his success with *Across the Continent* by opening *The Far West; or, The Bounding Fawn* at the same theatre in November 1871. At New York's Bowery Theatre in May 1872 *California; or, The Heathen Chinee* by J. Warwick dramatized the outcast "Wild Meg" in a play that also included Bret Harte western types including a gambler, a miner, and the Chinese, Ah Sin. The following season, the same play reappeared as *The Heathen Chinee; or, California in Its Youth*, but lasted only two nights. In June 1872 Albert W. Aiken wrote and acted in *Red Mazeppa; or, The Madman of the Plains* at Wood's Theatre.

In August Fanny Herring appeared at the Bowery Theatre in *Hazel Eye, the Girl Trapper; or, The Gold Hunters*, a play by Fred G. Maeder based on a Ned Buntline story from *New York Weekly*. Herring was born in 1832 in London, England.[36] Her father, Thomas Herring, was an English comedian and her mother, also Fanny, had acted at the old Bowery Theatre before moving to England with her father. After he died, mother and daughter returned to the United States. When Herring was fourteen, her mother also died, and the young girl gravitated to the only profession she knew, beginning her theatrical career in the chorus of New York's Chatham Street Theatre at $4 a week. She progressed to a general utility actress at double the salary and soon became a company member at the Brooklyn

Museum and Theatre at $10 a week. By the time of the Civil War Herring had played most of the standard female roles, including Shakespearean characters Portia, Ophelia, and Desdemona. After the war she found her niche in Bowery melodrama. Herring became the first female star of frontier drama, though, in truth, her frontier plays differed little from her nonfrontier plays.

In *Hazel Eye*, a Virginia gentleman, after learning of his wife's infidelity, takes his infant daughter to live in the West, and the play opens in the wilderness some years after that separation. The girl, called Hazel Eye, has grown into a beautiful woman while living with her father, known only as Trapper Guy. Although the story and play were written by the same two men – Buntline and Maeder – who wrote the first Buffalo Bill plays, the tone of *Hazel Eye* is remarkably different. Hazel Eye and her father live in harmony with nature and at peace with the local natives, who are their respected friends rather than buffoon-like targets for jokes and bullets. The Indians fear that whites encamped nearby want their land, but Trapper believes they are pursuing him and his daughter. He returns wounded from investigating the white strangers, and before he dies he gives Hazel Eye the key to an iron chest containing valuable papers. One of the whites, Captain Robert Norcross, arrives and declares that Trapper was slain by an Indian, but Hazel's native friends produce Norcross's bloody knife, and he is arrested for murder. Later, Norcross returns to the cabin and steals the iron box. Confusion ensues as Hazel Eye struggles to retrieve the chest until eventually she discovers there are twin Norcross brothers. In the end, the good twin helps Hazel Eye defeat the villainous brother and claim her just reward.

This play shows natives living peaceably, side by side with the white trapper and assisting Hazel Eye in her quest to find her father's murderer, while, just a few months later, Indians become the villainous foils in a Buffalo Bill play by the same author. With one hand Maeder generates sympathy and respect for the wrongly accused natives while with the other he induces laughter and derision. Clearly he used Indians simply as a dramatic convenience, for in neither case does he attempt to provide any cultural context.

A noteworthy feature of this and all Herring's shows was that she, a female, was the unquestioned star, and the plots reflected her central position. Hazel Eye is not passively captured and rescued. A skillful trapper and excellent shot in her own right, she leads the action, pursuing Norcross and her valuable possessions.

Despite the "enthusiastic welcome" that, according to a *New York Clipper* reviewer (August 24, 1872), greeted Fanny Herring, the notice for *Hazel Eye* was mostly negative. The writer had trouble keeping the brothers straight and asserted that "the characters are so lamely drawn and so utterly devoid of distinguishing characteristics the audience probably knew nothing thereof until told at the close of the drama." In addition to the loose construction the reviewer criticized extraneous dialogue and disconnected incidents. The writer found that the work declined after a decent first act until "the end, which seems only to have been obtained by sheer exhaustion on the part of the authors."

At the conclusion of a full, fair, and constructive review, the writer seemed compelled, like the *New York Herald* reviewer taking O. D. Byron to task, to blast the whole genre of frontier plays:

> This drama is of a class which of late has had an ephemeral existence . . . One object, which it is plain to see will be accomplished, must be attained, which will end the drama. Instead of accomplishing that in a legitimate manner, they approximate to it as closely as possible and then introduce a new series of incidents which makes the attainment desired as remote as at first. Such proceedings are often two or three times repeated.

Despite such critical notoriety for *Hazel Eye*, Herring maintained a lengthy career as one of the most popular actresses with New York's East Side audiences.

In her younger days Fanny Herring was known for her striking beauty, and she retained her youthfulness and energy so well that she played ingenues until almost the end of her career. After the popular success of *Hazel Eye*, Herring played numerous feisty western women in short sketches such as *Cal, the Cowboy*, *Arizona Sue*, and *Wild Ned*, all of which she wrote herself. In *The Tigress of the West*, in her play list from 1878 until 1887, Herring enacted a sympathetic native maiden. One of her particular specialties was taking on disguises or enacting more than one role, as she did in *The Female Detective*, in which she played six characters, and *Little Buckshot; or, Brought to Light*, in which she played Lillian Waters, Lillian Buckshot, and Little Buckshot.[37] *Little Buckshot*, also known as *The Boy Scout*, was one of Fanny's best-known pieces, and she kept it in her repertory from April 1881 to October 1892.

Critics praised Herring for her wide range of parts – ingenues, soubrettes, leading ladies, and even some male roles.[38] Like Chanfrau, Herring was a home-grown product, and when she died in 1906 at the age of seventy-four, obituaries displayed a genuine fondness, as if the writers believed she had not been given proper credit for what she had done when she was alive. The *Clipper* provided an extensive story and picture, and the *New York Dramatic Mirror* included pictures of Herring in six of her most famous roles. The *Brooklyn Daily Times* (May 21, 1906) wrote that "during her seasons at the New Bowery, no woman ever appeared on the East Side who attained a more enduring popularity with all classes of playgoers than Miss Herring."

The ultimate tribute, however, appeared in a six-inch remembrance in *Billboard* (June 16, 1906) under the title "Melodrama Versus Art." This item succinctly summarizes the highbrow–lowbrow approach at work. The first part of the article identified the unfashionable audiences of the Bowery, where "Art was an unknown quantity." The second part focused on Herring's orphaned predicament: although she aspired to more worthy drama, she settled for the safety of success in melodrama, and, once established, "she could not get away":

> At last opportunity was gone; age had set its seal upon her. Her career was rounded out in maudlin plays with tawdry accessories.
>
> Fanny Herring's early dreams of artistic portrayal and full dress first nights were never realized; yet they were never absent. Her beautiful home at Simsbury, Conn., was equipped with all the luxuries that gratify the aesthetic taste. Her library was as select as it was extensive, and it numbered several thousand volumes . . . her name and the plays she wrote and acted will live for many years in the traditions of the circles that patronize melodrama.

The implication was obvious: Herring was to be pitied because despite her artistic predilections – the reference to the library implants "highbrow" associations – she had been forced by her circumstances to labor on the illegitimate stage of melodrama.

Another performer ensnared by the sweet seductions of melodrama was N. S. Wood. Wood was a prodigy who played Hamlet at the age of eleven, although he modestly confessed, "I played 'Hamlet' – that is, I pronounced the lines, for I knew not what they meant."[39] By the 1878–79 season, Wood was a member of the company of New York's Wallack's Theatre, one of the leading stock companies in the country. Reviews praised him for his work in the difficult role of Anatole in *A Scrap of Paper*, and the *New York Mirror* featured him on its cover on May 31, 1879.

That week, Wood played a role that changed the course of his career. At the Bowery Theatre he undertook the lead in *The Boy Detective*, a part in which he enacted eight different characters. The *Mirror* (June 7, 1879) praised his versatility: "[W]hether as the town newsboy, the ancient mariner, the shrewd detective, or the highborn son, he is seen to constant advantage." On the other hand, the *Mirror* derided the play, claiming that it "contains more incongruity than sense and more sensation than either." Still, the audience loved Wood, and, apparently, Wood savored the adulation. When Wallack's revived *A Scrap of Paper*, Wood declined to reprise his work as Anatole, making what the *Mirror* later (December 2, 1882) labeled "the mistake of his life" in order to continue starring in sensational melodrama.

Wood's connection with frontier drama began the following season when he took on the title role of Lew Valleo, known as "Lightnin' Lew," in Maggie Weston's *The Boy Scout of the Sierras*, usually referred to simply as *The Boy Scout*, another piece that allowed Wood a variety of disguises and characterizations. Wood retained his popularity – he was featured on the cover of the *Mirror* a second time in December 1882 – but, like Fanny Herring, he was relegated to the ranks of melodrama and sank to performing his plays on variety stages interspersed with acrobats, singers, and dancing dogs.

Because he began working at such a young age, N. S. Wood remained active for many years, eventually becoming a venerable senior citizen of the stage. As late as 1906 Wood was still performing *The Boy Scout*, and in 1910 he toured as Shorty in Edwin Milton Royle's important frontier drama *The Squaw Man*.[40] As with Herring, disdain for the material he performed followed Wood to his grave. One publication summarized his career by noting, "what his career would have been had he not capitulated to the lure of melodrama one may only conjecture."[41]

Though her pedigree might have suggested otherwise, Alice Placide was another performer who willingly "capitulated to the lure of melodrama." A cousin to James and Lester Wallack and the niece of Henry Placide, one of the most gifted comic actors of the American theatre, Alice took naturally to the stage, and, by the mid 1860s, was playing Desdemona to Frank Mayo's Othello at the Boston Theatre. Then, in the early 1870s, she met Charles E. Emmett, who was performing in a company with Ned Buntline.

Emmett was a legitimate western scout.[42] Born in Kentucky in 1847, he had traveled west at the age of ten with his uncle, working for a fur company. Emmett served as an interpreter and scout with the army and carried mail on a two-hundred-and-fifty-mile route. He was involved in several battles and sustained serious wounds, including an arrow through his shoulder. In 1873, Buntline persuaded Emmett to go on the stage in *Dashing Charlie; or, The Scouts of the Plains*, and, while he was in the East, he met Alice Placide. They married in Philadelphia the following year, August 22, and suddenly his life became her vehicle.

That same year, they opened *Little Rifle; or, The White Spirit of the Pawnees* by James Barnes, which they toured successfully into the teeth of the depression. The pair provided an interesting combination. While he was the attraction, she was the actress. In the course of the Buffalo-Bill-like melodrama, Emmett rescued the young maiden, Little Rifle, from numerous desperate scrapes, including the obligatory abduction to an Indian village. A Wood's Theatre program from November 1874 makes clear the couple's relative theatrical positions, proclaiming "Miss Alice Placide supported by Chas. E. Emmett."[43] The *New York Herald* reviewer (November 17, 1874) noted that Placide "played the part of Little Rifle with much spirit, but Dashing Charlie's modesty amounted to tameness." Placide and Emmett played *Little Rifle* and *Dashing Charlie* into the 1880s, but their theatrical careers did not shine beyond that.

Other frontier productions came and went. In February 1873, at the Grand Opera House in New York, Augustin Daly tried unsuccessfully to duplicate his successful *Horizon* with *Roughing It* using many of the same conventions. In *Roughing It*, a young woman with a disapproving father runs off to the West with her beau. Their capture by a band of natives and subsequent rescue by army troops were the highlights of the play.[44] Daly employed the same title that Twain used for his satiric western travelogue, published in 1872, but the play borrowed little else from Twain's book. McCloskey tried another western play based on Bret Harte material, *Poverty Flat; or, California in '49*, at Wood's Theatre in August 1873, to lukewarm response. That same month, Wood's resurrected *Metamora* for a fresh production, and in October they told all the James Fenimore Cooper stories in *The Life and Death of Natty Bumppo*, starring longtime leading actor Edward Eddy. Niblo's also turned to Cooper's works during the same season, running *Leatherstocking; or, The Last of the Mohicans* for three weeks in February 1874, with J. B. Studley as the evil Magua and Fanny Herring as the noble Uncas.

Julian Kent brought his production, *Wild Bill, King of the Border Men*, which featured Kent fighting his trained bear Julia, to the Bowery Theatre in December 1875. The play was identical to Cody's *Life on the Border*, and

Buffalo Bill Cody and Texas Jack Omohundro immediately asserted their right to the play, which they called *Wild Bill; or, Life on the Border* and attributed to Hirim Robbins. In directly conflicting testimony, Kent circulated copies of depositions and receipts for rights to the show while Cody and Omohundro published documents that purported to sell the rights of the play to Cody and Omohundro for $600.[45] Kent ultimately triumphed, and he and Julia presented *Wild Bill* into the 1880s.

Daniel Boone, one of the more successful pieces of the mid 1870s, opened at the Bowery on November 3, 1873. Annie E. Ford, daughter of John T. Ford, who ran theatres in Baltimore and Washington, wrote the play, which focused on the famous backwoodsman leading a band of pioneers from Virginia to Kentucky. The plot detailed the trials and tribulations of the group as they confronted dangers from natives and British soldiers, and the *Clipper* (November 8, 1873) labeled it "one of the best dramas seen in this city in some time." *Daniel Boone* was thoughtfully staged. The *Clipper* for the following week (November 15, 1873) commended the exceptional scenery and lavished particular praise on the opening and closing acts, which used the entire depth of the Bowery Theatre stage, the largest in America. The first scene revealed a forest, and the last showed Mammoth Cave in Kentucky. "As the characters . . . in these scenes entered from the fly gallery and descended to the stage over a series of bridges or runs placed diagonally, the effect was grand and realistic."

J. P. Winter, who served his apprenticeship as a stock actor at the Bowery supporting such visiting stars as Buffalo Bill Cody, assumed the title role. Winter effectively claimed the character and the play as his own, enacting the role for at least nine seasons, and over one thousand performances.[46] Several years after Winter began performing Boone, the *New York Dramatic Mirror* (April 10, 1880) was still praising it as a "well-constructed melodrama" in which "a very fair representation of the historical Kentuckian is given."

An even more successful performer arrived in New York for the first time in early January 1874, when Frank Frayne brought *Oroloso, the Dead Shot* to the Metropolitan Theatre. Two weeks later he appeared at the Bowery, and the sketchy *Oroloso* had been expanded to *The Scouts of the Sierra Nevada*, credited to Frayne and J. J. Wallace.[47]

Frank Ivers Frayne created a spectacular form of frontier drama that incorporated live shooting stunts into the plots of his plays. Many individuals in nineteenth-century theatre traveled the country performing feats based on western activities such as roping or trick riding, but the most

Figure 7. Frank I. Frayne and his trained dog.

popular demonstrations featured shooting. A host of "marksmen," "sharp-shooters," "wing shots," "rifle shots," and "dead shots" entertained rapt audiences, shattering thousands of glass balls in the process.

Frayne was no mere exhibitor. He knew the stage, he had experienced the West, and he was an expert shot. He cleverly combined those ingredients to produce his unusual and popular shows. Frayne was born in Kentucky in 1839, and in the early 1850s he acted in Cincinnati and New Orleans. After the Civil War, dissatisfied with his progress in the profession, he headed west to the mining region where he became an excellent shot. He also taught his wife, Clara Butler Frayne, to shoot.

When Frayne returned to the East, he did so with a unique theatrical fare. Although he played in variety shows in the early 1870s, he quickly integrated his shooting tricks and trained animal stunts into fully plotted dramatic presentations, generally set in the West. For approximately twenty years, the Frank Frayne American Rifle Team thrilled the playgoing public with the same kind of shooting tricks and animal stunts that later excited generations of moviegoers in twentieth-century westerns. The tricks performed by Trigger and Bullet, the horse and dog of cowboy movie star Roy Rogers, were little more than updated and simplified versions of those executed by Frayne and his charges. Shooting stunts, which were easy to produce by editing film, were performed by Frayne with live ammunition. One of Frayne's more modest tricks involved extinguishing a candle with a bullet, and noted actor Otis Skinner recorded in his autobiography that he began his career in theatre with the Frayne combination playing a ranch hand who had a pipe shot out of his mouth.[48] The climaxes of Frayne's plays invariably spotlighted more complicated feats. In one he rescued an innocent man about to be hanged by cutting the rope with a bullet.[49] Frayne called another trick "the double shot." An actor put an apple on his head and sat in front of a device to which a gun was fastened. That gun pointed at a saucer on a shelf on the opposite side of the stage. Seated beneath the shelf, Frayne fired at the apple, splitting it and triggering the second gun, which in turn discharged its ball to shatter the saucer above Frayne's head.

Frayne's most daring stunt was called "the backward shot." In this trick Frayne shot an apple off his wife's head while he was turned backward, resting the rifle on his shoulder and focusing in a mirror. "The backward shot" figured in the climax of Frayne's most popular play, *Si Slocum*, as well as in the climactic moment of Frayne's life. *Si Slocum* was first produced in New York in August 1875. It was written for Frayne by Clifton W. Tayleure, and it employed the typical Frayne format, with shooting tricks at climactic moments. Early in the play Si Slocum and Vasquez work at the same business, and when Slocum accuses Vasquez of forgery, Vasquez plants stolen goods on Slocum. Both men lose their jobs, leave the city, and head west, where Slocum becomes proprietor of a ranch and an excellent shot. Vasquez tries to seize the property, and at the beginning of the last act Vasquez and his gang surprise Slocum's wife, Ruth, at the ranch. Vasquez binds Ruth to a tree and, when Slocum returns, Vasquez captures him and gives him one chance for freedom. In a transposition of the William Tell story, Vasquez demands that Slocum shoot an apple off his wife's head with a backward shot. Slocum succeeds, then quickly turns the tables on Vasquez and his men to emerge victorious.

Like many of the frontier drama imitations, *Si Slocum* lacked the specificity that can render even mediocre melodrama compelling to an audience.

It does not include the Harte-like details of local color that Daly strove for in *Horizon*. It lacks the poetic underpinning of *Davy Crockett* and the central connection with real events signified by Buffalo Bill. The ranch seems entirely generic without the slightest hint of an actual location. While Vasquez enjoys the distinction of being frontier drama's first Hispanic-named villain – at least in New York – he and his Mexican henchmen are sketched only as evil caricatures with no culturally defining characteristics. Mexican characters seldom appeared in theatrical mining camps or ranches even though letters, diaries, and other accounts indicate that Mexicans were a productive staple of western locales. When they did appear, they followed much in the mold of Vasquez, evil presences, Hispanic in name alone. *Si Slocum*, however, did not pretend to complexities of character development, but, like a modern movie with a surplus of explosions, relied almost entirely on its unusual shooting tricks.

Frayne was, of course, an extremely reliable shot, and made the stunts as safe as possible. Advertisements for the show proclaimed to the nervous that, although "the backward shot" looked dangerous, it was really quite safe because the actress wore a chain mail skullcap. Furthermore, the apple rested on a hat the actress wore, which placed the object some six inches above her head.[50] Still, despite the precautions, at one matinee performance while Frayne was performing *Si Slocum* before a packed Thanksgiving holiday audience on November 30, 1882, at the Coliseum Theatre in Cincinnati, tragedy struck. Ruth was played by Annie Von Behren, Frayne's fiancee after the death of his wife, who had played the part for five years, in 1880. On this particular afternoon, when Frayne pulled the trigger, an unusual explosion occurred. It burned Frayne's neck and face and blew the hammer spring and a screw that held the barrel in place into the audience. The blast deflected the barrel of the rifle downward, and two thousand three hundred people watched in horror as a bullet penetrated Annie Von Behren's head. Police arrested Frayne for manslaughter, but he was exonerated and resumed playing in 1883 after a respite of approximately four weeks. After this horrible incident Frayne abandoned his most dangerous shooting stunts, but he performed his somewhat tamer shows, such as *Kentucky Bill*, into the 1890s.

Captain Jack, Donald MacKay, and George Custer

Another phenomenon of the frontier drama of the early 1870s was the dramatization of current events ranging from western warfare to outlaw attacks. On the one hand, the use of historical material was common in the theatre. After all, two of the earliest American plays were William Dunlap's *André* (1798) and John Burk's *Bunker Hill; or, The Death of General Warren* (1797), which dramatized famous Revolutionary War incidents. Plays about Pocahontas, Daniel Boone, and battles of the War of 1812 and the French and Indian War also adopted historical material. What made the plays that emerged in the 1870s so unusual was the rapidity with which authors translated historical material into dramatic action.

The telegraph revolutionized news gathering, bringing stories to eager readers with overnight dispatch. News reporters battled for exciting scoops, and the frontier provided fertile ground for thrilling stories. When hostilities with the Modoc Indians broke out on the west coast in 1873, reporters flocked to cover the action. After the government opened the Modoc country in northern California to settlement in the 1860s, clashes erupted between settlers and the native population.[51] Authorities removed the Modocs and the Klamaths to Oregon, but the two tribes quarreled, and in 1870 a band of Modocs under subchief Kintpuash, known as "Captain Jack" to the whites, returned to California. For two years the group of about seventy-five warriors and their families passively resisted moving. After they were attacked in early 1873, they retreated to the lava beds south of Tule Lake, and there, from January through April, they held off repeated attempts to dislodge them. Eventually, the army forced them from their encampment, and the struggle ended in June 1873, with the capture of Captain Jack. He and three other leaders were hanged in October of that year.

In the early months of 1873, newspapers carried almost daily accounts of the Modoc War wired from California. Extensive maps detailed the movements of Captain Jack and his rebellious Modocs as well as the movements of a thousand soldiers and the activities of the Warm Springs Indian scouts under the leadership of Donald MacKay, who was of mixed white and Native American ancestry.

In May, even before the conflict was completely resolved, *Captain Jack of the Modocs* by John F. Poole opened at Wood's Theatre. Not long after the final resolution, in March 1874, the Bowery mounted *White Hair; or, The Last of the Modocs*. By November of that year at Wood's Theatre, O. D. Byron was presenting *Donald MacKay, the Hero of the Modoc War* with himself in the title role, while at the same time, just down Broadway, the actual Donald MacKay appeared at Niblo's with a contingent of twenty Warm Springs Indians in *Wild Cat Ned*, his version of the capture of Captain Jack. MacKay was still acting with his native performers in New York as late as January 1879, although by then his production was the old Cody play, *Life on the Border*, renamed *The Trapper's Daughter*.

Although MacKay was part Native American himself, his plays and others about the Modoc War chauvinistically celebrated the victory of the army over the rebellious Modocs. A *New York Mirror* review (February 1, 1879) of Byron's play, which by then had been retitled *The Hero of Mt. Shasta*, summarizes the Fourth-of-July patriotism of the fourth act:

> Lava beds rising one above another 'til they reach the flies were filled with painted Indians and supernumeraries clothed in the uniform of United States soldiers; guns, revolvers, pistols, firecrackers, and all manner of fire-arms belched out their contents 'til the stage and auditorium were filled with the smoke . . . a continuous fusillade from the prompt side, red fire lighted at intervals to make the surroundings more lurid, Oliver Doud Byron, the star, vociferating all kinds of heroics, a little dismal comedy introduced by way of contrast, a grand final clash in which soldiers, Indians, villains and others littered the stage, dead, dying, and triumphant, and in the center, by way of climax, Mr. Byron, with the rescued heroine, the American flag waving overhead – this went to make up a picture which, once seen, will not soon be forgotten.

Once again Byron featured revolvers and red fire – no romance here – and reinforced the sanctity of manifest destiny by waving the flag over the fallen tribesmen. The writer emphasizes that audience reaction to this spectacle differed along class lines: "The gallery was jubilant; the orchestra disgusted." That comment, however, intrinsically betrays that it was not only the lower classes that attended Byron's histrionics.

The best way for a reporter to cover action on the frontier was to accompany the troops, and that frequently occurred. When Custer met defeat at the Little Big Horn River, correspondent Mark Kellogg was among the dead. Custer's defeat occurred on June 25, 1876, but it was not reported in newspapers until after the Fourth of July celebrations.[52] Just six weeks after that, on August 14, Harry Seymour's *Sitting Bull; or, Custer's Last Charge* opened at Wood's Theatre, followed three weeks later by *Custer and His Avengers* at the Bowery. In March 1879, W. J. Fleming took the part of Custer at the Bowery in a play by A. R. Trumbull, which may have been rewritten from one of the earlier versions. Fleming played the fair-haired Custer at least until August 1891.[53] The Custer plays departed from the usual frontier fare in one important respect. The whites lost. No climactic rescue spared Custer and his men, which may explain why, despite several dramatized versions of the battle, none gained the prominence of other significant touring combinations.

Some of the plays based directly or indirectly on current frontier events and personalities gained immediate notoriety, but most of the productions featuring contemporary border incidents during the early 1870s were unable to translate currency into long-lasting success – the charismatic Buffalo Bill, of course, being the prime exception. More viable in this regard was Frank Mayo's attempt to uncover artistic inspiration from the older, more pastoral frontier of Davy Crockett – a frontier ripe with poetry and void of violence and aboriginal inhabitants. Taken cumulatively, the imitation border plays of Herring, Wood, Frayne, and others celebrated melodrama, not the frontier. Herring and Wood incorporated multiple disguises into their acting vehicles whether they were set on the plains or in New York. Frayne inserted the same shooting stunts and animal tricks whether the action took place in the West or in Russia, as in his *The Nihilists of St. Petersburg*. In the years to follow, however, playwrights learned from Bret Harte's local-color writing the value of specific locales and character idiosyncrasies, and, as a result, an array of distinctive frontier plays and personalities emerged to entertain American audiences.

3

Prominence: 1877–1883

The few plays of this kind which have been placed upon the stage represent perhaps nearly all that can be done with such simple materials.

The *New York Times* critique of *M'liss*, January 1879

JUST AS *HORIZON, ACROSS THE CONTINENT,* AND *Kit, the Arkansas Traveller* had established a firm foothold for frontier drama at the beginning of the 1870s, so, at the end of the decade, three well-received and well-regarded plays pushed border drama to a position of public prominence. The plays appeared in successive seasons: *The Danites,* credited to Joaquin Miller, premiered in 1877; *M'liss,* by Richard H. Cox, Clay M. Greene, and A. S. Thompson, opened in New York in 1878; and *My Partner,* by Bartley Campbell, debuted in 1879. Together they comprise three of the most successful touring productions of the last quarter of the nineteenth century. All three plays employ a mining camp setting rich in specific local-color detail, and all three lean more to the romantic and sentimental mood of *Davy Crockett* than to the red-fire action of the Buffalo Bill plays. The gunfire and activity-oriented drama did not disappear, however, as a cluster of productions in 1882 and 1883 about the exploits of the James gang demonstrates.

The successes of *The Danites, M'liss,* and *My Partner* followed on the heels of disappointing frontier plays composed by two of America's most distinguished writers, Bret Harte and Mark Twain, in 1875 and 1876. Despite those setbacks, however, all three of the later hits owed their spirit, their sense of detail, and in some cases their plots and their characters, to Bret Harte.

Bret Harte and Mark Twain saw the stage as a means to cash in on the popularity of their writings about the West. Augustin Daly persuaded Dion Boucicault to collaborate with Harte on a piece originally titled *Kentuck,* but

Boucicault found Harte "dilatory and erratic," and the partnership disintegrated, leaving Harte to finish the piece himself.[1] The well-regarded actor
Stuart Robson wanted a vehicle and was reported to have paid Harte
$2,000 to write a play for him, which became *Two Men of Sandy Bar*.[2]
Unfortunately, according to Robson, Harte had no understanding of the
theatre. "One act had seven scenes in it. Another time he had a quick change
of scenes, both of which were full-stage interiors; that is, the stage had to
be reset in less than a minute . . . [Harte would] get mad when told how
impossible it was."[3]

On July 17, 1876, *Two Men of Sandy Bar* opened at Hooley's Theatre in
Chicago. Based on "Mr. Thompson's Prodigal," the plot involves Sandy, a
generous young drunk living on the southern California ranch of Don Jose
Castro.[4] Sandy helps Don Jose's fiery daughter, Jovita, hide her clandestine
meetings with a secret lover, but Don Jose, thinking the lover is Sandy, fires
him. About that time, Alexander Morton arrives at the ranch seeking his
wayfaring son and accompanied by his loquacious legal adviser, Colonel
Starbottle. Morton believes that Jovita's secret lover, John Oakhurst, is his
lost son and invites him to San Francisco. The scene switches to Sandy Bar,
a little town in the mountains, where Mary Merritt teaches school. Sandy
and Mary are close friends, but their relationship is shattered when Mary
comes to believe – incorrectly – that Sandy is married. Disillusioned, Mary
leaves for San Francisco, where Oakhurst is now ensconced as the scion of
the Morton mansion. Eventually a ranch hand and Hop Sing, a Chinese
laundryman, bring the real son – Sandy – to the house. At the curtain
Oakhurst and Sandy, whose once strong friendship had been carelessly
destroyed, reconcile, Morton accepts Sandy as his son, Sandy is reunited
with Mary, and Oakhurst marries Jovita.

After its Chicago debut, the production continued to New York, where
it opened on August 28 at the Union Square Theatre. The critics derided it,
the complicated plot bearing the brunt of their complaints. The *Spirit of the
Times* (September 9) declared:

> [M]any of the characters are utterly superfluous . . . We do not attempt
> to give an account of the plot of *Two Men of Sandy Bar*, for the very excel-
> lent reason that, although we have seen the play twice, we have hitherto
> utterly failed to discover any.

The *New York Herald* (August 29), however, delivered the *coup de grâce*:

> Ever since he left California Mr. Harte has lived upon his reputation and
> has failed in his performances. He lost inspiration when he left the Pacific

coast and there's no stronger evidence of the fact than this play . . . we have never known so celebrated a writer to produce such a worthless work.

He has reversed the part of the sun. He rose splendidly in the west and has set in darkness in the east.

The drama is like Chaos. It is without form and void . . . This inconsequential, wandering, purposeless play insults the public and must be a humiliation for the author.

Such vituperative comments give pause. Did the anticipation of a play by so respected a writer generate an especially keen disappointment? Or were there other reasons behind the diatribe? An irate Robson initially insisted that the devastating reviews resulted from his refusal to pay bribes to critics. In a later interview, however, Robson confessed, "It was a bad play; it was very properly roasted."[5] Robson as Starbottle and Charles T. Parsloe as the Chinese laundryman provided the highlights of the production, but both played comic relief roles that interrupted the action even as they added comedy. Robson himself admitted in the same interview that, while Starbottle had wonderful lines, they ultimately disconnected the plot. *Two Men of Sandy Bar* eventually ran for five weeks in New York before touring the East and Midwest.

So successful was Parsloe in his comic caricature of Hop Sing that one year later Harte combined forces with Mark Twain to showcase Parsloe's comic Chinaman. The result of their collaboration, *Ah Sin*, opened in Washington, D.C., in May 1877, and moved to New York for a July 31 opening at Daly's Fifth Avenue Theatre. In the play, Ah Sin witnesses one miner attack another and discovers a blood-stained coat. The authorities eventually accuse an innocent mine owner, who is about to be hanged for murder when Ah Sin displays the bloody coat that exposes the guilty party. Ah Sin also reveals that he has been secretly hiding the injured – but still alive – miner.

Most people loved Parsloe's comic caricature, in which he repeatedly expressed his fear that he would go to hell with the phrase "Go helly." One of his prominent laugh lines involved a dispute between a Mexican couple, which Ah Sin described as "Melican man's wife give Melican man helly." The *New York Clipper* (August 11, 1877) called Parsloe "remarkable," noting, "He has copied quite faithfully the personal appearance, the effeminate voice, and peculiar gate [sic], and the pigeon [sic] English of the 'heathen Chinee'."

Not everyone, however, appreciated Parsloe's portrayal. The New York

Spirit of the Times (August 4, 1877) reacted to his work with a sensitivity that seems almost a hundred years ahead of its time. The paper called Parsloe's performance "incessantly ridiculous" and concluded:

> If Mark Twain supposes for one moment that this character, as enacted, is a correct portraiture of the Chinaman, he is mistaken. It is a reflection of the American burlesque of the Chinaman . . . It is a Bowery boy in a short gown, grinning, and mixing the dialect of Washington Market with the business of Tony Pastor's.

Parsloe's portrayal of Ah Sin is especially intriguing in light of Margaret Duckett's assertion that in "Plain Language From Truthful James," the poem that first introduced Ah Sin to the world, Harte underscores the prejudice and hypocrisy of the poem's narrator and his friend.[6] One wonders how Harte and Twain could have reconciled the poem's attempt to ridicule racial prejudice with the play's actual racial insensitivity. A comment by Twain biographer Albert Bigelow Paine is significant. Recognizing that Ah Sin was merely a caricature, he noted that some of the character parts in the play "if not faithful to life, were faithful enough to the public conception of it to be amusing and exciting."[7] In this regard, Susan Harris Smith's comments regarding the dominant prose–poetry hierarchy are germane, for neither Harte nor Twain gave the respect to dramatic writing that they did to their poetry or prose, and they readily compromised the essence of the character in their efforts to be theatrically entertaining.[8]

As they did with Harte and *Two Men of Sandy Bar*, critics faulted *Ah Sin* and its creators for loose dramatic construction. "The whole of the first act wanders about in a maze of rude talk till it stumbles on a murder," complained the *Spirit of the Times* (August 4, 1877). Like the keenly disappointed *Herald* reviewer writing about *Two Men of Sandy Bar*, the *Spirit of the Times* critic was particularly discouraged at how mediocre a piece the two great writers had produced:

> Both of these clever humorists have tried their hand singly at plays, and neither achieved what may be called a dramatic success. Their collaborated result is in some respects even worse than their individual efforts. Few plays of the American stamp can be mentioned whose literary execution is so bad, whose construction is so ramshackly, and whose texture is so barren of true wit, good taste, and the peculiar American humor for which both of these writers are justly celebrated.

Ah Sin played for five weeks in New York before embarking on a brief tour.

McKee Rankin, Joaquin Miller, and *The Danites*

On August 22, 1877, at the beginning of the theatrical season and just days before *Ah Sin* closed, *The Danites; or, The Heart of the Sierras* opened at New York's newly refurbished Broadway Theatre. The production that opened inside brought together two of the most extraordinary characters of American arts and letters. The man of arts was McKee Rankin, an actor and manager who, in the course of a long career, was called brilliant, charming, intelligent, fascinating, and virile; also a liar, a thief, a traitor, a Judas, and a deadbeat. The man of letters was Joaquin Miller, "The Poet of the Sierras," who was credited with writing *The Danites*, and who, during his lifetime, was hailed as "The Byron of the Rockies." He was also branded a liar, a horse thief, a jail-bird, a treasonous southern sympathizer, and a splendid poseur.

Arthur McKee Rankin was born in 1841 at Sandwich, Ontario, the son of a Canadian politician. After a quick stab at government work, Rankin turned to acting in the Ohio River valley at the end of the Civil War. He advanced to leading man for Louisa Drew at her Arch Street Theatre in Philadelphia, and by 1872 he was a lead actor at A. M. Palmer's Union Square Theatre in New York. He also played major roles at the venerable Chestnut Street Theatre in Philadelphia, where he met Joaquin Miller.

Miller was born in 1837, in Liberty, Indiana, as Cincinnatus Hiner Miller, but he spent most of his life in northern California and Oregon.[9] After a conviction for horse stealing and charges of assault with intent to commit murder, he abandoned civilization to live with the Modocs, where he fathered a daughter before returning to white society. Miller tried a number of occupations. He mined, he practiced law, he served as a judge for three years in Oregon, and he organized a pony express business. He edited a newspaper and a literary magazine, and he wrote poetry. Miller married an aspiring poet, Theresa Dyer, fathered two more children, and then divorced. In 1871, he visited London, where his long hair, flannel shirt, and above-the-knee western boots created a sensation. His first book of poetry, *Songs of the Sierras*, was published in London that year, and his semi-autobiographical *Life Amongst the Modocs* was produced there two years later.

In 1875, Miller published *First Fam'lies in the Sierras*, a story of a mining camp in the early West that imitates the successes of Bret Harte and Mark Twain. In Miller's story, a good woman arrives at the camp and immediately transforms the environment. Two mining partners vie for her affections until one wins out. Eventually, she bears a child in a scene reminiscent of

Harte's "The Luck of Roaring Camp." The story also includes a Chinese similar to Ah Sin.

In the dramatic adaptation of this story, a tale of Mormon revenge was added to the frontier romance. Suspicion surrounded the Mormons from the moment Joseph Smith founded his church in 1830, and it followed them to their sanctuary in the Great Salt Lake valley. During the years of oppression the Mormons allegedly established a secret group to wreak vengeance on their persecutors. This group, called the Destruction Company, the Avengers of the Faith, the Destroying Angels, or the Danites, reportedly sought revenge on the killers of Joseph Smith and on their descendants.

The play sprang from the gruesome story of a man named Williams, who participated in the jailhouse raid that led to Smith's death. Williams drowned a year after Smith's murder, and his wife and eldest son were slain soon after that. Their surviving children set out across the plains, but, one by one, two brothers and, finally, one last girl, Nancy Williams, disappeared, all, it was alleged, victims of the Danites. The inclusion of the Mormon violence turned out to be extremely timely, for in September 1877, just a month after *The Danites* opened, the government indicted Orin Porter Rockwell in Provo, Utah, for murders committed in 1858. In that incident, known as the Aiken massacre, Mormons killed six men they suspected of spying. Although the Aiken episode was entirely separate from the Danites' revenge, advertising copy for the play referred to both stories. In addition, the name Bill Hickman, one of the Danites in the play, comes from one of the men implicated in the Aiken murders.[10] Here, as in other frontier plays, the authors blended together various border names and incidents to provide an exciting mixture with a patina of authenticity.

The Danites focuses on a young woman, Nancy Williams, who disguises herself as Billie Piper to elude the Danites, who have butchered her family.[11] She takes refuge in a mining camp in the Sierra Nevada mountains, at the center of which is the Howlin' Wilderness Saloon, peopled with sundry mining types who supply local color. Charlie Godfrey boasts the ironic moniker of "Parson" because he can outswear any man in the camp, and Alexander "Sandy" McGee, played by Rankin, is a former wagon master. Washee Washee is the Chinese laundryman while Sallie Sloan and Henrietta Dickson, known as Captain Tommy and Bunker Hill, are the convenient females. Into this mix the author throws "The Widder," Huldah Brown, who arrives to educate the miners. As Sandy and the Parson compete for Huldah's affection, both become jealous of her attentions to Billie, whose real identity Huldah discovers and agrees to keep secret.

Eventually Sandy and Huldah declare their love while Captain Tommy and Bunker Hill pair off with other miners. Meanwhile, Danites Bill Hickman and Ezekiah Carter stalk Nancy.

At Sandy's cabin a year after he and Huldah marry, the encroaching influences of society are visible as the newly domesticated miners celebrate the first child born in the Sierras. The genial atmosphere dissipates, however, when the Parson, unable to live happily near the woman he loved so dearly, leaves the camp and the jealous Sandy orders Billie to stay away from his wife. In the final act the Parson returns from his self-exile to prevent the miners, urged on by Hickman and Carter, from attacking Billie. After the two Danites are recognized and summarily lynched, Nancy Williams steps out of her disguise and is reunited with a brother she had believed was dead, freed at last from the vengeance of the Danites.

The Danites' pursuit of the defenseless young woman gave the play a powerful conflict and a focus that *Ah Sin* and *Two Men of Sandy Bar* lacked. The terrifying pursuit of a young girl by agents of a mysterious conspiracy touched a raw sexual nerve, just as Zane Grey did years later in his classic western novel *Riders of the Purple Sage*, for the public viewed polygamy as a dangerous threat to proper moral values, and, in fact, the government outlawed the practice just five years after *The Danites* opened.

The threatening Mormons coupled with the joyful miners celebrating weddings and the first birth in the camp ensured a warm reception for the production. It played the Broadway Theatre for four weeks before it moved to the Grand Opera House on October 1 for two more. *The Danites* then embarked on a typical touring season through the East and Midwest, which proved so successful that Rankin added a supplementary jaunt to California in May and June.[12]

Rankin began his next season with two more weeks at the Grand Opera House in New York, and in January 1879 *The Danites* opened a four-week engagement at the elegant Booth's Theatre. In less than a year and a half, the play had become

> [t]hat best of American plays *The Danites* . . . It strikes a keynote of American life and character and combines humor, pathos, and poetry in agreeable proportions. One cannot conceive of anything more thrillingly and truly dramatic than the spectacle of a weak but noble woman pursued by the avenging, unsated, semi-religious fervor and fury of a mighty organization.

That this *New York Mirror* critic (February 1) finds religious violence directed against an innocent woman a "keynote of American life" testifies to the deep distrust Americans felt toward religious nonconformity, whether the religious practices were the alarming dances of heathen Indians or the promiscuous multiple marriages of the Mormons.

The *New York Clipper* called Miller's dialogue "excellent, ofttimes poetic," while the *Mirror* declared it "the best, probably, of any play of native authorship now before the public."[13] The same *Mirror* reviewer praised the "remarkable" distinctness of the characters and concluded, "There is not a 'climax' but what is effective, or a scene but what serves well its purpose."

Rankin's Sandy McGee combined bravery and a rugged exterior with a heart full of love and understanding in a performance that critics identified as a shining example of masculinity. "McKee Rankin's Sandy McGee," the *Mirror* critic wrote (September 1, 1877), "is a rendition of rough, uncouth, rugged, hardy manhood, which . . . is now as well-nigh perfect as may ever be expected." The writer for the *Clipper* agreed that Rankin "delineated his rough manly quality quite successfully, being tender and affectionate in his love making and leonine in manner when facing danger."

A talented cast enhanced the production. Reviews complimented Rankin's wife, Kitty Blanchard, for her work as the disguised Nancy Williams.[14] With her irresistible beauty and despite her slight lisp, Kitty Blanchard had first gained prominence as a comedienne at Selwyn's Theatre in Boston. She made her first splash in New York starring with Rankin in Augustin Daly's *A Flash of Lightning* in 1868, and on September 17 of that year the *Clipper* featured her on its cover. She married Rankin the following year, and in 1874 they achieved a major success at New York's Union Square Theatre with *The Two Orphans*, a sentimental melodrama in which McKee portrayed the swaggering Jacques Frouchard, while Kitty played Henriette, frantically searching for her orphaned sister. Kate Claxton rendered the blind sister, Louise, a part that became a signature role throughout her career, and romantic star James O'Neill as Pierre headed the powerful production.

Louis Aldrich, who played Charlie Godfrey, the Parson, also collected excellent notices. The *Clipper* (September 1, 1877) applauded his brusque love-making with Huldah, his tender farewell to Sandy and Huldah, his final, half-paralyzed *tête-à-tête* with Billie, and his courageous upsetting of the Danites' plans. The Chicago correspondent for the *New York Mirror* said Rankin was "overshadowed by Louis Aldrich, who makes the Parson really the star feature of the piece," an opinion that was regularly expressed.[15] So important was Aldrich to the show that he not only received a generous salary of $100 per week, but a percentage of the gross takings as

Figure 8. McKee Rankin as Alexander "Sandy" McGee in *The Danites*.

Figure 9. Kitty Blanchard as Nancy Williams in *The Danites*.

well.[16] Harry Pratt originated Washee Washee, but after *Ah Sin* closed Charles Parsloe, the definitive comic Chinese, replaced Pratt. As the *Mirror* critic wrote (May 10, 1879), "Parsloe's Chinaman is unapproachable."

Each act of *The Danites* presented a different location, exploiting the western landscape as well as any border play since *Horizon*. A miner known as "The Judge" referred so frequently to "this glorious climate of California" that the line became a catch phrase for the play. Sandy idealized the California terrain, comparing it directly with the Garden of Eden: "This 'ere is the edge of God-land."[17] Thus was the mining camp linked to the unspoiled utopia. Other touches of the local color that was so important to Harte's stories found their way into the sets. The opening scene of the wagon-train camp included rocks bridged by a log. Stone steps descended from stage-right boulders to a tree stump down right, and at left a campfire heated a coffee pot. Act III at Huldah's cabin featured a log house with a series of steps leading to a rocky precipice and a view of lofty mountains in the distance. In the final act Billie's secluded cabin stood in the foreground, with stumps and rocks providing a dense, rustic environment in front of a mountain background complete with a working waterfall. The water ran over oil cloth and a calcium spotlight enhanced the sparkling effect.[18]

Aldrich and Parsloe left *The Danites* after the second year to launch their own venture, but the play continued to attract audiences and in 1880 the Rankins took *The Danites* to England. Knowing what a sensation Joaquin Miller had created in London, Rankin hoped his play would, too. He was not disappointed as *The Danites* became the toast of the season. The play opened in April at Sadler's Wells Theatre, and transferred to the larger Globe Theatre in June. One London paper fairly gushed: "Thank you Mr. Rankin for one of the freshest and most artistic treats seen in London. Not to see *The Danites* would be to miss one of the most novel and welcome American plays ever transported to the London stage." British commentators credited *The Danites* with being the first American production to import a complete company, and audiences appreciated the performers speaking a uniform western dialect and working together as an ensemble.[19] After closing its London run with over one hundred performances, *The Danites* toured through England and concluded in Edinburgh, Scotland, in November.

Rankin and *The Danites* might have returned from their British engagement prepared to rise to even loftier theatrical heights. Instead, within a year Rankin had plummeted from the pinnacle of his success into a succession of personal and legal entanglements. First came marital difficulties,

which erupted in April 1881, and, although the Rankins temporarily reconciled, business problems with a play they were preparing for the 1881–82
season soon exploded.[20]

Rankin announced a new piece called '49 for the fall of 1881, claiming that
he had written it in collaboration with Joaquin Miller. Miller denied that,
branding Rankin "the most colossal liar and impudent thief that ever made
use of the practice of both without having the necessary skill of either."[21]
That was just the opening salvo. Rankin sued Miller and Andrew C.
Wheeler, who wrote theatrical commentary for the *New York Dramatic
Mirror* under the pseudonym "Nym Crinkle," for libel, and Miller, in return,
sought a restraining order to prevent Rankin from performing '49.[22]

In the course of the legal arguments, it emerged that Miller had not actually written *The Danites*, an accusation that had surfaced as early as February
15, 1879, in the *New York Mirror*. Rankin testified that he purchased from
Miller the right to adapt *First Fam'lies of the Sierras* for the stage as *The
Danites; or, The Heart of the Sierras*.[23] Rankin outlined what he wanted to an
obscure Philadelphia actor and writer, P. A. Fitzgerald, who then wrote the
script. Rankin said he had paid Fitzgerald $25 per act – a total of $125 – and
Fitzgerald's widow, who indicated that her husband, unable to make ends
meet, had committed suicide in November 1876 without ever seeing the
success of *The Danites*, supported Rankin's testimony.

Although Miller later published his own version of *The Danites in the
Sierras*, copyrighted it, and asserted his rights to it, he never denied Rankin's
basic contention. In fact, in a letter to the *New York Dramatic Mirror* of May
13, 1882 he admitted that Fitzgerald had "fashioned the American version"
of *The Danites*.[24] Miller was apparently quite comfortable selling his name
and his story, for he confessed elsewhere that even his autobiography, *Life
Among the Modocs*, was written by someone else.[25] An editorial comment in
the *Dramatic Mirror* (October 15, 1881) put the shabby dispute between
Miller and Rankin into perspective: "Who is the greater knave, the man
who sold his name for a certain sum to be palmed off as the author of a play,
or the other, who, by his own admission, paid for it?"

Although Rankin obviously thought it prudent to buy Miller's name for
his drama, he failed to keep up his royalty payments. That prompted Miller
to hound him from city to city to collect the monies due to him, and their
occasional meetings led to the dispute over '49.[26] Miller claimed he wrote
'49 for J. C. Williamson. When Rankin took *The Danites* to England, Miller
gave him the manuscript to deliver to Williamson, but, according to Miller,
Rankin stole it for himself instead.

Rankin, for his part, boldly asserted that "not a line or a word of the play of '49 has been written by Joaquin Miller." Rankin acknowledged that he had copyrighted a title – permissible at that time – as "'49 by Joaquin Miller the property of Mr. and Mrs. McKee Rankin." He even acknowledged that Miller gave him a manuscript of the play '49, which, according to Rankin, Williamson declined. Rankin, however, insisted that he completely rewrote the play.

Once again an editorial comment in the *Dramatic Mirror* seemed appropriate: given the problems Miller had incurred with royalties for *The Danites*, the *Dramatic Mirror* (October 8, 1881) reflected, it is "utterly incomprehensible to us how Miller could have consented to associate himself again with a man at whose hands he had received such shabby treatment."

Legal complications buffeted Rankin's career. In 1879 when he took *The Danites* to Indianapolis, the sheriff attached his scenery for bad debts.[27] In 1881 Rankin placed *The Danites* under the management of Brooks and Dickson to schedule bookings and handle financial matters. Rankin then forwarded all his debts to Brooks and Dickson, forcing the firm to void their contract with Rankin. "I have met many deadbeats in the world," Mr. Dickson stated, "but Rankin is the biggest of the lot."[28]

After the courts rejected Miller's suit for an injunction, Rankin opened '49 at Haverly's Fourteenth Street Theatre in New York on October 1, 1881. The prologue is set in 1857 and uses as its springboard the infamous Mountain Meadows Massacre in Utah, in which 140 travelers were attacked by Mormons and Indians, and all but a few children were killed.[29] In the prologue, Mr. and Mrs. Stuart die in the attack. Their black servant, Ned, escapes, and natives carry off their little daughter. The main action of the play takes place fourteen years later as the hero, Arthur Dennison, and the villain, Tom Bradshaw, try to locate the girl, now heir to a fortune. They trail her to a Nevada hotel, where, as in the Cinderella story, the proprietress Mississippi has a natural daughter, Belle, whom she spoils, and an adopted daughter, Carrots, whom she mistreats. Also instrumental in the plot is an old miner, '49, who discovers he is Dennison's father. At the climax of the action, Bradshaw tries to frame Dennison for a stagecoach robbery, but the townspeople uncover his deception and force him to marry Belle – a kind of fate worse than death – while the old black servant returns to identify Carrots, who claims her inheritance and marries Dennison.

Given the publicity generated by the disputes over '49, it is surprising the property proved to be of so little commercial value. The responses to its opening were entirely negative. The *New York Times* (October 2, 1881) summarized that hardly anything in the play "rises above empty mediocrity." The *New York Dramatic Mirror* (October 8, 1881) excoriated it as a "heterogeneous hodgepodge which takes the prize for being the very worst example of its class we have ever seen." It branded Rankin's execution "hard" and "metallic," summarizing that "from beginning to end, there's nothing to praise in his performance." Even Rankin's popular wife elicited criticism. A later *Dramatic Mirror* review (December 9, 1882) called her performance "undeniably clever," but observed that she was getting heavy and suggested gently that "she is a trifle mature for the part." The *Clipper* (October 8, 1881) commented that her appearing as the mother in the prologue made it confusing for her to play the daughter in later scenes. The Rankins apparently took the negative comments about the prologue to heart. Later advertising cards listing the scenes of the play omit the prologue, but they include an additional act, reuniting '49 with his long-lost wife.[30]

Although he continued to play *'49*, Rankin's problems only multiplied. In the fall of 1883 the Rankins bought Dick Parker's 1,900-seat American Theatre and reopened it as the Third Avenue Theatre. Despite such gimmicks as the introduction of female ushers, the venture failed. During Rankin's tenure as manager at the Third Avenue, he produced several unsuccessful frontier dramas. *Gabriel Conroy*, mounted in January 1884, adapted Bret Harte's only novel about travelers lost in a snowstorm in the Sierras. *John Logan*, by Joaquin Miller, closed in November 1884, after a week of bad business.[31] The title character is the son of an Indian and a French land speculator, who deserted the family and whose identity Logan is unaware of. In the end, the father and son reconcile, and the courageous Logan, in a rare departure for a mixed-race character in a frontier drama, wins the heroine.

Miller, who retained a popular reputation as a poet, tried again and again to produce plays, as if to demonstrate that he really could write a dramatic script. Unfortunately he proved just the reverse. Prior to the failure of *John Logan*, Miller had premiered *Mexico* at the Grand Opera House in 1879. The *New York Mirror* (February 15, 1879) wrote with indignation that the piece was "one of the most pitiable, puerile, and most inherently worthless pieces of dramatic claptrap which has encumbered the stage . . . Whatever pretensions as a dramatist Miller may have had are quite offset by this production." After *John Logan* Miller tried again with *Tally-Ho!*, which played the Mount Morris Theatre in February 1885. In that play Hank Monk, the singing driver of the stagecoach "Tally-Ho!," marries Rosie Lane, known as "The Rose of the Sierras."[32] When Rosie is discovered holding a bloody knife over a body, Hank, in characteristically noble and melodramatic fashion, confesses to the crime to protect her. The miners are about to string up Hank when they discover the real murderer. Hank's long, meandering narratives, intended for comic effect, proved simply tedious, and the production was no more successful than *John Logan* or *Mexico*.

Rankin's personal and professional life continued to deteriorate.[33] In 1891 Rankin tried a play called *The Canuck*, based on his Canadian background, but Niblo's Garden Theatre curtailed a projected two-week engagement because of bad business. Rankin also had a falling out with producer Charles Frohman when, according to Frohman, Rankin refused to cover losses on *The Golden Giant*, a mining-town play by Clay Greene on which they collaborated in 1886. On the personal side, Rankin bounced from one affair to another. He left his wife for a fling with future film star, Mabel Burt, and rumors circulated that his third daughter, Doris, who was raised by Kitty, was the child of another woman.[34]

Despite all his problems, Rankin, whose once handsome physique had ballooned to corpulence, managed one last improbable run at success. In 1893 Rankin recruited a young actress named Nance O'Neil for his company at the Alcazar Theatre in San Francisco, where he had taken refuge. Rankin recognized her extraordinary gifts and molded her into a star, first touring with *The Danites* in California and eventually showcasing O'Neil as the consumptive heroine of *Camille* and other melodramatic characters in national and world tours. Rankin exerted a Svengali-like influence on the emotional actress, who refused to perform without Rankin present. Yet, even with O'Neil, Rankin stumbled into complications.[35] A. M. Palmer accused Rankin of pirating Paul M. Potter's adaptation of George du Maurier's novel *Trilby*, in which O'Neil played the title role, and the courts enjoined him from using the play. Later, police arrested Rankin and O'Neil for copyright infringement of Hermann Suderman's *The Fires of St. Joan*. In 1904 in Boston, Rankin filed for bankruptcy, listing assets of only $100 and liabilities of $27,647, including a $12,309 claim by Nance O'Neil for salary and loans.

In his last years Rankin gained solace from his children. Rankin's eldest daughter, Phyllis, married actor Harry Davenport. His second daughter, Gladys, married actor Sidney Drew, an illegitimate son of Louisa Drew, the Philadelphia theatrical manager. His third daughter, Doris, married an equally famous member of the Drew–Barrymore clan, Lionel Barrymore. On occasion, Rankin acted in pieces with his daughters and his sons-in-law, who achieved the critical recognition that Rankin squandered.[36] When

McKee Rankin died in April 1914, at the age of seventy-two, the *Chicago Daily News* columnist Amy Leslie remembered the "wild, wonderfully fascinating and unreliable" actor (May 2):

> There is no man so picturesque today, no man so capable, no man so brilliant and probably no man of such startling genius who will leave so little to commend him to posterity. Somehow he always stacked the cards against himself and overplayed the game.

The *Los Angeles Examiner* (April 18, 1914) wrote an epitaph that could speak to ages of ancient performers:

> [T]he great too frequently live too long; the fickle public does not tolerate the burden of years. With advancing age comes the change from the dramatic to the vaudeville, then the change from . . . the "big" to the "little" time, and then the change to the no time.

Annie Pixley, Kate Mayhew, and *M'liss*

On June 10, 1878, the *New York Clipper* carried a small item stating that John E. McDonough had purchased the rights to a play called *M'liss*, based on a story by Bret Harte. The piece had enjoyed some success in Portland, Oregon, and San Francisco, and now it was to open on August 12, 1878, at New York's Grand Opera House, starring Katie Mayhew as the good-hearted, backwoods girl. Within a few days, the opening date was moved back and the leading lady changed. This time *M'liss* was advertised for the Grand Opera House for September 9, 1878, with Annie Pixley in the leading role and McDonough in the prominent role of stagecoach driver Yuba Bill. Katie Mayhew sued. She claimed she owned the property, and the courts enjoined the opening. An announcement soon followed that *M'liss* with Annie Pixley would debut on September 16 at Niblo's Garden Theatre, but Mayhew halted that production, too. *M'liss* finally opened in New York on September 23 at Niblo's. Katie Mayhew enacted the title role, with Charles J. Edmonds as Yuba Bill. But that was not the end of the battle over *M'liss*. Despite Mayhew's apparent victory, nineteen months later Annie Pixley emerged in the role of M'liss as one of the brightest stars of American theatre.

The struggle over the rights to *M'liss* indicates the chaotic state of copyright laws, contracts, and play "pirates" in the late nineteenth century. The battle over the play also highlights the very different careers of two talented actresses, both of whom became significant players in American theatre.

Moreover, the conflict between Mayhew and Pixley illustrates the power of the performer over the material, for it demonstrates how one actress gained prominence even with virtually identical material and even though the less successful actress enjoyed important legal advantages. Finally, *M'liss*, the play that provoked the legal jousting, exemplifies many of the conventions of frontier drama while containing several crucial variations on the usual formula.

Even before it was dramatized, Harte's story of the mountain waif had led a legally traumatized existence. Harte's original story, "The Work on Red Mountain," was published in the *Golden Era*, a San Francisco literary magazine, in 1860. The four-chapter story centers on the feisty young Melissa Smith, who lives in the mining town of Smith's Pocket with her father, Bummer Smith, a one-time miner and current town drunk. The girl, called M'liss, receives instruction from the schoolmaster, Mr. Gray. After the despairing Bummer Smith commits suicide, M'liss is placed in the home of the always correct Mrs. Morpher, where she is constantly compared with Mrs. Morpher's proper daughter, Clytie. Jealous of the schoolmaster's attentions to Clytie, M'liss decides to run off with a theatrical troupe. Mr. Gray saves her from that sinful fate by fighting the manager of the theatrical company, after which the schoolmaster and his young charge – M'liss is only about eleven by the end of the tale[37] – leave the town together.

Most of the frontier romances followed the model of *Davy Crockett* or *The Danites*, in which coarse, unlettered, but tender-hearted men such as Davy and Sandy McGee court better-educated, genteel women such as Eleanor and Huldah. *M'liss* reversed that usual formulation, for the charm of *M'liss* stems from the burgeoning, unspoken love between the educated schoolmaster and the passionate but unlettered adolescent girl.

The saga of the little girl from the mountains proved so popular that the the *Golden Era* asked Harte to extend the story. Harte produced ten chapters, which the *Era* published in 1863, but, deciding that the story could not bear greater elaboration, Harte "wound it up in disgust," ending the tale abruptly and inconclusively. Ten years later, in 1873, just after the public's enthusiastic embrace of the publication of Harte's stories, the weekly commissioned G. S. Densmore to augment Harte's previous material. Despite Harte's objections, the *Era* printed the extended version, and Robert M. DeWitt, a New York publisher, twice issued it as a novel before the courts suppressed the fraudulent publication.[38]

While Harte successfully sustained his right to the story as fiction, dramatic works fell under different rules, for the United States considered the dramatization of a story or novel a completely original creative act. So Katie Mayhew was acting entirely within the law when she innocently initiated the war over the dramatic rights to *M'liss* in April 1877 simply by purchasing a script.

Kate Mayhew was born in Indianapolis in 1853.[39] She began acting at the age of four at the Metropolitan Opera House in that city, and in 1864, as "la Petite Mayhew," she played Eva opposite Lotta Crabtree's Topsy in a dramatization of Harriet Beecher Stowe's powerful anti-slavery novel, *Uncle Tom's Cabin*. She worked in Chicago and St. Louis and toured with McKee Rankin's *Danites* before making her New York debut at Niblo's Garden Theatre in 1873. Her sister's poor health prompted Mayhew to move to California, where she bought a dramatization of the Harte story from Richard H. Cox.[40] She paid Clay M. Greene and A. Sisson Thompson to revise the script, and on Thursday, July 5, 1877, Mayhew tested her new play at the New Market Theatre in Portland, Oregon.[41]

A script entitled "*The Waif of Smith's Pocket*, a drama in four acts founded upon F. Bret Harte's sketch 'M'liss'" was printed by Francis & Valentine in San Francisco in May 1878, and entered for copyright a month later by Kate Mayhew Widmer.[42] That script mirrors accounts of the Mayhew production and owes at least as much to Densmore's continuation as it does to Harte's original story. Act I presents the town of Smith's Pocket and shows the Wells Fargo office, a blacksmith's shop, and a hotel. Juan Walters and "Mrs. Smith" arrive, plotting a nefarious scheme. Mrs. Smith knows that Bummer's wealthy New York brother has died, leaving Bummer a large estate, and she plans to grab the property before Bummer knows he has inherited it. The pair conspire to kill Smith while "Mrs. Smith" pretends to be his long-lost wife. They plan to get rid of M'liss by enticing her to join a traveling theatrical company run by an acquaintance named Morton, who encourages M'liss to join his company. The thought of being "handsomer and better off than Clytie" proves a powerful inducement, and M'liss decides to go until schoolmaster Gray intervenes. In Act II, at Smith's mining claim, Gray persuades M'liss to return to school by denying that he loves Clytie, and M'liss sings him a sentimental ballad. When Smith, bragging of a rich strike, ushers Gray into the mine, Walters ties up M'liss and stabs Smith as he emerges from the mine. Walters then gathers the miners and swears he saw Gray kill Smith. The miners are ready to hang the schoolmaster when M'liss, desperate to save Gray, claims that *she* killed her father, which brings the act to a startling curtain.

Act III employs a complicated set depicting both the interior and exterior of a log prison. The script notes: "The walls and roof to break and fire." Above the prison runs a log flume, also "made to fire and break." The trial of Gray is in progress as the act begins with Mrs. Smith claiming that she was separated from her husband and child ten years earlier. During a break in the trial, Walters leads a gang to torch the jail, but, as the friendly stagecoach driver, Yuba Bill, holds the mob at bay, M'liss helps Gray cut a hole in the roof and clamber onto the flume "surrounded by flame." As the men prepare to shoot the escaping schoolmaster, "the flume at back breaks, precipitating Gray and M'liss into chasm at back." The final act shifts to a New York mansion three years later, where Walters lives in purloined luxury with his female accomplice. Yuba Bill and a disguised Gray reappear to help M'liss – now eighteen and a boarding school graduate – regain her fortune and ensure that her father's murderers are brought to justice. Eventually the guilty parties are apprehended, and Gray and M'liss profess their love and prepare for marriage.[43]

The play differed markedly from Harte's short story. The affectionate relationship between M'liss and the schoolmaster remained, and the subplot of the theatrical troupe, ejected from the novel, reappeared in the play. The plot to kill Bummer Smith and the jail fire were adapted from the novel. The resolution deviates from the novel, but it is hardly more successful than Densmore's clumsy attempt, which paired M'liss with a San Francisco lawyer's son and married Gray to the lawyer's daughter.

In any case, the *Portland Morning Oregonian* (July 14, 1877) loved Mayhew's *M'liss*, calling it, "the most entertaining, laughable and intensely exciting piece we have ever witnessed." The writer waxed enthusiastic over Mayhew's portrayal:

> Voice, form, the vivacity and buoyancy of girlhood, all seem to blend harmoniously and to combine in the formation of the perfect, realistic conception of the author's fertile and ingenious brain. She is just such a strange and contradictory piece of femininity as Bret Harte has limned.

The *Portland Standard* (July 6, 1877), on the other hand, confessed to being "unable to see much merit in the plot," and objected that "little scope is given to . . . the artists to exhibit much fine acting."

A month later, Mayhew brought *M'liss* to the California Theatre in San Francisco, where the *San Francisco Chronicle* (August 6) listed Clay M. Greene as the author. San Francisco was not so receptive to the play as its northern neighbors. Reviewers were displeased to find that Harte's original young girl was already a mature teenager in the play, and the *San Francisco Daily Evening Bulletin* (August 7) observed that showing the murder in Act II detracted from the potential tension of the trial in Act III. The correspondent for the *New York Clipper* (August 25) blasted the play's "hackneyed" motives, criticized the feelings of the characters "which do not seem to us natural and truthful," and lamented the "morbid, feverish, unwholesome atmosphere through four long acts," yet summarized that "with all its faults, *M'liss* is the most artistic picture of California life we have seen upon the stage." Comments about Mayhew's performance suggested room for improvement. The *Chronicle* (August 7) wanted "more juvenility, more tenderness, more impetuosity, more spontaneity" and the *Daily Evening Bulletin* concluded: "The lights and the shades of the character should be carefully studied, her vivacious moods made more vivacious, and her glimpses of sentiment more shy and tender."

Encouraged by her engagements in Portland and San Francisco, Mayhew asked Greene and Thompson to revise the troublesome last act. Thompson rewrote the script, but instead of returning it to Mayhew, he sent a detailed contract and threatened that, if the contract were not signed immediately, he would sell the manuscript to someone else. Mayhew claimed that, although she thought the terms of the contract "oppressive," she signed it on February 7, 1878, to ensure her rights to the play.

Clay Greene, meanwhile, copyrighted a version entitled "*M'liss, a Romance of Red Mountain*, a drama in four acts based upon the novel of the same title by F. Bret Harte and G. B. [sic] Densmore, written conjointly with C. M. Greene and A. S. Thompson" on February 19, 1878, and then arranged a production with John E. McDonough in New York. McDonough asked Mayhew to come to New York and appear in *M'liss* in a production that he would manage and in which he would enact Yuba Bill. McDonough was so sure Mayhew would agree to his terms that he announced the opening at the Grand Opera House on August 12, 1878. Mayhew, however, refused the collaboration. McDonough then arranged for Annie Pixley to play M'liss, and he continued to announce the play – now with Pixley in the lead – for August 12 and then September 9 at the Grand. Mayhew's injunction, however, suspended the McDonough–Pixley production. McDonough tried to sidestep the injunction by shifting to another house, but a second injunction blocked *M'liss* the following week at Niblo's,[44] and, instead, Mayhew's version premiered there on September 23.

Neither the injunctions nor Mayhew's production thwarted McDonough's plans. He simply took his company elsewhere and opened his *M'liss* at Philadelphia's North Broad Street Theatre on October 7. He used a version very similar to Mayhew's, crediting Richard H. Cox as the author.[45] McDonough copyrighted that version, entitled *M'liss, Child of the Sierras*, on October 11, 1878, and three years later McDonough sent a typed copy of the script to the copyright office.

That 114-page script with "Property of Robert Fulford" – Pixley's husband, who played the villainous Juan Walters – typed on the front clearly represents the version played by Pixley and McDonough.[46] The basic plot and settings show few changes from Mayhew's version, with Act I in Smith's Pocket, Act II at the mine, and Act III at the jail, but Act IV changes the setting from New York to Sacramento. Characters and incidents are nearly identical to Mayhew's copy, although some names are changed: Morton, for example, becomes Templeton Fake. Most of the lines, business, and stage directions are also near duplicates.

Some differences do exist between the two scripts, however, particularly in relation to the way the villains effect their crime. The idea of a rich brother in New York is a clear plot line in the Mayhew script, whereas in the McDonough–Pixley version the villains focus solely on acquiring Smith's mine. The courtroom scene in the McDonough–Pixley version is more ludicrous than in the Mayhew script. On the other hand, the Mayhew script provides a more personable Yuba Bill, who makes frequent use of homespun, ironic humor. The McDonough–Pixley version enhances the character of the theatrical manager. When he entices M'liss to join his troupe, for example, he enwraps the young girl in a queenly theatrical robe, an effective bit of business that was featured in advertisements.[47] Differences also exist in the fourth act, with Mayhew's version set in New York while the McDonough–Pixley version takes place in Sacramento. While the resolution is somewhat different in the two scripts, both attempts are equally contrived and exposition-filled.

M'liss clearly belongs to the strain of frontier drama that emphasizes romance over revolvers. Like *The Danites* and *My Partner*, which was soon to follow, the action takes place in a mining camp and involves a false accusation. In *My Partner* and *M'liss* that accusation results in a trial. In *My Partner* the trial plays a decisive role and leads directly to the denouement. In *M'liss*, however, the trial comes in the third act, not the final act, and is replete with structural problems. Not only has the audience already seen who committed the murder and how, but the trial itself is interrupted, ultimately unresolved, and upstaged by the fiery jailbreak. That ineffective use of the conventional courtroom structure produced a weak final act that, despite repeated rewritings, merely recapitulated what the audience already knew.

Also like *The Danites*, *M'liss* featured a woman at the center of the action, and, although both women exhibit masculine behavior, they ultimately reaffirm traditional values. Nancy disguises herself as a male and works as a miner. Photographs show the character with a pickax and pan. Nancy, however, is never completely comfortable in her masculine role, and, when she reappears as a female at the conclusion, the effect is that of a butterfly freed from the confinement of a cocoon. M'liss exhibits "tomboy" qualities in her tree-climbing, her threats of violence, and her feisty independence. She is obviously torn in her feelings, however, as she is jealous of the conventionally beautiful Clytie and craves the attention of the schoolmaster. The fact that, given a mature actress, M'liss had to be played as a teenager rather than a *near* teenager meant that the tone of the play was very different from that of the story. The original story produces an acute sexual tension involving a very young girl. Clearly she adores her teacher, is jealous of his attentions to Clytie, and wants him to herself. Gray's feelings toward M'liss are equally complex. On one level he is simply a caring teacher and friend, but on another, especially after Smith's death, he becomes a combination father, protector, and potential lover for M'liss. The Pixley stage version conveys sexual temptation when the theatrical producer entices M'liss. When Gray intervenes, declaring, "Leave her to me," the producer insinuates that Gray just wants the girl for himself, which incites Gray to fight. While the sexual nature of this interaction is obvious whether M'liss is eleven or fifteen – her approximate age through most of the play – the youthfulness of the girl in the story evokes a more complicated, almost predatory transaction. The end of Harte's story produces a similar complication as the older man escorts the young girl into the sunset. The stage version, by contrast, translates M'liss from an untutored youth into a well-educated woman prepared for a conventional engagement.

It was immediately clear in the fall of 1878 that *M'liss* would be a hit, but it was not clear who would control the property. McDonough's company played three weeks in Philadelphia and then moved on to November dates in Maine, Rhode Island, and Massachusetts before a Thanksgiving engagement in Boston. Mayhew, meanwhile, went to Chicago where she opened at McVicker's Theatre on October 21, and as a former Chicago actress, Mayhew received a warm welcome. Chicago writers expressed reservations about the play itself – which led to another rewriting of the fourth act – but they praised Mayhew's work and defended her attempts to retain her rights to the play. Critics liked the parts of the play that adhered closest to Harte's original story. The *Chicago Daily Tribune* (October 27, 1878) compared the final act to "the unwinding of some trashy plot concocted by Oliver Doud [Byron]," and it lambasted parts wedged in from other Harte stories, such as "Mrs. Skagg's Husbands," and from Densmore's continuation.[48] "As long as the inspiration of Bret Harte's sketch is felt – as it is clearly in the first two acts – the drama is full of vivid poetic interest," the writer opined, "but when the playwright undertakes to contrive a sensational ending all out of his own head, the waif of Smith's Pocket immediately ceases to interest us . . . [and] Miss Mayhew . . . struggle[s] to preserve the outlines of a picture which has been disfigured by a clumsy hand."

The *New York Clipper* (November 2, 1878) and other papers praised the scenic elaboration at McVicker's with the Act I hotel and schoolhouse in the foreground and the Sierra Nevada mountains beyond. The arrival of Yuba Bill's stagecoach and four was described as "realistic and effective." The Mayhew script calls for actual horses, and George C. D. Odell states that Yuba Bill drove a real team on stage in the original Niblo's Garden Theatre production.[49] Reviews seldom mentioned the Act II setting at the mine, but Act III received generous accolades. The *Chicago Times* (October 22, 1878) described the log building stage left with the front constructed of painted gauze, which faded away to reveal the interior where the trial progressed. That scrim effect became quite common in theatre, but in 1877 the "dissolving view," as it was called, was still an arresting and warmly applauded device. The review also noted the log flume, which stretched across the stage in front of distant mountains and collapsed on cue to provide the startling Act III curtain. Act IV showed a parlor, which was switched from its original New York location to a stately San Francisco mansion, a conventional setting that attracted little attention.

Commentators praised Katie Mayhew for her earnestness and truthfulness. The *Chicago Daily Tribune* (October 27, 1878) called her "really brilliant," and described the impression she conveyed:

> Her childish artlessness, the unconscious revelation of her love for the schoolmaster, which is indicated always indirectly in her hatred of a fancied rival, the alternations of vehement passion, wayward caprice, tender, womanly affection, and filial devotion – combine to make up a portrait at once captivating to the eye and heart.

In addition to applauding her performance, the newspapers also took her side in the legal wrangling. The *Daily Tribune* accused McDonough of trying to "deprive" Mayhew of her rights, and the *Chicago Times* (November 10, 1878) and the *New York Mirror* (March 22 and 29, 1879) also criticized McDonough.

In an effort to strengthen her play, Mayhew ordered the ineffective fourth act to be rewritten once again, this time returning to Smith's Pocket on the day after Act III.[50] Although the *Chicago Times* (November 3, 1878) and the *Daily Tribune* (November 5, 1878) both found the new ending an improvement, the latter complained that "there is something still lacking to give an effective climax . . . [for] the curtain comes down upon the mere recital of a tame moral lesson."

In mid November 1878, Judge Lawrence rendered his decision in the New York suit for a permanent injunction against the McDonough production of *M'liss*. The judge determined that the issue was not one of copyright, which would have pushed the issue into a federal court, but rather one that concerned only the contract of February 7, 1878, between Mayhew and the authors, Greene and Thompson. Although the defense argued that Mayhew had broken her contractual arrangements and thereby forfeited her rights, Judge Lawrence sided completely with Mayhew and continued the injunction.[51] While a few of the terms in the contract such as "certainty" and "sharing limit" related to specific nineteenth-century staging practices, the gist of it provided that Mayhew could maintain her rights to *M'liss* if she played the work at least forty times each year and paid a minimum of ten dollars per performance. Or she could buy all rights for $5,000. It is clear why Mayhew thought her contract "oppressive." If she performed *M'liss* eight times a week through a forty-week season, she would owe $3,200. Even to buy all the rights for $5,000 was a stretch. Those were lofty figures at a time when rights to untried plays frequently sold for $100 or less. Mayhew's victory in the court, therefore, was a somewhat hollow one, for she could only sustain her rights at great cost.

Worse yet, the ruling applied only to the state of New York. Fending off play pirates in the nineteenth century was a time-consuming pursuit. The injured party had to travel to where the pirating company was playing and seek an injunction there. Often, by the time the complainant located an offending troupe, the pirates would have sailed off to fresh waters. Even if, as in this case, the plaintiff won an injunction, the artist would have to repeat that court action in virtually every jurisdiction. Protecting rights, therefore, was a bothersome and expensive business, which could only be justified if the stakes were high.

The stakes for *M'liss* were appropriately high, so, just eight days after gaining the favorable New York decision, Mayhew followed McDonough to Boston, where his *M'liss* was scheduled for a lucrative Thanksgiving week at the Gaiety Theatre, and she confidently sued again. Mayhew won a preliminary injunction, but this time the final decision was not so favorable. On November 25, Judge Colt of the Superior Court of Massachusetts ruled that the facts were too much in dispute, and he dissolved the preliminary injunction.[52] That action, which sanctioned McDonough's production in Boston, constituted a major victory for McDonough and Pixley and a stunning defeat for Mayhew.

Both groups continued to play *M'liss*. McDonough and Pixley visited Lawrence, Lowell, and Providence, and then returned to Philadelphia for Christmas week at the Walnut Street Theatre, clearly a step up from the tiny North Broad Street Theatre. The script of *M'liss* again provoked negative comments, but Pixley continued to impress. The *Philadelphia Evening Bulletin* (December 24, 1878) praised her "remarkable skill" in delineating the restless discontent of the heroine and compared her to Lotta Crabtree:

> She reminds one of Lotta in her methods. She is good-looking, animated, and full of grace in all her movements . . . She sings nicely and dances prettily, and of course she readily became a favorite with the audience.

The *Philadelphia Inquirer* (December 24, 1878) made the same comparison:

> Compared to Miss Crabtree, she does not suffer at all. Miss Pixley has a pleasing voice; she sings and dances well, and acts with excellent force and taste.

Barred from venturing into New York, McDonough in January reorganized his troupe to present *HMS Pinafore*, which had burst into prominence in England in 1878. This comic operetta by the prolific partnership of W. S. Gilbert and Arthur Sullivan produced one of the several ironies in the conflict between the two *M'liss* productions, for Annie Pixley became the first actress to perform Josephine in New York solely because her company could not legally play *M'liss* there. Mayhew's *M'liss* was booked into the Standard Theatre in New York for two weeks commencing January 6, 1879. She played only one. On January 15, McDonough's company moved into the theatre and staged the entirely unauthorized but perfectly legal New York debut of *HMS Pinafore* with Annie Pixley playing the lead.[53]

The struggle resumed as the two companies prepared for the 1879–80 season, but in the actress-to-actress competition for the role, Pixley emerged the clear winner. Although Mayhew received praise for her work, her abilities were unable to overcome the deficiencies of the script. The *New York Times* reviewer, for instance, liked the actress (January 7, 1879) declaring, "Miss Katie Mahew [sic] is a remarkable little actress . . . There was an irresistible charm about her . . . The utter absence of conventionality in her simple methods was especially noteworthy." And the *New York Mirror* (January 11, 1879) called her performance "a clever union of humor and pathos . . . very natural in its treatment." The play itself, however, elicited an odd mixture of praise and criticism, as if critics *wanted* to like it because they liked the actress or because they sided with her in her battle for the rights or just because they wanted to see successful American plays. Writers for the *Times* and the *Mirror* reflected all these reasons. The *Mirror* reviewer waved the flag by writing that "the play of *M'liss* as an American production can rank with the best in that embryonic list." The *Times* critic compared *M'liss* to *The Danites*, saying "intrinsically the two plays teach the same lessons – the heroism of untaught man and the idyllic purity of love nurtured amid the woodland of solitudes." The writer further noted with some insight:

> It is vain to enquire whether or not the Oakhursts and Yuba Bills of literature are real or fictitious personages; artistically their actual existence is a matter of no consequence. Are the novels of Cooper less interesting because we suspect that his Indians were, in most respects, creations of his poetic fancy?

Still, the critic disliked much about the play. The highlights were "submerged in a mess of interpolated talk" and Harte's best scenes were "rendered tedious and prosaic." The drama ruined the intimate scale of the short story because the playwrights were forced to "elaborate a certain number of incidents and characters which were artistically all that they could be." The *Times* reviewer concluded, with rather less perspicacity than was shown in the rest of the comments, that frontier plays had evolved as far as they could: "The few plays of this kind which have been placed upon the stage represent perhaps nearly all that can be done with such simple materials." Obviously the continued reconfigurations of frontier drama even through movies made a hundred years after *M'liss* such as *The Wild Bunch*, *The Unforgiven*, and *Dances with Wolves* give the lie to that evaluation.

Despite praise for her performances, Mayhew lacked the spark needed to overcome critics' reservations about the play and produce a resonating hit. Her acting, at least prior to her work in *M'liss*, had shown little potential for star quality. The *New York Times* (January 7, 1879) wrote that she possessed

Figure 10. Kate Mayhew in the title role of *M'liss*.

no "special dramatic power." In Chicago, according to the *Chicago Times* (November 10, 1878), she was known "if at all, simply as a competent young actress," and the same paper (October 22, 1878) called her performance as M'liss "a surprise," certainly a backhanded compliment. Mayhew was competent, even excellent, without being charismatic.

A second factor hindering Mayhew was that, although photographs show an apparently attractive woman, writers did not regard her as a striking beauty. Wilke's New York *Spirit of the Times* (January 11, 1879) referred to her as "comely . . . without being in the least beautiful" and the *New York Times* (January 7, 1879) observed that she had little "personal beauty." A writer for the *Portland Standard* (July 3, 1877) described her most striking feature, a mane of long hair that cascaded past her waist: "Her hair is a regular crown of glory, each rippling tress of which seems to shine with a light of its own, and to cover her rags and roguishness like a shimmering veil."

Third, Mayhew lacked something that Annie Pixley used to advantage – an excellent singing voice. Relatively few references addressed Mayhew's skills as a singer or dancer. The *New York Mirror* (January 11, 1879) indicated that she performed songs and dances for the miners in the first and fourth acts, but it called them "extraneous" and avoided comment on their quality. In California, the *San Francisco Chronicle* (August 7, 1877) chided that "her songs would have been better omitted."

Annie Pixley, on the other hand, overcame both script problems and bad publicity from the lawsuits. Pixley was born Annie Shea in Brooklyn in 1855.[54] After her father died, her mother moved west with Annie and three siblings. She married a California rancher named Pixley, whose last name Annie adopted, and in 1874 Annie married Robert Fulford, who often acted with her. In 1878, Pixley performed "The Widder" in *The Danites* with McKee Rankin and Gretchen in Joseph Jefferson's *Rip Van Winkle*.

Where comments about Mayhew's early performances as an actress are positive but constrained, those about Pixley suggest exceptional ability. Even while the legal tug-of-war clouded Pixley's production of *M'liss*, reviewers comfortably separated the actress from the play. In Chicago, one of Mayhew's most supportive cities, a correspondent for the *New York Mirror* (June 14, 1879) wrote disparagingly of McDonough while praising Pixley:

> Annie Pixley has unfortunately been handicapped by John McDonough and the bad play called *M'liss* . . . and therefore has not taken the front place she deserves . . . The sprite little actress is unquestionably one of the best soubrettes we have ever had here.

In another Chicago appearance, the play bore the brunt of the criticism, while the *Mirror* (December 13, 1879) showered Pixley with accolades:

> Miss Pixley is a delightful actress and singer, and illumines the bad play of *M'liss*. She is like a candle in a hollow pumpkin, and such talents as hers are wasted playing seconds to great and good John McDonough.

Annie Pixley had what Katie Mayhew lacked: good looks, an exceptional voice, and stage charisma. A Brooklyn writer for the *Dramatic Mirror* (May 22, 1880) noted that she possessed "a pleasing figure, an attractive face, a well-cultivated voice, and a wealth of animal spirits." A Cincinnati correspondent remarked on her "beautiful form" and another *Dramatic Mirror* reporter wrote of her "effervescence, dash and vivacity . . . added to a handsome face and a graceful figure."[55]

Figure 11. Annie Pixley in the title role of *M'liss*.

Pixley's singing was regarded as remarkable. The Cincinnati critic found her voice "far above the standard," and a St. Louis reporter enthused that "she sings like a bird with its heart full and its throat set to music."[56] The *New York Clipper* (April 3, 1880) declared, "As a vocalist she has no superior and possibly only a single equal on the dramatic stage."

Pixley also brought to the stage the special animation of a gifted performer. Variously described as "mercuriality," "vivacity," "effervescence," "magnetic powers," or "animal spirits," her dynamic performance style charmed audiences and prompted frequent comparisons with Lotta Crabtree and Maggie Mitchell.[57] A *Mirror* writer (March 27, 1880) described her acting vividly: "[Pixley] is graceful, quite prepossessing, and she has acquired a certain proficiency in speaking with that 'streety' accent peculiar to the kind of characters made popular by Tony Hart." Pixley clearly won the dramatic competition where it counted the most – on stage – and in February 1880, Mayhew gave in. The *New York Mirror* (February 14) carried the following note in its "Professional Doings" section: "The legal complications of *M'liss* are ended. Katie Mayhew has disposed of her interest in it to John E. McDonough." Once Mayhew sold her interest in *M'liss* to McDonough, Annie Pixley could play in New York. On March 3 she performed the role of M'liss for the first time in the state at Binghamton, and on March 22 she opened a hugely successful five-week engagement at the Standard Theatre in New York City. The *Mirror* (April 3) wrote of her popularity: "Pretty Annie Pixley is romping her way into the hearts of our theatre-goers, just in the same way Lotta did some years ago." The *Clipper* (April 3) noted that even during the religious holy week prior to Easter, considered one of the dullest for ticket sales, Pixley generated an increased attendance. After the standard complaints about the script, the paper lavished praise on Pixley:

> As an actress Miss Pixley possesses an abundance of mercuriality, is vivacious in style, quickly wins the sympathy of her auditors by her magnetic powers, and seems thoroughly in earnest in whatever she undertakes . . . in characters of the class portrayed by Maggie Mitchell or Lotta . . . she may eclipse the reputation of either of those artists.

Annie Pixley and *M'liss* became a major attraction. Critics in New York and Chicago hailed her as one of the finest soubrettes in America, and, just a year after her triumph in New York, the *Dramatic Mirror* declared, "Annie Pixley is probably the most attractive American star on the stage today, with one or two exceptions."[58] The same issue extravagantly labeled Pixley's

M'liss "[t]he most popular play on the American stage." It was not unusual for the company to gross over $5,000 per week, and the *Dramatic Mirror*, noting that Pixley's touring receipts consistently bettered those of Lotta and Maggie Mitchell, concluded: "The lady is esteemed by managers one of the best-paying stars in the United States."[59]

Throughout the 1880s Annie Pixley and *M'liss* reigned as one of America's most cherished attractions. The *Mirror* featured Pixley on its cover after her *M'liss* first opened in New York and again just fourteen months later – an unusual tribute to her popularity. The following year, August 19, 1882, Pixley graced the cover of the *Dramatic World*. Although she occasionally undertook other parts, including the title roles in Fred Marsden's *Zara* and A. C. Gunter's *The Deacon's Daughter*, it was her portrayal of M'liss for which she was famous, and by the time of her death in 1893 she had enacted it over two thousand times.[60]

Although Annie Pixley shone as one of America's brightest stars in the 1880s, misfortune dimmed the luster of her success. Pixley's mentor, John E. McDonough, died of throat cancer in February 1882.[61] Four years later Thomas Roland Fulford, Pixley's only child, died before he reached his teens. Pixley never fully recovered from that loss, and seven years later, on November 8, 1893, she died. In addition to a conventional obituary, the *New York Dramatic Mirror* editorialized: "Her M'liss . . . fell only a little short of greatness."[62]

Kate Mayhew's career went in the opposite direction. Not bound by any one character, she acted in more than five hundred roles in plays, movies, and on radio in a career that spanned over seventy-five years. She worked with virtually every major star in the late nineteenth and early twentieth centuries, from Maggie Mitchell, Lotta Crabtree, and Charlotte Cushman in her early days, through James O'Neill, John Drew, and Maurice Barrymore in her middle years, to Henry Fonda, Lillian Gish, and Philip Barry in her later years. She starred on radio as Mother on the CBS "School of the Air," and she last acted in the Alfred Lunt and Lynn Fontanne production of Jean Giraudoux's *Amphitryon 38* in 1937. In 1936 the "Broadway Associates" honored Mayhew at a luncheon where she was acclaimed "the oldest living actress."[63] She died in 1944 at the age of ninety-one.

The saga of *M'liss* continued even beyond Annie Pixley and Katie Mayhew. Barbara Tennant played M'liss in a 1915 film version that turned Bummer Smith's valuable property into oil wells. Three years later Mary Pickford starred as the young heroine in a treatment that closely followed the stage version. Universal filmed *The Girl Who Ran Wild* in 1922, a very different retelling of the story with Gladys Walton as M'liss, and Anne Shirley starred in a romantic 1936 *M'liss*. On stage, comedienne Nellie McHenry revived the piece in 1901, and the play was produced off-Broadway as recently as July 1976.

Louis Aldrich, Charles Parsloe, and *My Partner*

On September 16, 1879, Bartley Campbell's *My Partner*, the third major frontier play of the late 1870s, opened at the Union Square Theatre in New York. The partners of the title were two gold miners in love with the same woman, but the actual partners of the production were Louis Aldrich and Charles T. Parsloe. Aldrich and Parsloe spent two seasons with McKee Rankin and *The Danites* before striking out on their own. Despite their previous successes, however, getting *My Partner* to the boards proved a challenge, and only Aldrich personally reading the script to theatre manager Albert M. Palmer convinced Palmer to back the production.

Parsloe was born in New York on October 1, 1836, the son of an English actor. Adept at acrobatic tumbling and circus antics, he worked frequently with Frank Mayo and appeared in F. S. Chanfrau's original production of *Kit, the Arkansas Traveller*. His Chinese impersonation in *Two Men of Sandy Bar* brought him instant popularity and won him the title role in *Ah Sin*. He followed that with his success as Washee Washee in *The Danites* before teaming with Aldrich in *My Partner* to play Wing Lee, another Chinese laundryman.

Aldrich was born Louis Lyon on October 1, 1843, in Ohio.[64] As a child actor he was called the "Ohio Roscius" and the "Juvenile Wonder," and he played Richard III, Shylock, and Macbeth while still a teenager. He assumed the name Louis Aldrich when he joined R. G. Marsh's troupe of juvenile actors in 1858. After five years touring with Marsh, Aldrich performed at Tom Maguire's Opera House company in San Francisco, where, for the next three years, he learned from actors such as Junius Brutus Booth Jr. and Frank Mayo. Aldrich returned to the East in 1866 as a member of the Boston Theatre stock company, where he worked for seven years. In 1874 Aldrich acted in the company of Alice Placide and Charles Emmett in their frontier thriller, *Little Rifle; or, The White Spirit of the Pawnees*. During the next three seasons Aldrich served as leading man at Louisa Drew's Arch Street Theatre in Philadelphia, performed major roles for Wood's Theatre in New York, acted for John Ford's company in Baltimore, and occasionally made short starring tours. Then came his breakthrough with *The Danites*, where many reviewers regarded his portrayal of The Parson as the main reason for the success of the piece. Aldrich, the *New York Mirror* maintained, "was the real attraction."[65] *My Partner* provided Aldrich with his opportunity to test that assertion.

Author Bartley Campbell pinned particular hopes on *My Partner* as well. Campbell, born in Pittsburgh in 1843, had, like many authors, come to playwriting through journalism. He had written over a dozen plays before *My Partner*, many of them for Richard M. Hooley's Theatre in Chicago, including at least two – *Through Fire* in 1871 and *The Vigilantes; or, The Heart of the Sierras* in 1878 – with western settings. *The Vigilantes*, based on Harte's "The Outcasts of Poker Flat," served as a precursor to *My Partner* when Aldrich starred in it at New York's Grand Opera House. Still, while several of his plays had gained recognition, Campbell had failed to achieve any real success in New York.

Albert M. Palmer, the manager of the Union Square Theatre, showed little initial interest in Campbell's new play. According to theatrical agent C. R. Gardiner, Gardiner arranged for Aldrich to visit Palmer and read the play to him. When Aldrich arrived, Palmer said he could give Aldrich only ten minutes. Reluctant simply to leave the manuscript, Aldrich offered to read Palmer the first act and then leave the play. By the end of Act 1, however, Palmer was hooked. He delayed his appointment, listened to the rest of the play, and decided to open his 1879–80 season with *My Partner*.[66]

The rising curtain of the Union Square Theatre on opening night revealed the exterior of the Golden Gate Hotel in the mining district at the foot of Mt. Shasta in California.[67] Matthew Brandon, the proprietor of the hotel, has two beautiful daughters: Grace, who is fascinated by Sam Bowler, a former circus trapeze artist currently working halfheartedly at mining, and Mary, who, in the euphemistic words of one *New York Clipper* reviewer (September 27, 1879), is "more than fascinated and yet not quite married by" Ned Singleton. The nattily attired Ned graduated from an eastern college before heading for the mines to try his luck. Ned's partner in the mines is Joe Saunders, a plain-looking opposite to Ned. Unknown to Joe, Mary loves Ned. Unknown to Mary and Ned, Joe loves Mary, and when he discovers their secret affair he swears to the pregnant Mary – in a moving scene frequently depicted in advertisements for the production – that he will make Ned marry her. Unfortunately, Josiah Scraggs, bent on revenge against Matthew Brandon, overhears the conversation and sees in Mary's misfortune a way to hurt Brandon. Joe, distraught, severs his partnership with Ned and leaves their cabin, refusing to shake Ned's hand. Scraggs arrives and, hoping to embarrass Brandon by dissuading Ned from marrying Mary, he tells Ned that Mary has been Joe's mistress. As the infuriated Ned lunges for Scraggs, Scraggs stabs him and steals his gold. When the miners discover Ned's body, they first blame Wing Lee, but evidence points to Joe, and he is arrested. Months later in the parlor of the Golden Gate Hotel, Joe awaits the verdict of his trial. Meanwhile, Mary and Wing Lee return from a six-month absence, during which time Mary's baby died and Wing Lee cared for her. When Brandon demands that his daughter explain her absence, Joe tries to rescue her reputation by claiming that he and Mary were secretly married, and he declares his willingness to repeat the ceremony publicly. Although Joe confides to Mary that she does not really have to love him because he will probably be hanged soon, anyway, Mary now respects Joe's selfless courage and is more than willing to marry him. Just as the court announces its guilty verdict, Wing Lee arrives with a bloody shirt bearing Scraggs' name. A quick search of Scraggs' possessions uncovers Ned's gold, and the miners haul Scraggs to a nearby tree, leaving Joe and Mary to share a future together.

Two major subplots spice the play. One involves Mary's sister, Grace, who winds up with the former circus performer. The second features a blustering candidate for reelection to the legislature, Major Henry Clay Britt, who courts Posie Pentland, the spinster housekeeper of the hotel.

From the moment it opened, *My Partner* evoked powerful and positive responses. Reviewers praised virtually everything and everyone associated with the production. The *New York Mirror* (September 20, 1879) said Aldrich played Joe "superbly . . . displaying an amount of intensity simply marvelous." Later that same season (April 17, 1880), citing his "spontaneous and natural" style, the *Mirror* reviewer concluded, "There is an absence of all conventionality in Aldrich's acting that is delightful and refreshing." Aldrich made an unusual hero, for there was nothing dashing or handsome about him. Part of the appeal of the play lay in the fact that the "average Joe" emerged as the hero and won the heart of the girl he adored. Imagine a western movie where Ernest Borgnine marries the heroine. Although Ned initially attracts Mary, it is Joe who stands as the model of masculinity through Aldrich's "virile, manly performance." Ned was a fashion plate. Advertisements depict a clean-shaven dandy with plaid pants and a fitted coat carefully buttoned. Ned wears shoes rather than boots, and his hair is carefully trimmed. In a western male figure, even the fact that he is educated makes him suspect, for the well-schooled have little need to leave the East. Joe, by contrast, is a simple, untutored man. Rough and burly in appearance,

Figure 12. Poster for Bartley Campbell's *My Partner.*

he wears boots, a full beard, and long hair. His coat and collar hang open, like his heart. Joe repeatedly sacrifices himself for the woman he loves, and, in so doing, he symbolizes that the inside of a man is more important than the outside.

With Wing Lee, Parsloe undertook his fourth significant Chinese role, following Hop Sing, Ah Sin, and Washee Washee, and critics and audiences laughed at his antics. The *Clipper* reviewer (September 27, 1879) pointed out that Wing Lee's connection with the plot in *My Partner* duplicated that of Ah Sin in the Harte–Twain play, but it still said that his "work as the Chinaman can hardly be improved upon," and the *Mirror* (September 27, 1879) concurred: "In Chinese roles Mr. Parsloe is inimitable." Yet, while audiences laughed at his Chinese caricatures, legislatures debated ways to halt Chinese immigration, and in 1882, just three years after the premiere of *My Partner*, Congress passed the Chinese Exclusion Act to block further immigration. Just as audiences laughed at the representation of Indians in the Buffalo Bill plays while following the defeat of the tribes in newspaper articles, so audiences marginalized Wing Lee through their laughter even as they passed laws to ban him.[68]

In addition to Aldrich and Parsloe, the talented cast included Maude Granger as Mary and Minnie Palmer as Grace. Frank Mordaunt played Major Britt, and Henry Crisp was Ned Singleton. They, too, received commendation. Of Maude Granger's Mary the *Mirror* (September 20, 1879) wrote: "We do not know of any actress who could bring more intelligence, labor, and good looks to the depiction of the poignant woes and heartsore griefs of this woman."

The scenery also received plaudits, especially the first set with its distant view of Mt. Shasta, which the *Mirror* in the same review called "a genuine triumph." Bartley Campbell gathered the encomia he sought as the *Mirror* critic gushed:

> A good authority once said that Bartley Campbell displays more poetry in his writings than all other living dramatists combined. It is true. There are in *My Partner* lines of the tenderest and most unspeakable pathos, poetry as deep and full and genuine as the sounds wooed and wafted through a forest of pines and as redolent of the atmosphere of California as the streams which lave its valleys or the snows which crown its mountain heights.

My Partner exerted so powerful a hold on its audiences that within two years critics pronounced humble Joe Saunders "one of the greatest dramatic creations of the period." The play itself, meanwhile, became "the best drama illustrative of American life ever presented [in Boston]" and even "the best American drama by an American author ever written."[69]

Not everyone shared this unbounded enthusiasm. When *My Partner* visited Lewiston, Maine, in 1880, the Reverend J. Benson Hamilton railed at the illicit love affair. Mary Brandon, after all, winds up with the hero despite her fornication with Ned Singleton. Reverend Hamilton blasted the morality of the piece, declaring it indecent and un-Christian. The Reverend's attacks, the *Lewiston Weekly Gazette* dryly reported (October 8), inspired "a success that surpassed the most sanguine anticipations of the management."

By today's moral standards the righteousness of *My Partner* seems more laughable than touching. That Joe feels compelled to rescue Mary's reputation or that Mary meekly allows him to do so jars our modern sense of the equality of the sexes. That Campbell felt compelled to have Mary's baby die, as if to purge her sin through sacrifice, today seems callously moralistic. Perhaps, however, we might recall that even one hundred and twenty years after *My Partner*, the birth of a child to a single mother on a popular television series provoked national debate. In its time the moral dimension of *My Partner* – as the Reverend Hamilton's protest testifies – was *avant garde* in its implication that a fallen woman could gain happiness and return to the grace of society, prefiguring a similar redemption that appears in John Ford's *Stagecoach* sixty years later.

In addition to the titillation of its racy material, *My Partner* was a well-constructed melodrama that used its trial format much more effectively than *M'liss*. While a trial is a common feature in melodrama because it pits two sides so dynamically in opposition, it assumes special meaning in a frontier play. The trial provides a definitive manifestation of civilization and, as such, it represents the attempt not only to impose order on the action of the play, but also to impose society's order on the unruly frontier itself. As such, the trial was employed not only in *M'liss* and *My Partner* but in later plays as well, with variations such as the town meeting in *The Girl of the Golden West*. In *My Partner* the trial takes up fully half the play. Although the audience knows what happened in the cabin, they do not know how the truth will be discovered. Moreover, the action of the trial is carefully interwoven with the human elements of Joe and Mary's affection.

Although the trial symbolized society's regulation of the lawless wilderness, the institution arrived with mixed baggage, for the courtroom scenes also contained extensive comic elements. Joe's attorney in *My Partner* is the blustering Major Britt, and the Pixley *M'liss* courtroom featured Yuba Bill insulting Judge Beeswinger while the judge repeatedly fined Bill for contempt. The humor served as counterpoint to the tension of the melodramatic situations, but it also implicitly suggested that the law itself could be more than a little ridiculous. In a frontier trial, the characters were interested in the truth of the situation, not legal niceties.

My Partner created a sensation wherever it went. Aldrich, who openly shared his accounts with the public, informed the *New York Dramatic Mirror* that his first season grossed over $128,600 for 259 performances in thirty-five weeks. The theatres kept approximately $56,000, and Aldrich and Parsloe grossed over $72,000. Expenses, which included company salaries, printing, advertising, royalties, traveling, and baggage, totaled nearly $35,000, leaving the pair a profit of almost $38,000 to divide between them.[70] Profits increased in their second season. *My Partner* played 273 performances in thirty-seven weeks grossing nearly $130,000 and returning a profit of almost $41,000. The following year profits declined somewhat to about $35,700 despite a season of 293 performances over forty weeks because the year included a trip to the west coast, which entailed heavier travel expenses.[71] At a time when popular stars such as Chanfrau, Byron, Ned Harrigan, and Tony Hart earned from $10,000 to $20,000 in a season, Aldrich's figures place *My Partner* among the most profitable shows of its day.[72]

After five years Aldrich bought out his partner. Parsloe freely admitted that Aldrich possessed better business sense than he, and the rest of Parsloe's life bore that out.[73] The *Dramatic Mirror* claimed that Parsloe made $63,000 from *My Partner* before losing it all in shows and real estate. By 1892 Parsloe was reduced to suing his old partner for a $250 claim that the court threw out. Parsloe died destitute in 1898.

Like other performers identified primarily with one play, Aldrich searched for other vehicles. He seemed to have found one in a lighthearted piece called *The Editor*, which he wrote with Charles Vincent and which opened in May 1890. Aldrich played the congenial editor of a newspaper in Tucson, Arizona, whose visit to New York erupts into a spate of adventures. During his tour that year, however, Aldrich was trapped by a disastrous fire at the Leland Hotel in Syracuse, and his injuries impaired his health through the remainder of his career.[74]

Aldrich responded to his physical problems by channeling his energies into his already prominent philanthropic activities. In 1888 he had been a charter member with John Drew and Otis Skinner of the Edwin Forrest Lodge of the Actors' Order of Friendship, which assisted needy theatre people. He also worked with the Actors' Society, a forerunner of the Actors' Equity Association, to improve wages and working conditions. But Aldrich's efforts were primarily expended on behalf of the Actors' Fund of America, a benevolent organization founded in 1882 to assist impoverished actors.[75] Aldrich served as trustee and vice-president of the organization for ten years, and in 1897 became the first actor to be elected its president.

Perhaps recalling the plight of his one-time partner, Aldrich raised over $70,000 to establish an actors' retirement home, which opened in 1902 and still operates.

Aldrich's caring nature was well known among his professional colleagues and his audience. If audience members were purchasing a tarnished miscreant when they bought a ticket to see McKee Rankin, when they bought a ticket for *My Partner* they were buying the good-hearted Louis Aldrich as well as the good-hearted Joe Saunders.

Aldrich died June 17, 1901. He did not live to see the opening of the Actors' Fund retirement home in 1902 nor the movie version of *My Partner* made in 1909. Aldrich's contemporaries remembered him as much for his generosity of spirit as for his acting. After his death at the age of fifty-seven the *New York Clipper* (February 15, 1913) concluded that the man who created The Parson and Joe Saunders displayed many talents, but his acting did not reach the genius level: "As an actor Mr. Aldrich just escaped being great." The *Dramatic Mirror* (June 29, 1901) wrote, "It is as a broad, generous, noble philanthropist rather than as a capable actor that he will be best remembered."

Bartley Campbell's reputation soared after his success with *My Partner*. From 1879 to 1885 audiences made Campbell the most popular playwright in America, and one of the wealthiest. He amassed as much as $200,000 a year producing sentimental melodramas including *The Galley Slave* in 1879 and *The White Slave* in 1881.[76] The latter play contained Campbell's most famous dialogue. When the villain threatened to send Lisa, the heroine, to slave in the fields if she would not succumb to his advances, she defiantly proclaimed: "Rags are royal raiment when worn for virtue's sake, and rather a hoe in my hands than self-contempt in my heart." Such flowery, emotion-laden ornamentation made Campbell one of the most respected playwrights of the time. Campbell's heyday, however, was short-lived. His playwriting career ran just fourteen years, from his first work, *Through Fire* of 1871, to his last, the western-situated *Paquita* of 1885. In that brief time, Campbell wrote more than thirty plays, several of which depicted frontier subjects. *Through Fire*, also known as *Watch and Wait; or, Through Fire*, contained two acts set in the West sandwiched between two acts in New York. *Paquita* concerned an illicit affair between Jose Borosco and Hortense, the wife of Dr. Manuel Del Ray. When Paquita, Jose's jealous lover, learns of the affair and shoots Jose, the doctor, aware of his wife's infidelity, must choose between allowing Jose to die or saving his life. In the early 1880s Campbell ran New York's Fourteenth Street Theatre, but by 1885 his fortune had evaporated in the throes of a steep mental decline. By the spring of 1886 he was committed to the Bloomington Asylum, and by that fall he was confined to the Middletown Asylum, where he died July 30, 1888.

Jesse James

There were, of course, other frontier plays performed during the late 1870s and early 1880s besides *The Danites*, *M'liss*, and *My Partner*. Just as the real-life capture of Captain Jack and the defeat of George Custer had provided exciting stories, one of the most popular sources for dramatic material turned out to be the exploits of the James gang. Jesse was shot on April 3, 1882, and by the next theatrical season three different companies were presenting the story of the James gang to New York audiences. While *The Danites*, *M'liss*, and *My Partner* all shared romantic similarities, the Jesse James plays represent the action-packed line of border drama, with pounding horses and exploding six-guns. Furthermore, the James plays represent some of the few frontier pieces in which eastern institutions assume the villain's mantle.

The popularity of the James material is readily apparent. Newspapers throughout the country carried stories about the escapades of the gang. A series of letters purporting to be from Jesse himself and denying the crimes attributed to him further heightened public interest. Newspapers ran interviews with Zerelda Samuel, the boys' mother, who provided alibis for her sons. John Newman Edwards, a journalist with several Missouri newspapers, cultivated the saga of the James gang.[77] Jesse sent letters to Edwards, who became a prolific apologist for the James boys. His editorials cleverly denied the guilt of the brothers while praising the bravery exhibited in the crimes, and, harking back to *Davy Crockett*, compared the outlaws' actions to those of Sir Walter Scott's heroes.

The deeds of the Missouri outlaws, specifically the James brothers and the Younger brothers (Cole, Jim, Robert, and John), spawned books and novels from as early as 1875.[78] Edwards published *Noted Guerrillas; or, The Warfare of the Border* in 1877, and a raft of other books, dime novels, and illustrated weeklies about the James boys appeared even before Jesse's death.

Playwrights, managers, and actors were quick to realize the theatrical potential of the James brothers. In September 1882, Bunnell's Museum offered as its primary exhibit "The Ford Brothers, the Slayers of Jesse James."[79] New Yorkers flocked to see the pair, and in December they were featured at the New York Museum at 210 Bowery to extraordinary business.

In Missouri, Mrs. Samuel converted her farm into a showplace and charged curious visitors twenty-five cents to see Jesse's grave and memorabilia.

Theatrical companies mounted numerous plays about the James boys, at least three of which appeared in New York. Frank Lavernie claimed that he wrote his Jesse James play in 1880, two years before the outlaw's demise, and he and Sid C. France brought *The James Boys* to New York in late January 1883.[80] The appearance of Lavernie and France provoked spirited legal wrangling because James H. Wallick was starring at the same time in a Jesse James play by James McCloskey. Lavernie and France applied for an injunction to restrain Wallick and his producer, S. H. Barrett, from performing their play, *Jesse James, the Bandit King*, despite the fact that McCloskey had copyrighted his version of the story in February 1882, two months before James was killed by Bob Ford.[81] In January 1883, Wallick starred in the Barrett-produced work at Williamsburgh's Lee Avenue Academy and the Windsor Theatre in New York, while Lavernie and France performed at the Eighth Avenue and Bowery Theatres of Harry Miner and Thomas Canary.[82] Ultimately the courts refused to restrict the Barrett–Wallick version because, as the Massachusetts judge had ruled in the *M'liss* case, "the facts are so greatly in dispute."[83] The third play about the James brothers to entertain New York audiences followed on the heels of the Wallick and Lavernie–France productions. Henry Belmer's *The Outlaw Brothers, Frank and Jesse James* ran at the National in February 1883, and at the National and Park Theatres in November 1884.[84]

The Barrett production of *Jesse James, the Bandit King*, written by McCloskey and starring Wallick, proved the most successful dramatization of the outlaw's exploits. Wallick ran the show for more than a decade after its New York debut on January 29, 1883, at the Lee Avenue Academy of Music, and he revived it as late as 1902. Critical response ranging from condescending to castigatory recalled reactions to *Across the Continent* and the Buffalo Bill plays. The *Dramatic News and Society Journal* (February 6, 1883) sniffed: "If the management of this house [Lee Avenue Academy] intend to conduct it as a first-class theatre, it would be well to be a little more circumspect in the future and not present any more such sensational trash as it did last week." Yet, as with many of the frontier dramas, the presentation attracted the masses and even elicited a visceral reaction from some reviewers. Another summary in the same issue of the *Dramatic News and Society Journal*, reporting on the play's engagement at the Windsor Theatre just a week after the Lee Avenue showing, coupled artistic disparagement with a begrudging emotional attraction as the critic both condemned the play and recommended it. The writer began by admitting that he had expected to find a "top heavy house," that is, a theatre with the cheap gallery seats full and the more expensive and socially correct orchestra seats empty. Instead, he found standing room only at all levels, another indication that this play, like Byron's before it, appealed to diverse classes. He immediately declared, "The piece proved to be rot," but as the review progressed the writer allowed that the production was "better than people imagined," and concluded by admonishing that "the piece should be seen 'just for fun.'" Another reviewer in the same weekly (August 14, 1883), taking note of a huge, perspiring, fan-wielding summer crowd at the Windsor, mused on the play's undeniable popularity: "Nothing short of Equatorial temperature can keep theatre-goers from going to see what pleases their fancy." The appeal was still there even twenty years later to a reviewer who commented on Wallick's brief revival of *The Bandit King* in 1902, "The play carries with it an air of bravery and devotion, mingled with love for freedom, that wins for it the respect of an audience from the beginning."[85]

Several factors contributed to the emotional attraction of the James plays. For example, managers related the productions to real events by hiring individuals who had participated in the action or by using artifacts such as horses and guns connected to the James boys. While none of the companies boasted of the accuracy of the incidents in their plays, claims for people and paraphernalia associated with the actual events were regarded as significant factors. In advertising and in their court suit, Lavernie and France claimed to employ "the original horses of Jesse James."[86] For his part, Wallick bought full-page advertisements in the *New York Clipper* (July 1 and October 14, 1882) tracing the provenance of the James boys' guns and horses in his production.

Another feature of the plays that contributed to their appeal was their adaptation of various elements of the James legend. The activities of the James gang were clouded by political intrigues, personal motives, and Civil War animosities, all of which obscured the truth. Frank James, for example, was eventually acquitted of all charges against him. Still, whatever the facts, legend had already certified numerous deeds and misdeeds. Frank James had ridden with William C. Quantrill's guerilla band fighting for the Confederacy in the Civil War. During that time, legend asserted, Union sympathizers in Missouri harassed the family. Reportedly they bound and nearly lynched the boys' stepfather, Reuben Samuel. The boys' pregnant mother was abused and later arrested and imprisoned. Jesse, only a youth at the time, was beaten and eventually joined his brother under Bill Anderson, who inherited many of Quantrill's raiders. Later, after Frank and Jesse became fugitives, someone threw incendiary devices into the Samuels' house killing a half brother of Frank and Jesse and maiming Mrs. Samuel's right hand. Because investigators found a gun bearing the initials "P. G. G." – Pinkerton Government Guard – near the house, suspicion fell on that organization.[87]

The Lavernie–France production included a scene showing the hanging of Dr. Samuel. In McCloskey's script, the aged mother was killed by a bomb thrown into her house. In that version, Shapleigh, the villain, coveted the house and land, and his accomplice undertook the horrible act. When Jesse, alias Joe Howard, swore vengeance, Shapleigh accused him of the deed, which forced Jesse into hiding and a life of crime. One unique factor of the James legend was the sympathetic treatment given to men who fought for the Confederacy. In the Buffalo Bill plays only a few years earlier Confederate sympathizers were knaves. By creating the villainous Shapleigh, however, McCloskey avoided the uncomfortable implication that harassment by Union supporters had hounded the James brothers into retaliation.

In the Belmer production the brothers were already wanted when the curtain opened. Although the script provided no specifics regarding the harassment of the family, Frank refers to the wrongs done to his mother and asserts that "they made you a cripple for life" (1, iii). Such casual exposition indicates that Belmer assumed his audience would already know how Mrs. Samuel had been injured.

Another part of the James legend that found its way to the stage was the portrayal of the gang as modern Robin Hoods, stealing from the rich and giving to the poor while operating with courtesy, refinement, and honor. In the Belmer script Jesse prevents the robbery of a charming young lady while one of the tough gang members comments derisively, "He's always dead stuck on women."[88] Jesse himself boasts to the young woman that he takes from the rich and gives to the poor even if he is forced to rob "some heartless old millionaire." Later, Frank leads a stagecoach robbery in which he permits an old woman with a sick husband to keep her purse. As for the McCloskey–Wallick piece, a *New York Times* reviewer (March 24, 1885) commented that the hero was "a perfect gentleman, who wields the [B]owie knife in the sacred cause of virtue, and gets the drop on various persons for the protection of helpless female innocence."

The McCloskey–Wallick version included other incidents from the James legend. Advertisements in the *New York Herald* (February 4, 1883) referred to the Gadshill bank, Hot Spring stage, Blue-Cut train, and Kansas City fairground robberies, all crimes associated with the gang. While the names themselves created an immediate association – as with the use of McKandlass and Tutt in Buffalo Bill's plays – the production made little effort to capitalize on those connections by using local-color details. The Belmer production hardly mentioned specific names or incidents connected to the James legend other than Frank James' marriage to Annie Ralston and the final denouement of Bob Ford killing Jesse.

To further stimulate the audience the Wallick piece featured difficult equestrian specialties. Trained horses rescued a woman from a burning building, descended a staircase, and leapt through a window.[89] Horses also tore down reward bills, picked pockets, and shook hands. Wallick emphasized in his advertisements to prospective theatre managers that his horses were fitted with rubber shoes and that he carried a padded ground cloth to protect the stage floor.[90] The antics of the horses gave some critics ample opportunity to skewer the human performers. The *New York Times* (March 24, 1885) observed that most of the company "roam around and perform startling surgical operations on the English language," and added, "The two horses . . . perform their parts with much more intelligence than the majority of the human actors."

Although neither the McCloskey–Wallick nor the Lavernie–France version of the James story still exists, the Belmer version does, and, despite its connections to the James boys, the play devolves into a standard melodrama featuring ethnic stereotypes, contrived moral dilemmas, spectacular action, and overt conflicts between good and evil with large doses of punishment and repentance. The plot is fast and frenetic. Lawman Carl Greene and regulator Humpy Dick pursue Frank and Jesse through four lively acts. Those pursuits lead to a series of traps, near captures, captures, and escapes. Eventually Humpy Dick recruits the Ford brothers to corral the James boys, which leads inevitably to Bob Ford's shooting Jesse. Early in the play Frank and Jesse meet Mr. Ralston, a Pinkerton detective, and his daughter, Fanny. Frank falls in love with Fanny, and she eventually effects Frank's reformation.

Several of the characters present obvious stereotypes. Tim is a young, naive, and not very intelligent Irishman who carries much of the comic business of the play. When Frank robs a stagecoach, one of the passengers is the evil lawman Greene, disguised as a rich Jew. The archvillain, Humpy Dick, is, as his name implies, deformed. Jesse labels him a "misshapen specimen of humanity" (Belmer, ii, iii), clearly marking the stereotypical association of physical deformity with moral depravity. Calamity Jane, who appears in a subplot as a friend of the James boys, avoids usual stereotypes. A witty, self-assured widow, Calamity manages independently by running a mountain inn. Not only is she a shrewd businesswoman who immediately sets herself up as manager of a promising young prizefighter, but she is also sexually aggressive without being ridiculous.

Perpetuating one of the popular conceits underlying the James legend, the play presents Jesse and Frank as innocent victims of persecution, while their pursuers, Carl Greene and Humpy Dick, represent the epitome of evil. The play is rare among early border dramas in having villains associated with two of society's sacrosanct institutions – law enforcement and the railroad companies. The play also places the Ford brothers on the side of evil, although it draws a distinction between Bob, greedy for the reward, and Charley, who cooperates only reluctantly after Bob threatens him.

Jesse and Frank, portrayed in the play as in legend as criminals only because of persecution, provided an ideal real-life denouement for writers of melodrama. Since Jesse died while Frank was acquitted of all charges, the pair presented a forceful double ending with lessons in judgment and repentance. Jesse becomes the victim of his earlier crimes – whether or not they were committed in response to persecution – and even his final declaration of apology and repentance, in which he turns over his gun to Bob Ford and vows an end to his revenge, cannot save him from Ford's retribution. Frank, however, largely through the efforts of the pure heroine, receives salvation and forgiveness, as the final tableau showing the Capitol building of Independence, Missouri, with Governor Crittenden on the steps and Frank James surrendering his guns makes clear. The kneeling posture of the onlooking gang of outlaws reinforces the religious overtones of the surviving brother's reformation.

Public interest in the James story reached a zenith immediately after Jesse's death, but the dramas and exhibits retained enormous popularity for years beyond that. The James house in St. Joseph, Missouri, where Jesse lived and was slain, and the Samuels' farm in Clay County still attract inquisitive tourists. Frank James himself avoided the limelight for over fifteen years, but he appeared in minor roles in traveling stock productions from 1901 to 1905, and in 1903 he and Cole Younger assembled the James and Younger Wild West Show.[91] Another drama, *Jesse James, the Missouri Outlaw*, played New York's Third Avenue Theatre in 1902, and *The James Boys in Missouri* visited the same theatre a year later. Of course, dozens of films, plays, and television programs attest to the wide appeal of the James boys' story throughout the twentieth century.

Wallick proved an opportunistic performer, playing *The Bandit King* for over ten years. Although he originally went to great lengths to proclaim direct connections with the James brothers, he soon eliminated references to the authenticity of the trappings of his show. Furthermore, just as Buffalo Bill in his melodramas moved away from extremes of gunfire and toward more romantic plot lines, so, Wallick, too, de-emphasized the action of the play and accentuated its romantic aspects. In February 1883, Wallick billed his piece as *Jesse James, the Bandit King*. His advertisements referred to the exploits of the gang and claimed that his horses had belonged to the James boys.[92] The *New York Herald* (February 6, 1883) described the show as "a lurid, rip-roaring dramatic and equestrian sensation which packed the capacious Windsor Theatre last evening. Mr. James H. Wallack [sic] plays Jesse James with the trick horses once belonging to that distinguished outlaw." But by that summer, Wallick had shortened the title to *The Bandit King* and his advertisements in the *Herald* (August 19, 1883) stressed sentimental elements, promising that the show "is not a rough border drama, but a pure, simple western story of today, a thrilling story of the home fireside, which touches home in every heart." As Wallick severed the overt ties to Jesse James, reviews also ceased to mention the connection. In a *New York Times* critique on March 24, 1885, no mention whatever remains of the famous outlaws. Posters proclaimed *The Bandit King*, with prominent portraits of Wallick and his steeds. They featured an Indian maiden and a black-face comedian and illustrated scenes from the play, such as the escape on horseback through a window. Vestiges of the Jesse James origins still remained, however. The poster depicted the Kansas City robbery, one of the gang's most famous heists, and the name of the hero, Joe Howard, connected the play to Jesse James for those who remembered the "Mr. Howard" alias of the famed gunman.

Wallick added other western melodramas to his repertory, including *The Cattle King* in 1887 and *Sam Houston, the Hero of Texas* in 1890. His productions were immensely popular, with newspaper accounts describing "people turned away in droves" in Milwaukee, "the greatest number of people ever in a theatre in St. Louis," and extra police to control the crowds in Chicago.[93] Wallick parlayed those crowds into financial assets, which included "Holly Rood," a 350-acre farm in Orange County, New York, where he bred the horses he used in his plays. Unfortunately, like many others in the boom-or-bust theatrical business, Wallick squandered his fortune. In 1908 at the Commercial Hotel in Middletown, New York, near the farm he no longer owned, Wallick, in ill health and despondent over financial woes, shot and killed himself. He was sixty-three years old.[94]

Figure 13. Poster for *The Bandit King* by James McCloskey.

Different aspects of the frontier gained prominence at different times. *Grizzly Adams*, in which E. T. Goodrich starred in the early 1880s, dramatized the early trappers and traders. Mining camps presented their own distinct frontier environment in *The Danites*, *M'liss*, and *My Partner*. Army posts and conflicts with native populations represented another version of the frontier, as depicted in *Horizon*. Ranches and the cattle frontier appeared as a separate and late-blooming part of the western experience, spanning only about twenty years from 1865 to the mid 1880s. Near the end of that period, in August 1882, Harry Meredith's *Ranch 10* played Haverly's Fourteenth Street Theatre in New York and emerged as the first significant play set on a cattle ranch. Also called *Annie From Massachusetts*, this popular piece made use of old theatrical devices, which included having one actor play a dual role and putting a character in disguise. Act 1 is set outside Aunt Coriander Lucretia Smalley's Ranch 10 ranch house.[95] Annie of the subtitle is Annie Smalley, who is visiting her aunt to recuperate from lung problems. After Annie announces her engagement to Al McClelland, a cowboy at the ranch, Al writes to his twin brother, Tom, a miner in Colorado, inviting him to the wedding. Tom arrives just in time to be mistaken for Al and arrested for the murder of Silver Bud, an Indian maiden who worked at the ranch and was infatuated with Al. As Al searches for the real killer, Annie learns Tom's real identity and falls in love with him. Dressed as a man to make traveling easier, Annie goes after Al, only to find him severely injured in Tom's Rocky Mountain cabin, where he dies in her arms. The final act presents a comic courtroom scene reminiscent of *M'liss* and *My Partner*. The judge makes his assistant the prosecutor and appoints a local doctor as defense attorney, court clerk, and surrogate defendant. Eventually Annie returns and proves that Silver Bud was killed by her jealous suitor, Joseph "Red Bullet" Kebook. That revelation prompts Joe's arrest, and Annie and Tom are united at the final curtain.

In its use of one actor playing multiple roles and the cross-dressing disguise of another lead performer, *Ranch 10* employed typical melodramatic conventions. The West provided a convenient area in which to use such devices because of the ease with which old names could be discarded and new identities assumed. It was, as Bret Harte wrote in "Tennessee's Partner," a place where "most men were christened anew." In the West it made perfect sense for a character to don a mask or a new personality, just as The Lone Ranger would later do in episode after episode on radio and television. Disguise held two contradictory meanings, reinforcing the image of the West as a place for fresh starts, but also as a place of potential hidden danger, for villains could be disguised as well as heroes. Furthermore, when a woman switches to a man's garb – as Nancy Williams does in *The Danites* and as Annie does in *Ranch 10* – she also assumes a masculine self-sufficiency. There is no one else to take care of Nancy when she transforms herself into Billie Piper. The frail Annie from Massachusetts, by dressing in men's ranch clothing, physically reconfigures herself as the archetypal strong and independent western individual who actively pursues her desires, even though, in the end, she gladly returns to her approved female role.

Harry Meredith wrote the piece and played the brothers Al and Tom McClelland. While not one of the most significant of the frontier plays, it is notable as the recipient of one of the least prescient reviews ever accorded one of the border dramas. In a relatively positive notice on its first New York appearance at Haverly's Fourteenth Street Theatre in 1882, which praised its strong human interest and compact construction, the *New York Dramatic Mirror* critic opined (August 26):

> The possibilities of the western drama have about reached their limit, and for an aspiring dramatist to construct a piece that will contain any originality from material snatched out of the region lying beyond the Mississippi, is next to impossible. Bret Harte, Joaquin Miller, and Bartley Campbell have pretty much nearly exhausted the dramatic resources of the wild, wild west.

These conclusions, which perhaps rested more on the critic's wishes than wisdom, echoed comments from a *New York Times* review of *M'liss* more than three years earlier – and proved just as inaccurate.

By 1883 many major frontier dramas were well established. *Across the Continent, Davy Crockett, Kit, the Arkansas Traveller, The Danites, My Partner, M'liss*, and anything with Buffalo Bill in it drew huge audiences. In addition to those plays that quickly became standards, a wide variety of other frontier plays achieved popularity. The range of their influence may be gauged by looking at the month of February 1883. At the beginning of that month Annie Pixley enacted M'liss at New York's Grand Opera House, and then headed south toward Richmond. In that same month James H. Wallick performed McCloskey's Jesse James play at the Lee Avenue Academy and the Windsor at the same time that the Sid France and Frank Lavernie production of *The James Boys* held the boards at Miner's Bowery Theatre. At the end of the month Harry Belmer brought his piece on the same theme, *The Outlaw Brothers*, to the National. McKee Rankin and his contingent featured *'49* at the Lee Avenue Academy and the Grand Opera House before heading off to Chicago. Meanwhile, a second company authorized by Rankin and led by Lizzie May Ulmer played *The Danites* and *'49* in small towns in New England. Aldrich and Parsloe visited Providence, Rhode Island, and other northeastern cities, and on February 21 they celebrated the thousandth performance of *My Partner* at the Windsor Theatre in New York. Stepping away from his Davy Crockett characterization,

Frank Mayo used *The Streets of New York* when he followed Pixley and Rankin into New York's Grand Opera House, but he was impersonating his popular backwoodsman again when he traveled to Cincinnati and Pittsburgh. Oliver Doud Byron spent most of February playing *Across the Continent* in Delaware, New Jersey, and Pennsylvania, and he finished the month at the Opera House in Brooklyn. Buffalo Bill was being himself in *Buffalo Bill's Pledge; or, Twenty Days* in Massachusetts, Rhode Island, and New Hampshire, while Henry Meredith's *Ranch 10* company visited the Academy of Music in Cleveland and the Opera House in Louisville.

As the companies crisscrossed the eastern United States, they were also, in their manner, defining a new kind of American theatre. Bordman notes that *Davy Crockett* and other border dramas "contributed to the release of American playwriting from European shackles . . . [and] opened our stages to vistas alien to Europeans, to genuinely American scenes and themes."[96] That list of plays from February 1883 includes Mormons, Chinese, Native Americans, miners, scouts, and border outlaws. The cast of characters comment on the concerns of the day, from western warfare to polygamy to Chinese exclusion. Heroes range from the bellicose actuality of Buffalo Bill to the manufactured poetry of Davy Crockett and the adopted sentimentality of M'liss. Settings extend from California mining camps and the Rocky Mountains to cattle ranches, eastern backwoods, and the transcontinental railroad. While neither the characterizations nor the themes are especially complex, characters such as Buffalo Bill, Jesse James, and Davy Crockett and relationships such as that of Joe Saunders and Mary Brandon or that of M'liss and schoolmaster Gray suggest more sophisticated lines of development that frontier melodrama could follow. Before that occurred, however, a new competitor in the frontier drama category emerged in 1883 in the form of an elaborate exhibition known as a Wild West show.

4

Phenomenon: 1883–1892

People used to want me to dance – to play the banjo and do fancy steps. I said, "No – that is no fit thing for an Indian." It is beneath his dignity – dancing like a common street player.

Gowongo Mohawk, author and star of *Wep-ton-no-mah, the Indian Mail Carrier*

TRADE PAPERS SUCH AS THE *NEW YORK CLIPPER* AND THE *New York Dramatic Mirror* listed each year's touring combinations. Typically the roll included two hundred to three hundred companies, and in the 1880s usually fifteen to twenty of those companies specialized in frontier drama. A theatre manager in the 1880s could choose from Aldrich and Parsloe in *My Partner*, Byron in *Across the Continent*, Frayne with *Si Slocum*, Pixley in *M'liss*, Rankin in *The Danites* or *'49*, Wood in *The Boy Scout*, Wallick in *The Bandit King*, F. S. Chanfrau or his son, Henry, in *The Arkansas Traveller*, Mayo in *Davy Crockett*, Winter in *Daniel Boone*, Julian Kent and his bear in *Wild Bill*, Kate Purssell in *Calamity Jane*, Harry Meredith in *Ranch 10*, James Hardie and Sara Von Leer in *On the Frontier*, Charlie Emmett and Alice Placide in *Dashing Charlie*, Gowongo Mohawk in *The Indian Mail Carrier*, Joseph Dowling and Sadie Hasson in *Nobody's Claim*, Harry Mitchell in *Grizzly Adams*, Arizona Joe in *Black Hawks*, Buffalo Bill Cody in a variety of self-dramatizing vehicles, or any of a number of other border dramas.

Buffalo Bill's Wild West

Also during this period the patent medicine companies sent groups of seven to ten performers and Indians on the road to hawk their wares. The

Kickapoo Medicine Company – just one of many – sent out sixteen companies consisting of two or three comedians or rifle shots and four to six Kickapoo or Pawnee Indians.[1] Even with all that activity, there was room for something different. Buffalo Bill Cody's Wild West show is, without question, the most significant development of the 1880s, not only in the theatrical representation of the frontier but in a larger arena as well. The Wild West stands as a phenomenon in American entertainment, one of the most unusual, spectacular, and successful productions ever devised, and it spawned a raft of imitators. The Wild West shows represented the temporary triumph of action and gunfire over sentiment and romance in the depiction of the frontier. On one hand Cody's Wild West represented the past of a rapidly diminishing frontier. But in another way the Wild West as an entertainment vehicle represented a vibrant present in which American values were saluted both in the United States and abroad. Although Cody's Wild West proved controversial, attacked by reformers and historians for its use of Native Americans and for its depiction of the mythology of the westward movement, that did little to diminish its popularity. Like many successful enterprises, however, the future triumph of the Wild West show was not always obvious from its inception.

Several individuals suggested Wild West presentations, most notably P. T. Barnum, who in his autobiography outlined a production very like what became the Wild West show.[2] Even before an actual Wild West show existed, Cody had assembled diverse frontier entertainments. Between theatrical seasons he guided hunting parties of European noblemen and wealthy Americans, for whom he arranged demonstrations of roping, riding, and shooting. His presentations assumed added significance in 1882 when Cody staged a memorable Fourth of July celebration for his hometown of North Platte, Nebraska.[3] Called the "Old Glory Blow Out," the festivities featured roping and riding and proved so entertaining that Cody decided to form a show based on western skills. Though Cody was not the first to create such a display – demonstrations of frontier life and the exhibition of western animals occurred regularly in the East throughout the nineteenth century – his 1882 "Blow Out" led directly to the formation of his Wild West show, and his Wild West show exceeded in scale, in variety of attractions, in performance ability, and in theatricality anything of the kind that had previously been attempted. He was the first to unite historical frontier figures, representatives of native tribes, western animals, frontier activities, and dramatizations of border events on a large, outdoor scale involving hundreds of people.

In May of 1883 at the Omaha fairgrounds, Cody's new type of frontier entertainment made its inauspicious debut.[4] Cody joined noted sharpshooter Dr. William F. Carver to present "The Wild West," an outdoor extravaganza that combined extraordinary shooting and roping exhibitions with dramatic vignettes such as an attack on a stagecoach. That first summer the show toured to Springfield and Chicago in Illinois, as well as eastward to Boston, Newport, and New York. Although the show featured promising attractions, the venture was not successful. Cody and Carver did not get along, and the partnership disintegrated at the end of the outdoor season. The following year Carver teamed with Jack Crawford, "The Poet Scout," to create their own Wild West presentation. They competed directly with Cody for a while before the enterprise folded, and Carver drifted in and out of Wild West operations over the next decade.[5]

Cody's attempt at outdoor entertainment the following summer in partnership with Adam H. Bogardus and Nate Salsbury proved more successful. Bogardus, who had worked with Cody's show the first season, stood without peer as a rifle shot, although he bore no real connection to the frontier.[6] Salsbury had managed his own inventive musical comedy troupe, Salsbury's Troubadours, since 1875. Although he served as both performer and manager for the Troubadours, he acted only as a manager for the new entertainment, and the extraordinary success of the Wild West enhanced his reputation as a man with a flair for organization.[7]

Cody's Wild West was distinctly different from his plays, for the Wild West was shaped just as America's views toward its aboriginal inhabitants were undergoing a tidal change. In 1881 Helen Hunt Jackson published *A Century of Dishonor*, which documented America's mistreatment of its indigenous peoples. Her work touched a nerve, and reform groups including the Indian Rights Association, founded in 1883, sprang up to befriend native populations. Influential politicians and social reformers convened each year beginning in 1883 for the Lake Mohonk Conference, which exposed the plight of the first Americans and proposed strategies for improving their conditions. The reformers were not always in agreement and their plans did not always benefit the tribes ultimately, but the view of native populations as undeserving victims of white transgressions provided a new context for the appearance of reservation Indians in the Wild West shows. Furthermore, concerns about frontier warfare had diminished. Indians were largely confined to reservations posing no real threat to white communities, and therefore the public could afford to view Native Americans in a more compassionate light.

On one level the Wild West provided entertainment – a whole panoply of sights, sounds, and smells of the frontier. On a second level, however, in keeping with the changing attitude toward Native Americans, the Wild West provided – and promoted itself as providing – educational and cultural enrichment. Not only could patrons experience the sensations of the West, but they could also come into contact with people who created the history of the frontier. The effect was both panoramic and intimate. The scale of the production in the outdoor arena was vast, certainly much larger than the frontier plays that had been performed in conventional theatres. A small army of horses galloped at full speed around the outdoor arena while sharpshooters amazed spectators with tricks impossible to perform indoors. To nineteenth-century audiences it must have seemed that the scale of the West was being authentically recreated.

While the performances were panoramic, the backstage areas provided personal contact with the animals, the performers, and the representatives of history who appeared with the Wild West. The importance of this close-up aspect of the Wild West has never been fully appreciated, for the backstage area provided what amounted to a series of small, intimate performances. A ticket to the Wild West allowed patrons not only to watch the show in the arena, but also to wander the grounds. There they could stand close enough to touch historical figures such as Cody or Chief Sitting Bull and famous performers such as Annie Oakley. They could vicariously experience another culture as they saw tepees with Indians going about their normal routines. Of course, it was not obvious to casual patrons that the daily activities being performed in a relatively small section of Chicago, New York, or London must necessarily be different from a normal routine on the plains; and that the normal routine on the plains was virtually eliminated by the confinement of the reservations; and that the normal Wild West routine was now, in reality, that of being a paid performer. To such patrons, the animals as well as the performers provided interest. The grounds housed a menagerie, ranging from buffalo to elk to some of the finest horses most of the ticket-buyers were ever likely to see. In that pre-automobile era, superb horses held an interest akin to that of exotic sports cars for a modern audience. To put this backstage experience in perspective, a modern observer might think of the intimacy of touring an unusual or reconstructed area such as Colonial Williamsburg in Virginia combined with the special closeness of getting an autograph from a famous sports hero.

In only its second year Cody's Wild West included an impressive array

Figure 14. Backstage at the Wild West: an Indian cast member washing hair, about 1910.

of people who brought first-hand western experiences to the audiences. In addition to Cody himself the production featured William "Buck" Taylor, immortalized as the first cowboy hero in Prentiss Ingraham's dime novel, *Buck Taylor, King of the Cowboys*; John Y. Nelson, a scout and guide with a Sioux wife; Con Groner, a former sheriff who had broken up the Doc Middleton gang; and Johnny Baker, "The Cowboy Kid," a shooter, roper, and rider without equal. Still, despite the notoriety of the headliners, even in the second season success was not assured. After the summer of 1884 the company headed south for fall dates and a winter in New Orleans, where torrential rains tormented them. The venture remained so precarious that Bogardus dropped out of the operation after the second season.

The fortunes of the Wild West turned dramatically during the third season in 1885. First and foremost, Annie Oakley joined the company. Called "Little Sure Shot," the diminutive sharpshooter from Darke County, Ohio was a consummate performer. Nate Salsbury, demonstrating his managerial acumen, made her one of the first acts in the show. She looked so innocent and unthreatening as she strode out into the arena and she projected such a warm and friendly demeanor that she immediately put the audience at ease, especially since her rifle was loaded with reduced charges to accustom the patrons to the explosions of the gunfire.[8] Cody and Salsbury also arranged for the famous Sioux chief, Sitting Bull, to join the Wild West, and, though he only toured for one season, that season proved a turning point and the first of many enormously successful ones for the Wild West: in five months, the show played to a million people and netted $100,000.[9]

By the following year, 1886, the Wild West had achieved solid prosperity. It played for six months at Erastina, a summer resort on Staten Island, with weekly attendance frequently at 100,000 to 150,000 people.[10] In the winter Salsbury made another important decision. Rather than packing up the show as they had done before, he booked Madison Square Garden, and he hired the finest theatrical talent of the day to redesign the huge production for indoor performances. Steele MacKaye, an inventive writer and manager, composed a script called *The Drama of Civilization*, which celebrated manifest destiny through the emergence of civilization on the primitive frontier. Matt Morgan, one of the finest scenic artists of the time, designed backdrops and settings, and Nelse Waldron, a technical wizard, constructed mechanical effects, including huge steam-driven fans that blew leaves across the stage to simulate a prairie cyclone.[11]

Emboldened by their New York success, Cody and Salsbury laid plans to take the show to Europe. Salsbury, who had continued to manage and perform with his own Troubadour company, finally retired from that group in 1887 to devote all his time to the burgeoning responsibilities of the Wild West. Characteristic of Salsbury's management was his skill in linking the Wild West with major events that attracted throngs of people to the vicinity where they were performing. The trip to England coincided with Queen Victoria's Golden Jubilee in 1887, which celebrated fifty years of the monarch's reign. Salsbury had thought that a display of western Americana would be a hit in Europe, but even he could not have imagined the extraordinary passion with which England and eventually all of Europe embraced the Wild West.

Salsbury, duplicating a practice from his Troubadour days, courted and hosted well-known personalities, thereby tacitly and sometimes overtly gaining their approbation. In New York, Mark Twain, P. T. Barnum, and Thomas Edison attended and endorsed the show. In England, performers Henry Irving and Ellen Terry and politicians including prime minister William Gladstone toured the grounds at Earl's Court even before the first public performance. Word spread quickly that this American contingent constituted something original, and on May 5, 1888, Cody and Salsbury presented a special performance for Albert Edward, the Prince of Wales, and his entourage. A command performance for Queen Victoria herself followed. Subsequently, another command performance entertained members of royal families from all over Europe who had arrived for the Queen's celebration. During that performance, King Leopold of Belgium, King George of Greece, King Christian of Denmark, and King Albert of Saxony, plus England's Prince of Wales rode into the arena in the Deadwood stagecoach, an incident that provided years of valuable advertising copy. The Wild West settled in London for nearly six months of extraordinary popularity. The show then continued for another six months in Birmingham and Manchester before returning triumphantly to the United States in May for a summer engagement at Erastina.

Encouraged by their reception in England and reinforced by their contacts with many of the royal houses of Europe, the Wild West returned to Europe only a year later in 1889. Once again employing Salsbury's strategy of going where the people were, the tour opened with a lengthy engagement at the Exposition Universelle in Paris, most famous for the creation of the Eiffel Tower. It continued through southern France, Spain, and Italy, before moving on to Germany and central Europe, playing Innsbruck, Munich, Vienna, Berlin, Dresden, Leipzig, Bonn, Koblenz, Frankfurt, and Stuttgart.

After a break for the winter the operation resumed its travels in 1891 with stops in several more German cities. Eventually the Wild West headed to the Netherlands and then on to Great Britain, where it played half a dozen major cities before an indoor engagement for the winter in Glasgow. The final year of the tour saw the Wild West revisit London, where Queen Victoria requested a special performance at Windsor Castle.[12] After the three-and-a-half-year triumph the show returned to the United States in late October 1892.

Certainly no American entertainment group up to that time had ever enjoyed the magnitude of success abroad that accompanied the Wild West. Even today, over one hundred years later, it would be hard to think of another American production that received such acclaim in Europe. As a cross-Atlantic success story, the Wild West is rivaled only by the phenomenal American reaction to the Beatles in the 1960s.

The Wild West show returned to an America primed to celebrate the four-hundredth anniversary of Columbus' arrival in the New World. Unlike the five-hundredth anniversary, which occasioned serious divisions and questions of cultural conflict, the quadricentennial was an unabashed celebration of America's growth, strength, and emergence as an international power. The acceptance of the Wild West in Europe accentuated those sentiments, for patriotic Americans saw in Cody's success an Old World acknowledgment of contemporary American values.

The Columbus celebration reached its pinnacle in Chicago at the extravagant Columbian Exposition. Once again Salsbury scored a managerial coup by leasing grounds near the main entrance of the Exposition. Over twenty-seven-and-a-half million people attended the Columbian Exposition; the Wild West attracted six million patrons to its arena and made almost one million dollars.[13]

In 1894 the Wild West played mostly in the New York area, but the season was not without difficulties. Salsbury contracted an illness that limited his day-to-day participation in the enterprise, and that forced a deal with James A. Bailey, who also controlled the Barnum and Bailey Circus, "The Greatest Show on Earth." Whereas Salsbury preferred to site the show in key cities for extended stays, Bailey's strategy was to send the Wild West to the smaller cities it had never played before, and in 1895 he routed the show to 131 stops in 190 days over nine thousand miles. The following year the Wild West visited 132 sites and covered ten thousand miles.[14] Although the show flourished financially during the Bailey years, the extensive traveling took its toll on equipment and performers. A train wreck in 1901 seriously injured Annie

Oakley and killed over one hundred horses. A year later, just as the Wild West was about to begin its final European tour, Salsbury died.

Although the European tour scored another hit, the four-year grind from England to Scotland through Paris and across the continent exhausted the troupe. Additional problems arose in 1906 when, as the show returned to the United States, James Bailey died, leaving his financial interest to a panel of relatives. Cody still owned a third interest, but disastrous investments in Arizona gold mines, Nebraska cattle ranching, patent medicines, and other projects left him deeply in debt. Over the next several years, as part of the Bailey estate and then in partnership with Gordon W. "Pawnee Bill" Lillie, the show produced steady returns, but Cody's financial difficulties always undermined his plans for retirement.

Cody tried several times to cash in on the new phenomenon of moving pictures. He created the Buffalo Bill–Pawnee Bill Film Company in 1910 to make a movie of his adventures. In 1913 he formed the Col. Wm. F. Cody (Buffalo Bill) Historical Picture Company, and, in conjunction with the Essanay Film Company of Chicago, Cody filmed a two-hour epic called *The Indian Wars*. Shot on some of the original locations, including the actual Wounded Knee site, the movie recreated highlights of Cody's career and the Sioux wars, such as the Battle of Summit Springs, Custer's Last Stand, Cody's fight with Yellow Hand, and the killing at Wounded Knee. It featured actual participants in the events, from General Nelson Miles to Cody himself, as well as Sioux from the Pine Ridge Reservation.[15] *The Indian Wars* did not receive wide distribution, however, and like so many of Cody's enterprises it failed to bring him the financial return he anticipated.

Instead, Cody found himself bound to the saddle to repay his creditors. His "Farewell Exhibitions" stretched into 1911, then 1912, and 1913. By September 1913, business had degenerated so badly that the show was sold at auction, and for the following two years it was incorporated into the Sells-Floto Circus as Cody labored like an indentured servant to pay off his debts to the show's owners. In 1915 Cody appeared with Sells-Floto in 366 shows in 183 days over a route that spanned nearly seventeen thousand miles, and he did not miss a single performance.[16] Finally rid of his debt to Sells-Floto, Cody switched to "The Miller Brothers' 101 Ranch Real Wild West" for the next season, which proved to be his final tour. That show played its last performance of the season on November 4, 1916, and just over two months later, on January 10, 1917, Cody died. By the time of his death probably more people throughout the world had seen Cody in person than any other man or woman who had ever lived.[17]

The success of Cody's Wild West was not without controversy. Even during its glory days, critics complained about Native Americans appearing in such presentations. Though some of the carping was political – who was connected to whom and which troupes were able to secure the services of the most notable chiefs – much of the agitation was philosophical, with entrepreneurs and social reformers clashing over the image of Native Americans that should be presented to the public. Reformers feared mistreatment and exploitation of the native performers, but even more they feared that the shows would encourage loose habits, provide bad company, and emphasize heathenish, martial behavior. They wanted, instead, to project a comforting image of short-haired Native Americans attending schools, learning, and becoming farmers. Historians at the time and throughout the twentieth century objected to the showcasing of particular incidents and native traits at the expense of others. They believed the Wild West shows defined a false picture of the westward movement as the triumph of civilization over savagery and perpetuated demeaning stereotypes of barbaric Indians.[18] Gretchen M. Bataille and Charles L. P. Silet even asserted that the native performers in Cody's Wild West show were the theatrical equivalent of "the stage Irishman and the comic Jew." This statement more accurately reflects the treatment of Indians as objects of laughter in the early Buffalo Bill plays, as the Wild West show displayed a far more sympathetic image.

Recently L. G. Moses has offered a revisionist view that the Wild West shows provided money, cultural opportunities, and adventure for natives who were eager to leave the oppressive conditions of the reservations for the life of a performing Indian.[19] No doubt the native performers had better incomes than those compelled to farm unsuitable reservation lands, and Moses makes a persuasive case that Cody did at least as much for assimilation of native peoples and mutual understanding between whites and Native Americans as any government program. Moreover, as part of a Wild West contingent, natives were allowed to be "Indian" – retain their long hair and dress in traditional modes – in a way that was being denied them on their own reservations. According to this reading, Cody became a "cultural broker," to use Margaret Connell Szasz's helpful terminology, allowing whites and Native Americans to experience each other.

It is not easy, one hundred years after the event, to understand the phenomenal success of the Wild West, but the reasons are there. First, the exhibition boasted many genuinely talented performers with remarkable skills. It was a treat to see Johnny Baker lasso a steer, to watch Annie Oakley shoot a hole through a playing card, and to applaud Buffalo Bill as he rode his picturesque white horse and blasted glass balls from the sky. The show also included several spectacular scenes. Who could resist the thrill of two dozen Indian ponies circling a wagon at full speed with war whoops filling the air? As the wagon was set ablaze, the smoke and the crackle of the fire filled the arena before the blaring bugle signaled rescue by the thundering horses and exploding guns of the cavalry. Extant motion picture footage of Buffalo Bill's Wild West depicts the attack on the Deadwood stage and the Battle of Summit Springs, and even in this primitive, soundless early film the sense of action is palpable.[20] Equally impressive are the filmed shooting stunts of Johnny Baker, fancy riding and roping tricks, and bucking horses. One movie depicts the Grand Entry with Buffalo Bill introducing the show, and even at an advanced age he seems almost one with the horse. The film also records Cody talking in sign language with Iron Tail, which reinforces the idea of the Wild West as educational "cultural broker" and the notion that a primary attraction for patrons was intimate proximity to frontier icons. These short clips provide a shadowy hint of how extraordinary the show must have been in its prime.

By the early 1890s Cody and Salsbury had carefully developed and arranged the attractions of the Wild West. The large-scale events included the Indian attack on a wagon train described above, a buffalo hunt, an attack on the Deadwood stagecoach, a display of pony express riders, and a re-enactment of Custer's defeat at the Little Big Horn. Annie Oakley, Johnny Baker, Cody, and other performers exhibited shooting skills. Riders performed a carefully choreographed square dance, and other equestrian acts featured participants from various countries wearing native costumes. In their variety these acts highlighted the touchstones of the frontier: a connection with historical events and individuals, displays of skill, distinctive props and costumes, a menagerie of animals, and dramatic conflict, all confirming a vibrant and righteous American dominance.

Even with its spectacular elements, Salsbury carefully cultivated the Wild West as a wholesome entertainment with educational benefits for the entire family. Except when the Wild West played indoors, part of the thrill of attendance involved walking the grounds, seeing the cowboys, natives, horses, buffalo, and perhaps even Buffalo Bill himself. Later, Salsbury recruited Cossacks, European soldiers, Argentine gauchos, and Mexican vaqueros to ride with his American groups as he attempted to present "the whole subject of horsemanship." Even the dogged insistence of publicist John M. Burke on calling the production "The Wild West Exhibition" and his reluctance to use the term "show" emphasized education rather than performance.

The Wild West also had talent behind the scenes. A superb manager, Salsbury was smart enough to stay in the background and allow the spotlight to fall on Cody and the other performers, even though Salsbury had a low regard for Cody personally. "A partnership with W. F. Cody certainly is a picnic, as it is viewed in Hell," he once wrote. Although Salsbury arranged glowing publicity about Cody, his frustrations and, perhaps, jealousy emerged in his private writings, where he once said that Cody's "overweening vanity . . . leads him to think he is a Tin Jesus on horseback."[21] Whatever his personal feelings about Cody or the other performers, Salsbury surrounded them with talents such as Matt Morgan, Nelse Waldron, Steele MacKaye, and John M. Burke, who, despite his overblown verbiage, was nevertheless a remarkable publicist. While it was Cody who headlined the Wild West, it was Salsbury who recruited the talent that made the show work and orchestrated the orientation toward education and family values. It was Salsbury who engineered the Wild West tours, who placed the show in London for the Queen's Golden Jubilee, in Paris for the Exposition Universelle, and in Chicago for the 1893 Columbian Exposition. And, finally, it was Salsbury who insisted on thorough rehearsals and high-quality production standards.

Two other reasons for the success of the Wild West are linked. One was the vicarious thrill that audiences received from personal contact with men and women who played a legitimate part in the development of the West. Cody's exploits were well known, and they continued even after he launched his theatrical career. In 1890, for example, while his show huddled in winter quarters in Europe, Cody returned to the United States to make arrangements for reservation Indians for the spring season and immediately became embroiled in a historic episode. Nelson Miles, concerned about the Ghost Dance phenomenon that had aroused the emotions of the Sioux, sent Cody to talk to Sitting Bull.[22] Before Cody had a chance to see the chief, however, Sitting Bull was killed in a violent confrontation, which culminated in the infamous Wounded Knee Massacre. Although Cody played no active part in the Ghost Dance episode, the fact that he had been sent for enhanced his reputation as a man in the middle of the historic events of the West.

Allied to the vicarious thrill of close contact with famous people of the frontier was a nationalistic pride in what was considered the continuing march of white civilization and culture across the breadth of America. The presentation, of course, reinforced popular bias, as it cast Indians as attackers and whites as prey. The fact that Europe, too, embraced these ideas in wild excitement over the frontier exhibition provided an additional source of patriotic pride.

In a very real way the Wild West dramatized not only America's past but also its present. Buffalo Bill, Sitting Bull, John Nelson, and the various other Indians, scouts, and cowboys who rode into the arena embodied a factual link to frontier events and the fast-receding westward movement. But the show itself epitomized the present, for wherever in the world something important was occurring, the Wild West seemed to be there, from Victoria's Jubilee in London to the Exposition Universelle in Paris to the 1901 assassination of President William McKinley at the Pan-American Exposition in Buffalo. In that sense, the Wild West represented not just a relic of a bygone mythology of the frontier, but a piece of the current and ongoing history of its time. In the last fifteen years of the nineteenth century, nothing better represented the contemporary emergence of American might and values to the world than this mythic reformulation of the country's westward movement.

Other Wild West shows

Buffalo Bill Cody began the genre, but his was not the only Wild West show. In fact, in his study of the genre, Don Russell lists over one hundred Wild West enterprises.[23] Cody's original partner, William F. Carver, started his own show after his split with Cody, and the two shows dogged each other over many of the same routes. Eventually Carver took his "Wild America" company to Europe, once again following in Cody's footsteps, and then employed his company in spectacular melodramas in Australia and the United States. In between his Wild West and his "Wild America" days, Carver worked for circus entrepreneur Adam Forepaugh. Forepaugh recognized a good thing when he saw it, and in 1887 he established the "Forepaugh and Wild West Combination," which included Carver and featured a dramatization of Custer's Last Stand.

Gordon W. "Pawnee Bill" Lillie, an interpreter for the Pawnees in Cody's 1883 show before striking out on his own, also made a large mark in the Wild West field.[24] Pawnee Bill proved an able manager, eventually merging his show with Cody's in 1908. One of Lillie's featured shooters was his wife, May Manning, who was born in Pennsylvania and graduated from Smith College before she married Pawnee Bill, took up shooting, and became

"Miss May Lillie," a prize-winning rifle shot. Other acts included Lillie's brother, Albert, a rider and roper, and the Apache chief, Geronimo, the best-known member of Lillie's contingent. Lillie's productions featured dramatizations of the Mountain Meadows Massacre, the Massacre at Wounded Knee – which was certainly not called a "massacre" then – and Custer's Last Stand. Overall, Lillie hired as many as three hundred people and used two hundred horses, but his attractions could not match those of Cody's. Unlike Carver, who challenged Cody's show head to head, Lillie wisely avoided direct competition. He prospered by filling the void while Cody electrified Europe, and when Cody returned to the United States from his triumphal European jaunt for the 1893 season, Pawnee Bill headed to Europe.

Yet another man who began his career with Cody – Buck Taylor, the King of the Cowboys – tried his own show, "Buck Taylor's Wild West," in 1894 but it did not succeed. Colonel Frederic T. Cummins put together a show that specialized in Native Americans. With close connections to the Bureau of Indian Affairs, Cummins assembled expositions that included representatives from as many as fifty different tribes. At one time or another he employed Oglala Sioux chief Red Cloud, Nez Perce Chief Joseph, and Apache chief Geronimo. Another notable in Cummins' entourage was Martha Jane Canary, better known as Calamity Jane. In 1907 Cummins took his Wild West and Indian Congress abroad, and they toured England and the European continent for four years.

One of the better-known Wild West shows developed from the huge Oklahoma ranch of George W. Miller.[25] After his death his three sons – Joseph C., Zack T., and George L. – built the 101 Ranch to a vast spread of over one hundred thousand acres. The exhibitions the brothers produced at the ranch were so well received that, beginning in 1905, the Millers decided to take them on the road. Their performing stars included Bill Pickett, the black Texan cowboy credited with inventing "bull dogging," where a rider leaps from a horse and wrestles a steer to the ground. Another featured attraction was Iron Tail, the man on whom the bust on the "buffalo nickel" was based. Iron Tail previously toured with Cody's show, but he appeared with the 101 Ranch show from 1913, when the nickel was first minted, until his death in 1916. The 101 Ranch also emerged as a leader in the development of movie westerns through relationships with Thomas Ince and William Selig.

"The Miller Brothers' 101 Ranch Real Wild West" toured successfully throughout the United States and Canada, and in 1914 journeyed to

England. It was an inauspicious time. The show enjoyed enormous popularity, but when the First World War broke out, the British government impressed their horses and vehicles for the war effort. Eventually the troupe returned to the United States, reassembled the show, and continued it through 1916 when it featured Buffalo Bill Cody making his final tour. The 101 Ranch show profited financially, but the First World War supplanted it and signaled America's shift from its own western heritage to a European outlook. The brothers revived their show in 1925, but the depression doomed it, and the 101 Ranch Wild West folded its tent again in 1931. Even after that, Zack Miller resurrected the show on an occasional basis and toured it as late as 1949.

Zack Mulhall, who left St. Louis to set up a ranch in Oklahoma, led another family Wild West group. "Col. Zack Mulhall's Wild West" featured his son, Charley, and his daughters Agnes and Lucille. Lucille exhibited such extraordinary skills as a roper and rider that pundits invented the word "cowgirl" to describe her. The Mulhalls were always more of a contingent than a full-fledged Wild West company, but they did appear at Madison Square Garden and at other major venues, including the St. Louis World's Fair in 1904. Later, Lucille joined the 101 Ranch show, sharing the bill with Cody in 1916. Among the young stars who toured with the Mulhalls was Tom Mix, who also worked with the 101 Ranch and whose later cinematic fame eclipsed the popularity of the Wild West stars. After years of Hollywood celebrity, in 1935 Mix put together his own Wild West company – "The Tom Mix Circus and Wild West" – which toured for three years.

Perhaps the most famous performer to emerge from the Wild West shows – aside from Cody himself – was Will Rogers, who toured intermittently with the Mulhalls from 1899 to 1905.[26] He also appeared with Cummins' Indian expositions, in Australia with the "Wirth Brothers' Circus," and in South Africa with "Texas Jack's Wild West Circus," operated by "Texas Jack" Omohundro's adopted son. Will Rogers, who was part Cherokee and was raised in the Indian Territory that became the state of Oklahoma, possessed extraordinary talents with a lasso. Even today, it is hard to watch early movies of him tossing separate ropes around different parts of a galloping horse without thinking that someone must have used trick photography. Rogers eventually took his skills to the vaudeville stage, where he discovered a voice. His rambling commentaries about politics and current events turned out to be even more entertaining than his rope tricks, and Rogers settled in as one of the wisest and most quotable commentators on the contemporary scene.

In their last days, most of the Wild West shows were incorporated into circuses, where they were reduced to a sideshow shadow of their former grandeur. The last attempt at a full-sized Wild West show was "Colonel Tim McCoy's Real Wild West and Rough Riders of the World," which debuted in April 1938. This major enterprise played several large cities including Washington, Columbus, and Cincinnati. Tim McCoy could lasso eight horses at one toss, but he failed to lasso customers. The vogue for the large, outdoor western extravaganza was over, and in less than a month McCoy's venture folded.

Frontier drama in the theatre

While the Wild West shows constituted the most significant contribution to frontier drama in the 1880s, other more conventional performances remained popular and continued the presentation of frontier drama in traditional theatre settings. Sadie Hasson and Joseph J. Dowling brought *Nobody's Claim*, by Edwin A. Locke, to the New York area in 1883 and continued it for at least ten years.[27] The complex melodrama opens outside the Soaring Angel Tavern and Hotel in Yellowstone country, where Dell McWade wins a rifle contest and, rebuffed by Lillian Haywood, plots to halt a train and rob her wealthy father. Meanwhile, Ward Devereaux is trailing Rahl Mendoza's band of outlaws, who disguise themselves as owls. When one of the gang tries to send a wire to alert Mendoza, Devereaux shoots through the telegraph lines to prevent the transmission. Inside the barroom of the Soaring Angel, Devereaux announces that he is also seeking Joseph Brent because the worthless land he left behind him in San Francisco sixteen years earlier, dubbed "nobody's claim," is now worth millions. The action shifts to Bitterwood Cut, where McWade and his henchmen attempt to stop the train by displaying a red lantern. Devereaux, however, discovers the scheme, and, as McWade and the wildly dressed owls wait for the train to brake, Devereaux hangs out a white lantern and the train roars safely past. Later at the owls' hideout in a sawmill, Devereaux learns that McWade is really Mendoza and that he has kidnapped Lillian. As Devereaux tries to free her, he finds himself trapped in the burning mill until Madge, a mysterious friend of the outlaws, helps him to escape. Eventually Devereaux tracks the owls to a cave where he rescues Lillian, and Madge is unveiled as Joseph Brent's daughter and heir.

Joseph J. Dowling, an expert shot, had been working with frontier scripts for several years before he hit the right combination in *Nobody's Claim*. In

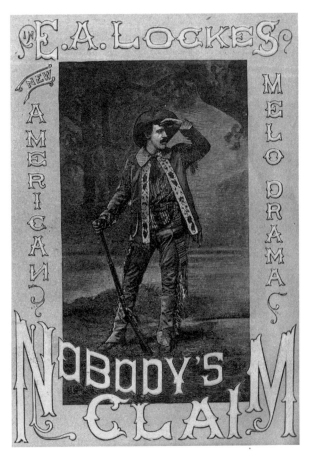

Figure 15. Joseph J. Dowling and Sadie Hasson from an advertising pamphlet for
E. A. Locke's *Nobody's Claim*.

October 1877, at the Olympic Theatre in Brooklyn and at the Bowery,
Dowling performed Frank-Frayne-like stunts, shooting an apple from an
accomplice's head with his back to the target and cutting the rope of a hanging
man with a bullet in *The Texan Avenger*. After their success with *Nobody's
Claim* Hasson and Dowling returned less successfully to a western mining-
camp setting in *The Red Spider* in 1890, and in 1901 Dowling combined with
J. O. Stewart on yet another play of western intrigue, *Roxanna's Claim*.

On the Frontier, by Annie Lewis Johnston, combined a typical melodramatic story with elements of the Custer massacre. First performed in
Philadelphia in November 1887, it played in New York in January 1888, and
appeared there as late as 1903. The plot involves Jack Osborn, his mother,

Figure 15. (*cont.*)

and his cousin, Katie O'Rorke, who live in a cabin in the Black Hills, not far from an army post.[28] Jack leaves his mother and Katie with Rose Austin, daughter of the fort commander, to join the troops in pursuit of hostile natives. As the troops trail Indians, they discover the remains of Custer's defeat. While they are away, Bill Morley, who incited the renegades, kills Jack's mother and kidnaps the young women. The troops eventually trap the Indians in their village and defeat them, and Jack catches Morley and rescues Rose and Katie. Throughout the play, Blue Flower, a princess of the Hassawa tribe and an expert shot, protects Jack from several serious scrapes. In the end she is revealed as the youngest daughter of Colonel Austin, who was kidnapped as a baby and grew up believing herself to be one of the tribe.

Sara Von Leer and her husband, James Hardie, played the lead roles of Blue Flower and Jack Osborn. Von Leer, born in Mobile, Alabama, in 1855, was a granddaughter of the British-born star of Boston theatre, Mary Ann Duff. A petite, emotional actress, she achieved little success until she teamed with Hardie in the Johnston melodrama. Hardie, born in Edinburgh in 1846, emigrated to the United States in his youth and first acted in San Francisco in 1867. Hardie moved east in 1872 and appeared in a variety of supporting roles over the next dozen years. He first paired with Sara Von Leer in 1884, and a year later they married and formed their own company. After positive reaction in the United States they took the play to England, where they scored a remarkable success with *On the Frontier* and a French melodrama called *Two Little Vagabonds*. They eventually developed successful managerial careers, building and managing theatres in Liverpool and Manchester and sending touring productions throughout the English provinces. Hardie died in 1905, after which Von Leer returned to the United States, where she died in 1916.[29]

The respected drama critic Brander Matthews joined George H. Jessop in the production of a frontier play in 1887. Jessop had previously touched on western material in his *A Gentleman from Nevada* in 1880, using the formula of transplanting a westerner into a sophisticated social milieu. The first act is set at a Nevada railroad station, where English Jack, a villainous English dandy and gambler now living in the West, shoots Alfred Egerton, a member of a vacationing family of British aristocrats.[30] The remaining acts shift to Egerton Park in England where Christopher Columbus "Kit" Galt, a staunch westerner, visits Alice Egerton, whom he had befriended at the station. Galt helps Alice's brother to avoid a blackmailer, brings English Jack to justice, and ends up with Alice.

A Gold Mine, the new Jessop and Matthews offering, which opened in Cincinnati in 1887, reprised Jessop's earlier effort. John T. Raymond enacted the lead role of California miner, Silas K. Woolcott, a part that comedian Nat Goodwin inherited when Raymond died just a few days after the opening. Woolcott travels to London to sell his mine, and there the play contrasts the earnest Woolcott with several haughty British characters. In the end Woolcott sells his mine to Sir Evarard Foxwood to rescue Foxwood's son from financial ruin. Foxwood contemptuously dismisses the foolishness of the uncouth American, but Foxwood's sister, realizing that Woolcott has made a sacrifice for her nephew, falls in love with the good-hearted man. Both of Jessop's plays mined the long-established American tradition of the hypocritical, morally bankrupt British aristocracy.

Another play that featured a western man in an eastern setting was *The Westerner*, by Edward Rose, which first played in New York at the Windsor Theatre in March 1892.[31] Jim Errol is another "gentleman from Nevada," who arrives in New York to pursue the heroine, Mary Lawton. Jim saves Mary's father from disastrous speculations in mining stocks and thereby wins the hand of his love.

From Buffalo Bill's company of Sioux and Pawnee to Donald MacKay's Warm Springs Indians, many touring productions employed Native Americans, but the first production to attract attention because it starred a native performer was a five-act melodrama called *Wep-ton-no-mah, the Indian Mail Carrier*, and the actress, who also wrote the play, was Gowongo Mohawk.[32] For at least twenty years Mohawk toured her play throughout the United States and Great Britain, and every time she set foot on the stage she challenged boundaries of ethnicity and sexuality. While she challenged some boundaries, however, she conformed to others.

Gowongo Mohawk was born on the Cattaraughs Reservation near Gowonda in western New York, a descendant of the Senecan chief, Red Jacket. Her father, Ga-na-gua, an elder of the tribe, sent his daughter to a seminary school in Painesville, Ohio. There, she said, she developed an interest in drama and a powerful individualistic streak. She began acting in the late 1880s, just after she completed her schooling. She married Charlie Charles while she was performing with the Michael Strogoff company, and together they wrote a play in which she could star.[33]

The plot of *The Indian Mail Carrier* is rather conventional, and the setting of the play illustrates one of the ways in which Mohawk conformed to the tenor of her times, for, despite the fact that she was an eastern Indian, she set the action on a western ranch. Colonel Stockton owns the ranch, and there the brave Wep-ton-no-mah saves Stockton's daughter Nellie from a stampede. That incident demonstrates one of Mohawk's unconventional choices, for she played the heroic male role. When Nellie rejects the advances of evil Spanish Joe and speaks admiringly of Wep-ton-no-mah, the infuriated Joe tries to shoot Wep-ton-no-mah but unwittingly kills his father Ga-na-gua, instead. (The part of Wep-ton-no-mah's father was played by Mohawk's own father, from whom the character took his name.) Wep-ton-no-mah signs on as a mail carrier at the nearby fort, thinking he can use his freedom to travel to track down his father's murderer. After several near misses, Wep-ton-no-mah finally corrals Spanish Joe and defeats him in a vigorous knife fight.

The use of a "Spanish" character as the villain continued the association of Hispanic characters with evil. In *Nobody's Claim*, Edwin A. Locke had also given his villain a Hispanic name – Rahl Mendoza – and, as in Mohawk's play, made no attempt beyond the name to supply a cultural dimension or ethnic background. In *Nobody's Claim* the action takes place not in California or the Southwest, but in the far northern Yellowstone area, and Mendoza adopts the un-Hispanic alias of Dell McWade. Gowongo Mohawk followed that lead by making the culturally undistinguished "Spanish Joe" her villain.

Although the plot was stereotypical, Mohawk staked out less conventional territory in several ways. The colonel, for instance, describes to his daughter the procedures of the roundup in a passage that provides realistic and instructive detail. At one point he explains the reason for "dugouts," the underground log lean-tos into which the ranch hands ride in case thunder or lightning stampede the cattle. The opening scene immediately signified another difference between Mohawk's play and a typical western melodrama. As they assist with the roundup, the Indians in this play enjoy an amicable relationship with whites and are clearly an integral part of the society. The economic interplay between the whites and the tribe is even more vividly presented in the second act at Ga-na-gua's camp, where Spanish Joe bargains for ponies.

Joe's killing of Ga-na-gua, who was played by Mohawk's own father, provided another interesting perspective. That Joe shot Ga-na-gua thinking he was Wep-ton-no-mah seems to be a comment on the idea that, at least to Spanish Joe, "they all look alike." Furthermore, Mohawk shows the dying Ga-na-gua tenderly cradled in Wep-ton-no-mah's arms, and this touching scene between two native performers was certainly a first for the American stage.

Yet another way in which Mohawk's production was peculiar was her own limited time on stage, especially for a featured actress. The title character hardly appears in the first act. At one point Wep-ton-no-mah rides past on his horse, but even his rescue of Nellie from the stampede is narrated rather than shown. Reviews of Mohawk's performance may explain her restricted stage time. Although reviewers credited her with "a truly magnificent contralto voice," one critic commented that she speaks with "a singularly pronounced and idiomatic" accent, and another wrote that she "reads her lines in a sort of monotonous chant."[34]

By producing her own material Mohawk made a declaration about her status as a Native American in a white society and, more particularly, about her status as a Native American within the specifically white, European theatrical tradition. She acted, she said, because she loved the stage – a prime reason for a performer of any background. She also wanted to protest wrongs done to Indians and the manner in which Indians were portrayed on the stage. She stated:

> People used to want me to dance – to play the banjo and do fancy steps. I said, "No – that is no fit thing for an Indian." It is beneath his dignity – dancing like a common street player. I saw an Indian dancing in variety once, and it was a shameful sight . . . He looked so out of his element. I said, "Look at that. Is that pretty or natural?" Ah! It was ugly and pitiful.

A third reason for her work was her desire "above all things to prove that the Indian is capable of the highest civilization." In other words she was using the European paradigm of theatre to validate Native American worthiness. Other Indians, she claimed, "are very proud indeed of me, and look upon me as a person whose business it has become to show the white people that the Indian is not a savage."[35] During this period politicians and social reformers hotly debated the assimilation of Native Americans, and the educated Gowongo Mohawk, making her living in the European theatrical tradition, certainly stood as a living exemplum of successful assimilation.

Many plays – *The Danites* and *Ranch 10* are two examples – disguised female characters as males. Not only was such cross-dressing a common theatrical device, but it made particular sense for a character trying to blend into a male-dominated frontier setting. A female performer actually playing a male role, however, was more unusual. In this case, especially because of stereotypes of native maidens, Mohawk's decision to play a male role is as striking as her determination to star as a Native American. The stereotype for the native maiden was to befriend and love white males. Rather than conform to that stereotype Mohawk cast herself in a typically male position. One reason may have been her physical appearance. She was described as "very tall" and "wonderfully muscular."[36] One review relates how she "flings a stalwart ruffian over her shoulder as though he were an orange."[37] A more potent reason for her choice of roles may have derived from her own active personality. She liked to ride, rope, fire guns, and shoot arrows. She decided to enact a male role, she said, because she wanted to do something "wild and free" and thought playing a male role would allow her greater opportunity for riding and wrestling.[38]

Although Mohawk played the role of the heroic male avenging the death of his father, the play avoids the typical pairing of hero and heroine. Mohawk's own history of marrying a white would appear to confound a reluctance to pair a Native American with a white partner, but perhaps she refrained from a conventional ending because she was a female playing a male.

In the drama Mohawk enacted a hard-riding, knife-fighting male, but in interviews she emphasized more traditionally female attributes. Writers described her as "graceful" and commented that she made all her own clothes and costumes. She wore European-style clothing that nevertheless reflected her heritage: a blue serge dress was trimmed with brass balls and another gown was decorated with bead work.[39] The images in a publicity collotype send striking and obviously calculated messages. The actress sits with legs crossed wearing the masculine fringed leggings appropriate to her male character and suggestive of her native background. An American flag draped on a table beside her declares her patriotism, and handguns, spurs, holsters, and bullets lie prominently on the flag, silently proclaiming both her physical skills and the action-oriented material in her plays. She signed her photos "Aboriginally Yours, Gowongo Mohawk."

Mohawk performed in at least one other play, *The Flaming Arrow* by Lincoln J. Carter, in which, as in *The Indian Mail Carrier*, she played a male hero in love with a colonel's daughter. *The Indian Mail Carrier*, however, remained Mohawk's staple vehicle, and she toured it as late as 1910. In 1893 she took the play to England, where, like many of the American frontier melodramas, it received positive responses during its two-year swing through London, Liverpool, and other provincial cities.

Another woman who starred in a frontier role was Kate Purssell, who played Calamity Jane in Ned Buntline's *The Queen of the Plains*. Buntline occasionally tried to recreate his Buffalo Bill success with other melodramas, and his Calamity Jane play seems especially derivative. Just as Buffalo Bill seeks revenge on his father's killer, so Calamity Jane seeks to avenge the murder of her mother. Featuring trained dogs and horses, *The Queen of the Plains* played in the New York area between 1888 and 1894.

One of the most elaborate frontier dramas ever presented was *The Scout*, which starred William F. Carver, Cody's ex-partner in the original Wild West show. In 1891 Carver and his "Wild America" troupe were at the Cremorne Gardens in Melbourne, Australia, when Alfred Dampier engaged them to perform a play written by Dampier and Garnet Walch. The resulting extravaganza, *The Scout*, played through the spring and summer at Dampier's Alexandra Theatre.[40]

The Scout tells the story of John Marvel and his two daughters, one of whom was abducted by Indians at the age of five. The other daughter,

Figure 16. Gowongo Mohawk, "The Only American Indian Actress," in a publicity portrait.

Brenda, is spirited away by Mark Vosper and his native accomplices. Vosper wants the girl to marry him so he can claim her father's fortune. Brenda finds her sister at the Indian village, and both women are ultimately rescued and returned to their father through the unstinting efforts of Carver, "the evil spirit of the plains," who is engaged to Brenda.

As its main attraction the piece featured a remarkable stunt. At one point Carver, fleeing a band of pursuers, rode his horse across a bridge suspended about twenty-five feet in the air. When the bridge snapped, the horse plunged twenty feet into a huge tank of water representing the Rio Grande River, then surfaced and swam to the shore amid a hail of gunfire. Carver, meanwhile, grabbed and clung to the dangling bridge before the natives captured him.[41] The vast tank at the back of the stage was forty feet long, twelve feet wide and nine feet deep, and the plot concocted a variety of uses for the water. Carver paddled a canoe in one scene, and in another he hurled a villainous warrior over a precipice and into the tank. For the climactic scene the Indians tried to swim away from capture while the cowboys rode into the water after them.[42]

Carver's group also performed a second Dampier–Walch script, *The Trapper*, which played variations on the same idea as *The Scout*, but there is no evidence that Carver ever performed it in the United States. In *The Trapper* Carver rescued a woman from a villain pretending to be her father. Once again the water tank played a pivotal role as a storm in the final act precipitated a landslide, which propelled Carver and his horse from a high, narrow ledge down into the water.[43] In one of the highlights of *The Trapper* a tree-branch snare yanked the villain upside-down into the air. Although the pieces were well received on account of their spectacle, the acting was clearly an afterthought. The *Melbourne Age* commented: "[W]e give Dr. Carver credit for making no pretense to histrionic ability, and he is justified in so estimating his claims to Thespianship."

When Carver returned to America, *The Scout* impressed New York audiences as it had those in Australia. In November 1892, his new vehicle played four weeks at Niblo's Garden Theatre with eight performances each week for the first two weeks and eleven performances each week including five matinees per week for the remainder of the run. The *New York Dramatic Mirror* (December 12, 1892) labeled it "the most stirring border drama yet devised," and within the next year *The Scout* played eleven more weeks at various New York area theatres.[44]

The most startling moment of Carver's drama – the leap of the horse into a tank of water – reappeared almost a century later at the climactic moment of a seminal western movie. At the end of Sam Peckinpah's *The Wild Bunch* (1969), which helped to redefine screen violence, several horses and riders descend into the Rio Grande in slow motion as a bridge explodes.

Extraordinary exhibitions dominated the dramatic presentation of the frontier in the 1880s and early 1890s. The various Wild West shows, of course, were the predominant factor, but even the plays, such as *The Scout* with its troop of Indians, its shooting, and its spectacular incidents, and *The Indian Mail Carrier* with its native star, are more the product of exhibition than of traditional dramatic concerns for character and plot. In the 1890s and through the turn of the century, however, a new wave of frontier plays emerged. Almost all of them lined up at the opposite end of the spectrum from the loud and boisterous Wild West shows and *The Scout* in that they emphasized romance over gunfire. They also imparted a new importance to the literary values of frontier drama and to the theatrical elaboration of those values.

5

Respect: 1893–1899

I could not believe in the white man; the Indian could not believe in me.
John Swiftwind in *Northern Lights* by James Harkins and Edwin Barbour

IN 1893 CHICAGO HOSTED THE COLUMBIAN EXPOSITION, A
gigantic celebration of the four-hundredth anniversary of Columbus' discovery of North America. Situated on 666 acres at Jackson Park, the
Exposition featured canals, fountains, and glistening white buildings.
Coming at almost the end of the nineteenth century, the Exposition
recalled Chicago's own frontier past, but, more importantly, it looked
forward to a new, industrialized century. Thus the Columbian Exposition
of 1893 interlaced America's past and its future. It also wove together several
significant strands in the tapestry of frontier drama.

Directly across the street from the main entrance of the Exposition, Nate
Salsbury secured a site for Buffalo Bill Cody's Wild West show. The Wild
West was just returning from its celebrated trip abroad where it had played
command performances before the kings and queens of Europe. The show
was about to embark on its most lucrative American tours, taking its vision
of the frontier to every corner of the country.

Nearby, an obscure historian delivered an academic paper at a conference
scheduled to coincide with the Exposition. His name was Frederick Jackson
Turner, and his paper, "The Significance of the Frontier in American History,"
put forward the thesis that free land available on the western frontiers and the
settling of that land had developed the particularly American values of equality, practicality, and democracy.[1] Turner pointed out that the government, as
a part of its 1890 census report, had declared the frontier officially closed. Just
at the time when the theatrical presentation of the frontier was achieving its
greatest popularity, the actual frontier was inexorably shrinking.

At a Chicago theatre, frontier drama of a more conventional, indoor variety also visited the city in that Exposition year. One of David Belasco's greatest hits, the military romance *The Girl I Left Behind Me*, shifted to Chicago almost as soon as it opened in New York, and another significant border piece, Augustus Thomas' *In Mizzoura*, premiered in Chicago just a few months later. As Turner's essay reexamined westward expansion and Cody's Wild West redefined western experiences, so, too, the Belasco and Thomas plays signaled new literary and production directions in frontier drama.

Beginning in 1893, with productions of *The Girl I Left Behind Me* and *In Mizzoura*, frontier drama began to acquire a literary respectability and attain a highbrow production status. These changes continued throughout the 1890s and into the twentieth century with Thomas' *Arizona* (1900) and *Colorado* (1901) and the dramatization of Owen Wister's *The Virginian* (1904), and they culminated in 1905 and 1906 with *The Squaw Man* by Edwin Milton Royle, *The Girl of the Golden West* by Belasco, *Strongheart* by William C. deMille, *The Three of Us* by Rachel Crothers, and *The Great Divide* by William Vaughn Moody.

One change represented by these productions was that frontier plays began to be written and produced by significant artists of the American theatre – or at least by those who were on their way to becoming significant artists – rather than by those who were regarded as fringe participants. In addition, some of those involved with the productions, especially the writers, arrived with refined social pedigrees, as graduates of Harvard, Princeton, and Columbia, and these gave their productions an immediate cachet of respectability.[2] Furthermore, the plays received first-class productions for extended runs at major New York theatres. Frontier drama evolved from being a part of the touring combination scene with seasons in New York to being an integral component of the permanent New York theatre world.

The composition of the players also changed. Featured performers in these productions were primarily standard stock actors and actresses rather than frontier performers or personages. They seldom possessed a birth certificate from a western territory or personal frontier experience. They were likely to perform frontier characters one month and lords and ladies in European drawing rooms the next. As a result, the plays became associated more with their authors than with specific performers.

The literary value and dramatic skill represented by the scripts also evolved. While the plays continued to rely primarily on moral dilemmas as touchstones for the plots, they exhibited more causality in plots, greater depth of character, more sophisticated language and dialogue, and more symbolic thematic motifs. Sometimes villains displayed glimmers of virtue, while even the heroes and heroines exhibited flaws. The subject matter also shifted as the public turned its attention to new problems. Assimilation of Native Americans replaced warfare as an overriding issue, and influences from the larger world began to impinge on the plays of the frontier. Suddenly the stories concerned not only cowboys, soldiers, and miners, and not only Americans, but also such international factors as America's relations with Cuba and Spain.

Additionally, productions from around the turn of the century revealed a new attitude on the part of the critical establishment toward frontier plays, with critics regarding them as major events worthy of extended coverage. In some cases the productions and the reporting on the productions displayed an ironic belittling of earlier, less sophisticated frontier drama – ironic in the sense that, while the newer plays were dramatically more advanced, they were also less directly connected to the actual events and personages of the frontier.

The plays of this period also marked a wholly unintended transition to the new medium of film, which emerged at the turn of the century. The West provided inspiration for scores of early movies, and numerous theatrical scripts provided material for the developing film industry. In addition to the gift of dramatic material, frontier plays also supplied several performers who emerged as stars of the new cinematic medium.

Change was also apparent in western art, which mirrored the development of western drama. Whereas earlier frontier art by artists such as George Catlin, Karl Bodmer, and Albert Bierstadt had primarily described native activities, representatives of various tribes, and striking landscapes, later artists emphasized action and dramatic story-telling. Frederic Remington's work shows a clear movement toward theatrical, narrative situations. His *Fight for the Waterhole* (1901) and *Fight for the Stolen Herd* (1908–9) freeze moments in the midst of ongoing, violent conflicts, and even the titles augment the narrative aspects of those paintings. Remington's sculpture, such as *The Mountain Man* (1903) or *The Outlaw* (1906), emphasizes action by removing all physical background and all reference outside the figure itself. The riders depicted in these works have no specific names, no surrounding environment. They ride in no specific place or time. They do, however, confront obstacles such as a steep decline or a bucking horse, and those obstacles set the figures into writhing action.

Charles Russell was concerned with detailed authenticity in his artwork, but he, too, stressed dramatic action. *The Hold Up* (1899) depicts the robbery of a stagecoach, and *The Cinch Ring* (1909) presents a mosaic of activity with one man rolling on the ground, a second man cocking his rifle, and two riderless horses straining majestically.

Charles Schreyvogel was another prominent artist of western images who emphasized action in his works. In *The Fight for Water* (1909) Schreyvogel paints a montage of vigorous western conflict with one warrior tumbling from his horse, a second struggling on the ground beside his downed steed, another horse rearing, and several guns and rifles blasting. Such images reinforce the accusation that Schreyvogel learned to draw the frontier by watching Buffalo Bill's Wild West show. So powerful was the influence of this theatrical production that Brian Dippie asserted, "No western artist after the 1880s was unaffected by [Cody's] presentation."[3]

David Belasco and *The Girl I Left Behind Me*

In the theatre world the multiple changes that frontier drama was about to undergo began rather inauspiciously with the production of *The Girl I Left Behind Me*, by David Belasco and Franklin Fyles, which opened on January 25, 1893, at Charles Frohman's new Empire Theatre in New York. This theatre itself represented a major departure in New York's theatrical landscape. The opening of the Empire inaugurated the shift of the theatrical district northward from Union Square to the Times Square district, and the Empire housed Frohman's operations until his death aboard the *Lusitania* in 1915.

The Girl I Left Behind Me represents a transitional phase for several reasons. For one, when the Empire Theatre opened in 1893, Frohman and Belasco – both of whom would eventually become dominant players in the theatrical game – were just beginning to emerge as talented and significant theatre men. Frohman, through his Empire Theatre stock company, developed such stars as Maude Adams, Julia Marlowe, William Gillette, and Ethel Barrymore, and helped to originate the Theatrical Syndicate, which controlled theatre throughout the United States at the turn of the century. But in 1893 Frohman was known simply as an aggressive and energetic young manager with one major hit, Bronson Howard's *Shenandoah* in 1889. Frohman's risk-taking is apparent not only in his opening a theatre so far north on Broadway, but also in his selecting a play by an American author with a frontier setting as his initial production, when most producers would have chosen an adaptation of a European play.

When *The Girl I Left Behind Me* opened, Belasco was thirty-nine years old, and he knew something about the West. He was raised in a theatrical family, his father, Humphrey Abraham Belasco, having worked as a pantomime performer in London before gold fever drove him to California with his wife, Reina Martin. Belasco was born in 1853, not long after his parents' arrival in San Francisco where Belasco's father opened a store. In his mid teens Belasco began working at Maguire's Opera House, and within a few years he had gained a reputation in San Francisco, Virginia City, and along the west coast. In those years he worked with James O'Neill and James A. Herne and secured the long-lasting friendship of the young Charles Frohman. In 1882 he moved to New York as stage manager and dramatist for the Madison Square Theatre, and two years later he switched to Daniel Frohman's Lyceum Theatre.

In 1887 Belasco collaborated with Henry C. DeMille on *The Wife*, a comedy about a man forced to win the affection of his uncaring wife, and this became Belasco's first significant success. Belasco and DeMille followed that with other hits, including *Lord Chumley* (1888), which starred E. H. Sothern as a young English lord, *The Charity Ball* (1889), and *Men and Women* (1890). DeMille, a native of North Carolina and a graduate of Columbia University, had written the frontier melodrama *The Main Line* with Charles Bernard in 1886, but he reached the zenith of his brief career in his sprightly collaborations with Belasco. DeMille died in 1893 at the age of forty-three.

In 1892 Belasco began working with Franklin Fyles, a native of Troy, New York, and the drama critic of the *New York Sun*, on *The Girl I Left Behind Me*. The plot entwines two stories, one concerning a conflict between the army and the neighboring Blackfeet tribe, and the other involving a love affair between a soldier and his general's daughter.[4] At the outset of the play everyone at a small army post in Montana in 1890 is preparing for Fourth of July festivities. Kate Kennion, the daughter of the general of the post, is engaged to marry Lieutenant Morton Parlow, although she really loves Lieutenant Edgar Hawkesworth. Also at the post is Lucy Hawkesworth, Edgar's sister, who loves Private Jones. Dr. Arthur Penwick, a Canadian visitor to the post who is investigating the way Americans treat the native population, falls in love with Wilbur's Ann, an outgoing country girl who lives on a nearby farm. Penwick and Wilbur's Ann provide much of the humor in the play and some of the most charming scenes. Another important character is Major Burleigh, who became an embittered Indian hater when his wife deserted him for another man; Burleigh actually says, "The only good Indian is a dead Indian."

The primary Indian of the play is Ladru, an intelligent and bitter Blackfeet chief known as Scarbrow because of a wound he received from General Kennion in a previous battle. When Kennion forbids the Blackfeet to hold a Sun Dance, Ladru and the other chiefs vow revenge. After a scouting party of army troops is ambushed, Parlow blames the incident on Hawkesworth's cowardice. As the Fourth of July dance at the fort progresses, the soldiers discover the telegraph line has been cut, and Hawkesworth rides to the next post for help. While he is gone, Ladru threatens to massacre everyone in the fort except Kate, whom he plans to take for himself. Soon thereafter the screaming Blackfeet attack the fort. As the soldiers' resistance crumbles, Kate pleads with her father to shoot her rather than allow her to suffer "the worst [fate]." In a scene that anticipates an identical moment in John Ford's *Stagecoach*, Kennion is about to shoot Kate when she hears the bugle of Hawkesworth arriving with the cavalry. The rather anticlimactic final act is set at the general's home near the fort. As the wedding between Kate and Parlow commences, Burleigh enters with a picture of the man who seduced his wife – Parlow. Parlow departs in disgrace while Kate and Hawkesworth are united, as are Penwick and Wilbur's Ann and Lucy and Private Jones.

Belasco was not known as an especially original writer – most of his plays were either collaborations, adaptations, or dramatizations of previously available material – and *The Girl I Left Behind Me* is a good example of this. Although the play was certainly successful, critics noted the authors' borrowings from previous works, including the use of the interrupted telegraph message, Kate's plea to be killed rather than captured, and her clairvoyant perception of the sound of the cavalry bugles before the arrival of the troops. The *New York Times* critic (January 17, 1893) pointed out that the attack on the garrison was similar to Boucicault's *Jessie Brown; or, The Relief of Lucknow*, and the arrival of the cavalry recalled the rescue of Snorkey from the railroad tracks in *Under the Gaslight* or the hero from the sawmill in *Blue Jeans*. However, the *New York Dramatic Mirror* reviewer (February 4, 1893) concluded, "it must be admitted that whatever the authors have borrowed, they have borrowed well."

More damaging than the borrowing from the *Dramatic Mirror*'s point of view was that the appropriated plot devices showed their contrivance: "Many of the threads of plot indicate unmistakably that they were spun to suit the exigency of a subsequent situation." A Washington writer, who reviewed the production in that city just prior to its New York debut, criticized the "wooden soldiers, hysterical women, and . . . incredible Indians" improbably attacking an armed fortification.[5]

On the other hand, the *Dramatic Mirror* praised the directness of the dialogue, indicating that there was hardly "a superfluous line in the text," an opinion shared by the *Times* critic, who called the language simple and direct. Furthermore, the devices Belasco employed to accentuate the tension of the situation clearly worked. The *Times* concluded: "More forcible, moving melodrama than the second and third acts of his new play we have never seen." The *New York Herald* (January 26, 1893), despite complaints about the "comparatively tame" last act, went even farther, declaring *The Girl I Left Behind Me* "one of the best dramas yet produced by American playwrights, if not the best."

Two years after it opened in New York, *The Girl I Left Behind Me* played for over one hundred performances at the Adelphi Theatre in London.[6] Although generally well received, the production occasioned a lengthy and biting critique from George Bernard Shaw, which is as illuminating for Shaw's opinions regarding melodrama in general as for his comments about the play.[7] "A really good Adelphi melodrama," Shaw wrote, "is of first-rate literary importance, because it only needs elaboration to become a masterpiece . . . Unfortunately, a really good Adelphi melodrama is very hard to get." He does not find it in *The Girl I Left Behind Me*. Shaw labeled the Belasco–Fyles effort "a very bad [melodrama]." Like his New York counterpart, Shaw pointed out that the authors adapted their dramatic climax from *Jessie Brown; or, The Relief of Lucknow*, which, he added, provided such a powerful dramatic situation "that it is hardly possible to spoil it, though the authors have done their best." Shaw continued: "Instead of being natural and sincere, [the play] is artificial and sanctimonious. The language, which should be vividly vernacular, is ineptly literate." As for the characterizations, Shaw concluded:

> The characters, instead of being consistent and typical, are patched and rickety, the author's grip constantly slipping from them . . . The hero, assaulted [by his antagonist], ingloriously brings down the curtain with a stage villain's retort, "You shall rrepent – thiss – bblow". . . As to Kennion, the sympathetic general, I cannot believe that even in the army so incapable a man could rise to high command.

Despite Shaw's criticism, *The Girl I Left Behind Me* recorded an enormous success, enhancing the reputations of Belasco and Frohman.

If the script was not a literary masterpiece, Belasco at least knew how to write effective melodramatic moments and his staging was a leap forward in building emotional tension. The *Times* reviewer noted the contrast in

Act II between the "gayety [sic] of the ball and the developing tenseness of the situation," which was precisely Belasco's intent, for he writes in the script, "There must be a strong contrast between the gaiety of the ball and the gloom of danger hanging over the Post."[8] In this act, Belasco counterpoints a waltz and a quadrille with the announcement of the ambush of the soldiers and the discovery of the severed telegraph line. He employs music equally well elsewhere, as when he calls for the melancholy "Soldiers' Farewell" to underscore a romantic parting and the spirited "Du Da Day" to enhance an angry confrontation between Parlow and Hawkesworth. The *Herald* particularly praised Belasco's use of sounds and chants to suggest the approaching Blackfeet. Yells, drums, and rifle fire accentuated the attack, and in the midst of the frenzied sounds and action Belasco, again for contrast, has Kate quote lines from the burial service.

Noted for his realistic staging, Belasco emphasized graphic and telling details in *The Girl I Left Behind Me*. Dust and grime clung to the costumes. Real water at a well accommodated drinking and hand washing. A practical oil-burning chandelier made of bayonets adorned the barracks in Act II. The settings – Act I at sunset, Act III at dawn, and Act IV at twilight – provided opportunities for the lighting effects Belasco loved. Belasco also knew how to tease his audience with light sexual innuendo, in this case through the use of petticoats. When Dr. Penwick washes his hands, Wilbur's Ann flirtatiously offers her petticoat for him to dry them. When Private Jones lies wounded, Lucy selflessly tears a strip from her petticoat for a bandage. Although these racy actions occasioned some criticism from reviewers, they no doubt titillated the audience.[9]

It is perhaps unfortunate that Belasco's staging skill weighted the melodramatic moments at the expense of other thematic concerns, for the linchpin of the plot – the general's refusal to allow the Sun Dance – sprang directly from contemporary issues. A decade earlier in 1882 the Secretary of the Interior, Henry M. Teller of Colorado, had ordered the Commissioner of Indian Affairs to end "savage and barbarous practices" on the reservations, and he singled out "the old heathenish dances such as the sun-dance." Ten years later in 1892, the year in which Belasco and Fyles wrote the play, Commissioner of Indian Affairs Thomas J. Morgan issued regulations threatening any Indian who participated in the Sun Dance with loss of rations and imprisonment.[10] The Indian dancing also irritated a deepseated white revulsion, for while white society generally accepted dancing as a social refinement, it viewed Indian dancing as a practice associated with the devil.[11] In the play the chiefs' anger over the apparently arbitrary denial of their right to dance seems entirely justified. Thematically, the refusal to allow the Blackfeet to dance provides a striking counterpoint to the carefree dancing by the whites in the stockade, especially as that dance celebrates America's birth, which became, in effect, a tragedy for America's aboriginal inhabitants. That thematic statement, however, is eventually overwhelmed with sentiment as Ladru reveals his conventional villainy and the play deteriorates into melodramatic pathos.

The Girl I Left Behind Me ran for over two hundred performances in New York, an especially remarkable accomplishment given that only two months into its run Frohman moved the original company to the Columbian Exposition in Chicago, where the ironic contrast between the prohibition of the Sun Dance and the whites dancing in celebration of their country's birth went unnoticed in the hoop-la of the Columbus quadricentennial. The play retained its popularity throughout the 1890s, with more than one hundred additional performances in various theatres in the New York area and numerous touring productions. The Kalem Company in 1908 and the Box Office Attraction Company in 1915 produced film versions. Franklin Fyles continued to write for the *New York Sun* and for the stage, and he enjoyed particular success with a Civil War piece, *Cumberland '61*, in 1897. In 1901 Fyles returned to a western setting in *Kit Carson*, which featured the frontier hero leading a band of settlers across New Mexico while the villain incites natives to attack the group, and six years later, working with Ralph Stuart, he plowed essentially the same ground in *At the Rainbow's End*.

Augustus Thomas and *In Mizzoura*

In the summer of 1893 a play opened in Chicago that, like *Kit, the Arkansas Traveller*, straddles the boundary of what constitutes border drama. *In Mizzoura* by Augustus Thomas starred the well-known comedian, Nat C. Goodwin, who had commissioned Thomas to write a script that would give him a more serious role. Thomas was to become the dean of America's playwrights, arguably the most famous American dramatist before Eugene O'Neill, but in 1893 Thomas, like Frohman and Belasco, was just beginning to forge a reputation. Born in 1857, he grew up in St. Louis, worked as a railroad clerk for several years, and ran unsuccessfully for public office.[12] Fascinated by the theatre, he wrote several short comedies and formed his own troupe in 1883. Known as the Dickson Sketch Club, they toured primarily in the Midwest until 1885 without notable success. For the next few years Thomas turned to journalism, working as a reporter in St. Louis and

Kansas City. He continued to write plays, however, and in 1889 he moved to New York to market them. He met with little notice until 1891, when Albert M. Palmer produced *Alabama*, a romantic play about reconciliation between the North and the reemergent South. *Alabama* enjoyed immediate acclaim, and Thomas followed it with the comedy *Colonel Carter of Cartersville* in 1892. Still, in 1893 Thomas was merely an emerging playwright.

Nat Goodwin, on the other hand, already enjoyed a well-established comic presence. Born in Boston in 1857, Goodwin rocketed to fame at an early age in a series of frothy burlesques performed with his first wife, Eliza Weathersby. A slight man – he only weighed about one hundred and fifty pounds – Goodwin projected a boyish look and a mischievous charm. Amy Leslie called him "the greatest comedian America has ever produced. A brilliant, spontaneous talent . . . deliciously volatile, magnetic, and original."[13] Goodwin, it seemed, would do virtually anything for a laugh. He was famous – some would say infamous – for making direct asides to members of the audience and for trying to break up fellow actors. Eventually he also gained notoriety for a scandalous and dissipated private life. After Eliza Weathersby died suddenly in 1887, Goodwin married and divorced four times, apparently unable to find a replacement for his first true love. In his 1919 obituary, the *New York Evening Post* (January 31) labeled him "wayward, impulsive, and reckless."

By 1893 Goodwin craved acceptance as a serious actor. He had previously had some success playing a sympathetic miner in *A Gold Mine* by Matthews and Jessop, and now he turned to Augustus Thomas for a vehicle. *In Mizzoura* premiered at Hooley's Theatre in Chicago on August 7, and, a month later, on September 4, it opened at the Fifth Avenue Theatre in New York. The play achieved what Thomas and Goodwin hoped: it was a successful production, and audiences and critics for the most part accepted Goodwin in the more serious role of sheriff Jim Radburn.

Thomas' play combines rural simplicity with several border elements. The setting is Pike County, Missouri, a state in transition from border outpost to urban gentility. Only eleven years before Thomas wrote his play the James boys were still robbing banks and trains, and only eleven years after Thomas wrote his play St. Louis ushered in the twentieth century with an astonishingly modern World's Fair. By 1893 Missouri's major cities – even St. Joseph and Kansas City, the jumping-off places for points west – had lost many of their distinctive frontier traits, but the rural areas retained a border quality, which Thomas accentuated by having his sheriff wear a pair of six-guns. While Thomas' play evokes a constant tension between rough border impulses and the encroaching civilization of the town, critics certainly perceived its frontier flavor. They called the sheriff a "Westerner," and referred to the play as a "backwoods" drama, "a study of Western life," and a reproduction of "Southwestern life."[14]

Set in the town of Bowling Green in Pike County, Act 1 shows the combined living room, dining room, and kitchen of the rather ramshackle Jo Vernon household on a hot June evening.[15] Mrs. Vernon and her daughter 'Lizbeth are ironing. Mrs. Vernon gets so hot she sends to the local drugstore for a beer, which is available only by prescription since they live in a dry county. Both the proximity of the town and its law prohibiting alcohol reflect the presence of society. A second daughter, Kate, is another reminder of sophisticated society. She has just returned home from several years of schooling and, feeling stifled in the backward town, she has become fascinated by an urbane newcomer named Travers, who wants Kate to elope with him. Also attracted to Kate is the sheriff, Jim Radburn, played by Goodwin, who wears two large revolvers and has shot fifty people, but never killed anyone. Radburn paid for Kate's education, but Kate is unaware of this and treats him coldly because he seems to epitomize the unrefined small town. When Travers is implicated in a robbery and wounded, Kate shelters him. The sheriff discovers his hiding place, but, instead of shooting him, Jim, out of love for Kate, gives Travers his horse and allows him to escape. The final act brings news that Travers has been killed in a nearby town while making his getaway. Some townspeople are angry at Jim for releasing Travers, but they nevertheless reelect him for another term as sheriff. The play ends with the suggestion that Kate, now reconciled to living in Pike County, will accept the gallant sheriff.

Although the plot of the play remained rather conventional, the characters, the humor, and the sentiment propelled it to popularity. The *New York Times* critic (September 5 and 10, 1893) astutely realized that, despite Goodwin's burning desire to gain recognition as a serious actor, *In Mizzoura* was primarily a comedy in the same vein as the works of Mark Twain. Only as comedy, the writer noted, can "we accept as a heroic act the liberation of a thief and murderer by a law officer because a certain girl thinks she loves the fellow." Several scenes reveal Thomas' sharp comedic sense. Jo Vernon, the town blacksmith, tells his helper Dave that he will not consent to his marrying his daughter 'Lizbeth until he gets a steady job, but, at the same time, Jo keeps him so busy that Dave has no time to look for a better job. The halting charm and innocence in the burgeoning love between Dave and

'Lizbeth is both funny and touching. The *Times* critic (September 10) said of their courting that there was "no better scene in modern comedy," only to add that the scene where the mother tries to prevent Kate's secret assignation with Travers might be even better. In that scene Thomas takes a simple, rather melodramatic confrontation between mother and daughter and turns it to comedy by placing Jo Vernon in the middle of the two women's pleas. Caught between his love for his daughter and respect for his wife's demands, the befuddled Jo becomes the butt of the scene.

In *In Mizzoura* Thomas demonstrated his fine eye for the telling sentimental moment, such as the entrance of the sheriff, cradling an injured dog. Thomas loved such props. He once wrote, "If you use a property once, use it again and again if you can," for in that way, he believed, the props became visual elements that bound the play together.[16] Thomas followed his own advice here, for, at the end of Act II when Kate rejects Jim's overture of marriage, Jim turns and caresses the dog as the curtain descends.

This conclusion to Act II evidences another characteristic of Thomas' writing, namely, his use of the sentimental anticlimax. While most authors sought to end an act with a dramatic flourish and a riveting tableau – Belasco was a master of that – Thomas showed more interest in characters' reactions to a dramatic announcement. The end of *In Mizzoura* contains no theatrically satisfying embrace between the hero and heroine, but merely the expression by Kate that she will stay in Bowling Green and the implication that she and Radburn will eventually come together. In that way Thomas allowed the audience to complete the story in their minds rather than providing the final picture for them. Thomas' fondness for the anticlimactic moment affects other scenes besides those at the ends of acts. When the sheriff finds a drop of blood and suspects Travers is hiding in the cupboard, he does not draw his guns and threaten. Rather, he casually straddles a chair and waits for Travers to emerge.

Thomas effectively mixes positive and negative qualities in his characters. Kate, the heroine, is overly proud. Travers, the villain, behaves admirably in providing information to free an innocent man, and he sacrifices his chance to escape for what appears to be a sincere love for Kate. Some of Sheriff Radburn's actions, especially his allowing Travers to escape, are highly questionable.

Finally, Thomas utilized realistic detail in his settings, plots, and characters. Two crucial threads in the plot of *In Mizzoura* came from Thomas' days as a reporter. In 1884 he wrote a newspaper article about a farmhand who anonymously paid the expenses for a young, half-Indian girl to attend school, only to be rejected later because she wanted to marry an educated man. Another time he covered the robbery of an express train by a man named Jim Cummings. When the manager of the train was jailed as an accomplice, the apparently fair-minded robber wrote letters to newspapers declaring the man's innocence.[17] These two ideas form the backbone of Thomas' plot.

As he prepared the script Thomas retraced the robber's route and visited Bowling Green. There he watched a blacksmith fix a wheel, and he incorporated that action into his play. The naturalness of welding a wagon tire on stage as the rest of the action unfolded drew frequent comment. Thomas also watched as the blacksmith's assistant shaped wood with a drawknife, and that young man became the model for Dave. On his trip Thomas gathered atmospheric details such as the burning of odious-smelling dog fennel to ward off mosquitoes. The use of such realistic, local-color incidents provided a patina of nature to Thomas' work and justified the opinion of the *New York Times* (September 5, 1893) that the play was "written in a fresh vein of humor and sentiment."

The play proved successful for Goodwin as well. The same *Times* review called his performance "finely conceived and carried out with dignity and skill." Other accounts were even more positive. *Harper's Weekly* (October 28, 1893) enthused that "one has to go back to [Joseph] Jefferson [as Rip Van Winkle] for as perfect a performance of an American part." Despite the accolades for his work in *In Mizzoura*, Goodwin was only partially successful in his attempt to transform himself into a serious actor, with his highpoint coming in 1899 when he starred in Clyde Fitch's *Nathan Hale*. At the turn of the century Goodwin and his third wife, Maxine Elliott, appeared in several successful pieces, including *When We Were Twenty-One* (1900), and another play with a western motif, Fitch's *The Cowboy and the Lady* (1899). The pair separated in 1902 and divorced in 1908, and Goodwin's career declined precipitously until his death in 1919.[18]

The All Star Feature Corporation filmed *In Mizzoura* in 1914 with Burr McIntosh as Jo, Raymond Bond as Jim, and William Conklin as Travers. Five years later Noah Beery played Jo with Robert Warwick as Jim, Robert Cain as Travers, and Eileen Percy as Kate in a Famous Players–Lasky Corporation production.

Both *The Girl I Left Behind Me* and *In Mizzoura* represented advances in the writing and production of frontier plays. Belasco's careful and elaborate staging provided all the outward trappings of first-class drama, and Thomas' use of local-color detail, anticlimactic scenes, and characters with mixed motives gave new direction to the genre. Both plays contain character motifs. The bitterness that infects Ladru and Burleigh provides bookends to the action in Belasco's play. In *In Mizzoura* Thomas evokes the impression that the backwoods land itself impacts Kate's lonely ennui. Furthermore, Kate's infatuation with the outlaw Travers to the point of shielding him from capture establishes a new model for a daring, independent-minded woman that is repeated again and again.

Assimilation, train robberies, cowboys, and ladies

While *In Mizzoura* and *The Girl I Left Behind Me* flourished, theatre in general foundered on the terrible depression that rocked the country in 1893. In April 1892, The *New York Dramatic Mirror* recorded 277 companies on the road. A year later, in March 1893, the number declined to 248. Ten months later the roll had dwindled to 220 companies, and by April 1894, the *Dramatic Mirror* listed only 186 touring companies. In the space of less than two years nearly one third of the major touring operations had simply disappeared. The 1893–94 season was, in the words of the *Dramatic Mirror*, "the most disastrous known to the theatre in this country," with estimates that sixty percent of performers had either lost jobs or suffered pay cuts.[19]

Even in the worst of times, however, managers presented plays, including several frontier dramas produced during the 1890s. Bret Harte's writings continued to furnish material for adaptations. Charles Frohman produced a one-act version of *The Luck of Roaring Camp* at his Empire Theatre in New York in May 1895. Dion Boucicault, apparently picking up where he had left off with the ill-fated *Kentuck*, was to write the adaptation with Ben Teal. According to Teal, Boucicault finished the draft of the first act, but died before completing the projected second and third acts. Frohman decided to present Act 1 as a unit just as Boucicault had written it, but the attempt was not successful.[20] Harte material also provided inspiration for Scott Marble in June 1894, at New York's Fourteenth Street Theatre, where he presented *Tennessee's Pardner*, a variation of *M'liss*, in which a confidence woman and her accomplice try to wrest a dead man's gold from his daughter and rightful heir. Bret Harte himself still hoped to cash in on the theatrical possibilities of his stories, and in 1896 he collaborated with T. Edgar Pemberton on *Sue*, based on Harte's "The Judgment of Bolinas Plain." *Sue* opened at Hoyt's Theatre in New York on September 15 and, though only moderately successful, it proved to be Harte's most fruitful dramatic effort. Ironically, while Harte's stories supplied materials for countless plays, in this piece Harte seemed to take his cue from the success of Thomas' *In Mizzoura*. Sue is an ingenuous western girl whose selfish, overbearing father, Silas Prescott, forces her to marry Ira Beasley, an older man she does not love. She resigns herself to a monotonous existence on Beasley's farm, but three years into their marriage a circus acrobat named Jim Wynd enters her life. Like Kate in *In Mizzoura*, Sue is fascinated by this wanted man. Mesmerized by his tights, his spangles, and his apparently exciting life, she hides him in the barn and protects him by flirting with the sheriff, which infuriates her jealous husband. While attempting to escape, Wynd shoots the sheriff at the very moment that Beasley, jealous of Sue's attention to the sheriff, also fires at him. At a comic trial scene in the last act, Sue loses respect for Wynd when he tries to frame her husband. The play ends with Sue and her husband gaining a new and sounder basis for their marriage. The production played less than a month in New York, and then continued on tour. As with all of Harte's forays into the world of theatre, critics questioned his dramatic technique, citing the "extraordinary number of soliloquies," the "palpable lack of movement," and the "curiously inexpert" construction. The engaging Annie Russell played the title role and gathered rave reviews. The *Illustrated American* (October 24, 1896) called her "attractively fresh and girlishly pretty," and, as much as the script, the "irresistibly charming" performance of Annie Russell helped the play achieve its modest success.

The first play to focus on the character of a Native American caught between his culture and that of the whites was *Northern Lights*, by James Harkins and Edwin Barbour, which played New York in 1895.[21] Although the Ghost Dance phenomenon and the Massacre at Wounded Knee still lay ahead, by the mid 1890s warfare between whites and native tribes was fundamentally settled and the struggle for control of Native Americans had moved from the battlefields to the schoolhouse, where the major question of the day was that of assimilation. White reformers, the self-proclaimed "friends of the Indian," viewed education as the primary tool for acculturation. Men like Herbert Welsh and Henry Pancoast, founders of the Indian Rights Association in 1883, and Episcopalian Bishop Henry B. Whipple saw assimilation as the saving alternative to ultimate extinction or eternal reservation dependency. In the 1870s the educational thrust for Native Americans moved from reservation schools to off-reservation boarding schools favored by progressive white educators as a means to separate natives from tribal influences. Native Americans began attending Hampton Institute in 1878 and a year later Carlisle Institute opened in Pennsylvania.

Figure 17. Annie Russell in the title role in *Sue*.

These schools attempted to stamp out native culture by cutting students' hair, dressing them in western clothing, and giving them western names. The experiments commenced with great optimism and at first seemed to yield positive results as the number of such schools grew to twenty-four by 1898. But by then a sober reassessment had replaced the initial idealism as native students returned to their reservations and resumed traditional behavior, thwarting the dreams of the reformers.

While Belasco's Ladru had shown some of the acculturation conflict by rebelling against his education, *Northern Lights* became the first of several plays to address directly the changing views regarding assimilation. The play is built around two stories. One involves the anemic and cowardly Wallace Gray, the son of an army colonel, who is befriended by John Swiftwind, a Sioux studying to be a doctor. The second plot line centers on Sidney Sherwood, a medical doctor who attempts to poison his invalid wife and marry another woman before Swiftwind uncovers his scheme. The action, set at the time of Custer's defeat in 1876, takes place at Fort Terry, Montana, where Colonel Gray is in command. Swiftwind is the post surgeon, but, despite his successes, he fails to find acceptance in either the white or the native community. When he learns of an impending attack on the fort, Swiftwind must decide where his allegiance lies. At the end Swiftwind dies heroically, lamenting, "I could not believe in the white man; the Indian could not believe in me." In his demise, like Metamora and numerous other native characters before him, Swiftwind epitomized the paradox of native people as viewed through the perspective of white authors. Failure to assimilate left the Indians backward, primitive, and unable to function in the coming century, while assimilation left the characters adrift, exiled from both cultures. In the first plot, Wallace finally redeems himself in the eyes of his father and the woman he loves when he rescues the fort from the attack. *Northern Lights* recorded forty performances after it opened at New York's American Theatre just before Christmas in 1895 and then toured successfully for several years. Another play that dealt with issues of assimilation was *The Indian* by Lorimer Johnstone, which played at the People's Theatre in September 1897, and used the theatrical device of one actor playing the dual role of two Indian brothers, the westernized Rex Sterling, and his tribal double, Red Feather.

Cultural assimilation of a very different sort was featured in an unusual farce comedy based on the differences between ranch life in Texas and political life in Washington that opened at New York's Madison Square Theatre on January 8, 1894. The author, Charles H. Hoyt, was already a well-known comic writer. Born in New Hampshire in 1860, Hoyt aspired to West Point, but when he failed the physical examination he turned to cattle ranching, journalism, and, eventually, play writing. He gained success with *A Bunch of Keys* (1882), which kept characters dashing about a hotel like a Feydeau farce, and *The Brass Monkey* (1888), which made fun of superstitions. His fluffy musical comedy *A Trip to Chinatown* (1891) established a record for a consecutive long run with 657 performances. By the time *A Texas Steer; or, Money Makes the Mare Go* opened in 1894, Hoyt was a noted writer, a wealthy man, and a respected member of his community, having been elected to the New Hampshire legislature.

Hoyt put his personal experience from ranching and politics to good use in *A Texas Steer*. As James Kirke Paulding had done in *The Lion of the West*, Hoyt placed homespun western figures among the corruptions of the big eastern city. Unlike Paulding, however, Hoyt turned the tables and ridiculed the habits of the unrefined westerners while allowing his good-natured border family to adopt the suspect morality of the East.

In Hoyt's play, cattle king Maverick Brander is elected to Congress through the efforts of his social-climbing wife and daughter and despite his refusal to stand for office.[22] Hoyt, himself no stranger to legislative habits, wielded a sharp, satiric knife when it came to politicians, as seen in this biting exchange between Brander and his unwanted campaign manager:

> BRANDER: I'm an honest man! What do I want in Congress?
> YELL: We want a few honest men there.
> BRANDER: Well, I won't be the one to go first.[23]

Similarly, after Brander resigns himself to his election and moves to Washington, he hires a private secretary who boasts of his ability to support any side of an issue:

> INNITT: I can write a speech on any side of any question
> BRANDER: What has become of your conscience, sir?
> INNITT: I've lived in Washington all my life.[24]

One lobbyist pushes Brander to support a proposal for a $20,000 building in a notoriously immoral Texas town. When Brander balks at the inhabitants' seedy reputations, the lobbyist claims that all the town needs is "some good society and a little more rain," prompting Brander to reply: "Some good society and a little more rain – that's all Hell needs."[25] As with Will Rogers, Hoyt's commentary and his dramatic situations are as appropriate to today's politics as they were a hundred years ago. Brander reacts with a comically suspicious homophobia when a valet tries to help him undress. Confronted with a forward female lobbyist, Brander acquiesces in her request for a kiss, and then she blackmails him with a photograph of it. After Brander has adapted to life in Washington, three of his old cronies arrive from Texas and wreak drunken mayhem at an elegant dinner party. Their obnoxious antics embarrass the Branders and make them repent their own uncultured behavior. Thus the Branders accept the mores of their new home, and Hoyt mocks the conventional model of the honest, good-hearted West versus the greedy, corrupted East by deriding the unsophisticated excesses of the Texas bumpkins.

Other frontier plays of the decade included *The Great Northwest*, with future film star William S. Hart and Minnie Dupree, presented at the American Theatre in New York in August 1896, and *Madeline of Fort Reno*, a romantic military drama starring Pawnee Bill and May Lillie, presented in June 1897. Scott Marble's *The Heart of the Klondike*, an Alaskan gold rush story performed in November 1897, apparently renamed an earlier Marble play, *Heart of the Rockies*, copyrighted the previous year, in which villains salt a mine to con a speculator.[26]

Three frontier plays during this period used the railroad for inspiration: *The Limited Mail* by Elmer E. Vance, first produced in October 1890, and performed for several years on tour; *The Pacific Mail*, adapted by Paul M. Potter from Tom Taylor's *The Overland Route*, which recorded forty-eight performances in 1894; and Scott Marble's *The Great Train Robbery*, which first played New York in October 1896. Whereas the transcontinental locomotive in *Across the Continent* was a new phenomenon, by the 1890s the railroad was a fixture of civilization in the West with five separate transcontinental lines. None of the plays follow the lead of the Jesse James plays in representing the railroad as an oppressive institution. In all of them, as in *Nobody's Claim*, the railroad is a positive icon representing communication, freedom of movement, and the power of the nation. Like a fort, the train was an outpost of civilization to be protected by the hero or heroine. Elmer E. Vance's *The Limited Mail*, billed as "a comedy drama in four acts," contains extraordinary melodramatic devices and some effective character interactions in addition to several deft comedic touches.[27] The play begins at a small way station of the Union Pacific railway in Redwood, Arizona, where Nellie Harland lives with Zeke and Nancy, who adopted her as an infant. Nellie loves Charlie Morton, the conductor of The Limited Mail, who travels to San Francisco to care for his wealthy, bedridden uncle. While he is away John Giddings courts Nellie, whom he knows to be Morton's

Figure 18. Poster for *The Great Train Robbery*.

uncle's secret daughter and heir. Feeling trapped, Nellie dons men's clothes and takes a telegraph operator's job at lonely Floodwood Cut, where she spoils Giddings' plans to crash and rob the train. Her heroism reunites her with Charlie, the conductor of the train, and leads them to unravel Giddings' evil actions and solve the mystery of Nellie's birth. Vance's play included a bit of everything, including original songs.

Also worth noting is the production of Scott Marble's *The Great Train Robbery*, which provided the title and inspiration for Edwin S. Porter's classic 1903 movie western. Marble's play involves a complicated plot in which the villain, Dan Hollis, recruits a young, jilted lover, Sam Carter, who works in a Wells Fargo office in Kansas City, to assist him in a robbery.[28] In what must be one of the first uses of electronic bugging on the stage, Hollis surreptitiously plants a telephone receiver in the office of William Bennett, the express superintendent, to show Carter that his beloved Alice, Bennett's daughter, really loves Tom Gordon. Stung by his rejection, Carter joins Hollis to get revenge on Bennett and his daughter by stealing a fortune in gold set to be shipped out on the next express. The explosive third act reveals a telegraph office in the Wichita Mountains. There Hollis and Carter surprise the telegraph operator, tie him up, and cut the wires. They display a red light, and the engine, with whistle blaring and steam spewing, grinds to a halt. Then, in the most spectacular moment of the play, they dynamite the express car, blasting open the door and side walls. They escape with the money while their Indian accomplices abduct Alice, who was a passenger on the train. In the final act, Tom Gordon and his friends track down Hollis and Carter and rescue Alice and the money in a climactic shootout.

Thomas Edison was so enthralled by the play that he arranged for his Edison Studio to prepare a filmed version. Porter's one-reel, eight-minute adaptation necessarily diverged from Marble's lengthy original. Essentially, Porter began with Marble's third act, the attack on the train. The villains in the movie enter the station and tie up the telegraph operator. They attack, halt, and rob the train and then make their getaway. After the telegraph operator is discovered, a posse pursues the robbers, capturing them as they are about to divide their ill-gotten loot. Along the way Porter includes snips of specialty acts in a barroom, a variation on Marble's Act II in the Never Shut Saloon. Porter's explosion of the safe in the rail car is tame, but his ground-breaking outdoor camera work made the attack on the train a riveting scene. The juxtaposition of the play script and the film provides an instructive lesson in cinematic adaptation, for Porter did in eight minutes what Acts III and IV of the play took over an hour to do, and movies have been "cutting to the chase" ever since.

The decade closed with an attempt by Clyde Fitch to cash in on the lucrative market for western drama despite the fact that Fitch had little familiarity with the West. Fitch was born in New York in 1865 and graduated from Amherst College. By the time he wrote *The Cowboy and the Lady*, Fitch was well established with plays such as *Beau Brummell* in 1890 and *The Moth and the Flame* in 1898. Some of his most popular and highly regarded works, however, including *Captain Jinks of the Horse Marines* in 1901 and *The Truth* in 1907, followed after the turn of the century. Like Augustus Thomas in *In Mizzoura*, in *The Cowboy and the Lady* Fitch was writing a part for Nat Goodwin, as he had done the previous year with *Nathan Hale*. Goodwin's co-star was the attractive and able Maxine Elliott. The result, a play more about flirtations than frontiers, opened at New York's Knickerbocker Theatre on Christmas Day of 1899 following a healthy American tour but a disappointing London run. Set at Teddy North's Colorado ranch, the play revolves around two triangular love affairs. The mixed-blood cowboy Quick Foot Jim tells the philandering newcomer George Weston, a married man, to stay away from his girlfriend, Molly Larkins. Meanwhile Weston's vivacious wife Jessica carries on an overt flirtation with Teddy. When Weston is murdered, Teddy and Jessica each think the other committed the crime. As Teddy is about to be convicted, Molly implicates Jim, who impulsively shoots her and then, grief-stricken, confesses to killing Weston, which frees Teddy to unite with Jessica.

It was certainly no accident that the first name of Fitch's shy cowboy echoed that of the popular Spanish-American War hero and western romantic who would soon be elected the twenty-sixth president. Nor was it mere chance that his last name signified that he was originally from a region other than the West. Unlike the typical frontier hero, but very like Teddy Roosevelt, Teddy North was an eastern gentleman who proved his prowess on the range. Fitch's modest cowboy and the casual humor of the ranch prefigured the far more successful Virginian of Owen Wister, who was to emerge in narrative and dramatic form just after the turn of the century. For instance, when Teddy tells the ranch hands that a young girl will be staying at the house as his ward, he orders them to avoid swearing and places a box on the porch into which a twenty-five-cent fine is to be placed for every violation. Thereafter, the swearing, the circumlocutions to avoid swearing, and the abruptly interrupted oaths become a running gag. After Jessica Weston revives following her rescue from a fall, she coyly promises to the assembled ranch hands a kiss for the unknown man who saved her, to which Teddy replies, "You might kiss us all around, on the chance o' hittin' the right one." Jessica's testimony in the courtroom scene turns into a touching, almost intimate courtship as Teddy, gently declaring his own affections, asks her personal questions, which she answers under oath directly to Teddy. Despite such positive aspects, *The Cowboy and the Lady* lacked the melodramatic highlights of *The Girl I Left Behind Me* and had little sense of the impact of the environment on character that infused *In Mizzoura*. It recorded forty-four performances, failing to duplicate the success of *In Mizzoura* as Goodwin had hoped. That feat remained for another Augustus Thomas play, *Arizona*, which was already pleasing audiences in Chicago. Within a year, *Arizona* would spark a whole new rage for frontier plays, and eventually it would not only equal but surpass the success of *In Mizzoura*.

6

Dominance: 1899–1906

We both came out of nothin' an' we met, but, through loving, we're goin' to
reach things now – that's us! We had to be lifted up like this, to be saved.

Ramerrez to Minnie in David Belasco's *The Girl of the Golden West*

IF *IN MIZZOURA* QUALIFIED AS A SUCCESS, AUGUSTUS THOMAS'
next frontier drama, *Arizona*, amounted to a blockbuster. Through the 1890s
Thomas wrote plays revolving around politics (*The Capitol*, 1895), historical
events (*Colonel George of Mount Vernon*, 1895), and rural sentiments (*The
Hoosier Doctor*, 1897). In 1897 he traveled to Fort Grant, Arizona, searching
for a story. Charles Frohman paid for his trip to the West in return for an
option on the finished product – and then Frohman inexplicably rejected
what was to become the largest grossing production in American theatrical
history up to that time.[1] *Arizona* not only turned Thomas into a wealthy
man, it also reignited enthusiasm for frontier drama both on stage and on
the screen.

Arizona

Arizona opened at Hamlin's Grand Opera House in Chicago on June 12,
1899, and forever altered the perception of frontier drama. It quickly became
one of the most highly regarded plays ever written by an American author
as well as the most financially successful. The combination of respect and
money signaled the arrival of frontier drama on the center stage of
American theatre, and the major New York producers spent the early years
of the twentieth century trying to duplicate the success of *Arizona*. Within
just a few years several other distinguished border plays by notable authors
emerged that were as good or even better than *Arizona*. In plot, character,

theme, and attitude, these productions represented a leap forward in the ideas that infused border plays, and this led to the emergence of the American frontier as the dominant subject matter of American drama. As prominent easterners journeyed to the West and wrote of their experiences, the conflict between proper eastern beliefs and forthright but violent western attitudes emerged as a recurring motif. The plays addressed complex issues such as assimilation, women's rights, and interracial sex and marriage, but authors invariably found ways to dodge the troubling implications of these issues or to paper over the seriousness of the problems.

After a successful run in Chicago, *Arizona* played throughout the United States for a year before its much anticipated New York debut at the Herald Square Theatre on September 10, 1900, with Kirke La Shelle and Fred R. Hamlin as producers. Besides the publicity generated by the Chicago opening and the nationwide tour, Thomas sparked additional interest by publishing the script. The distribution of a script as a piece of literature was a relatively new phenomenon; earlier theatre practitioners had been reluctant to publish scripts for fear of unauthorized productions. In the last years of the nineteenth century, however, the literary value of scripts acquired new importance with the publication of innovative European drama by such authors as Ibsen and Shaw. The general availability of the script of *Arizona* had the effect of increasing the public's desire to see the production.

Arizona begins in the courtyard of Henry Canby's Aravaipa Ranch, where the troop of the Eleventh United States Cavalry is camping for the night.[2] Canby, the owner of the ranch, speaks in a distinctive, racy manner replete with ranching expressions. His strong personality is matched by his younger daughter, the strikingly independent and well-educated Bonita. Lena Keller, daughter of a sergeant of the troop, works at the ranch, and she has fallen for the roguish Captain Leonard Hodgman, by whom she has an illegitimate child. Despite her troubles, Tony Mostano, a high-spirited vaquero at the ranch, adores her. Other primary characters include Colonel Frank Bonham, an elderly man in charge of nearby Fort Grant, and his beautiful young wife, Estrella, Canby's older daughter. The hero is Lieutenant Harry Denton, a gallant soldier who has been like a son to the colonel. Dr. Fenlon, surgeon for the troop, and Miss MacCullagh, a schoolteacher, provide comedic diversions.

Just as Dr. Fenlon and Miss MacCullagh represent the dramatic equivalent of Dr. Penwick and Wilbur's Ann, so Estrella recalls Kate Vernon. Educated in San Francisco, Estrella is bored by life at the isolated fort and yearns for the excitement of the city. Her listless marriage to the sixty-year-old Bonham augments her restlessness. In a series of scenes after the troop arrives at the ranch, Denton woos Bonita, and then Hodgman courts her as well. After Bonita exits, Hodgman turns his attentions to Estrella, awakening her dreams of escape from the lonely desert outpost and convincing her to take her valuable jewelry and run away with him to New Orleans. Denton interrupts their elopement and forces Hodgman to surrender the jewels, but when the colonel returns unexpectedly, Denton, to spare Estrella's reputation, allows the colonel to think he stole the jewels, and then resigns from the army. Canby hires Denton to oversee his ranch, and after Denton successfully leads a contingent of volunteers in the Spanish-American War, Canby agrees to allow him to marry Bonita. Tony and Lena also plan to wed. When the soldiers bivouac at the ranch on their way to the war, Hodgman is wounded during a confrontation with Denton. Initially Denton is charged, but ultimately Tony confesses that he shot Hodgman when he discovered the captain had seduced Lena and then deserted her. As the colonel is about to leave for the war, Estrella confesses her relationship with Hodgman and begs her husband's forgiveness, but he rides off to the war promising only to see her when he returns.

Critics praised the intelligent construction of the play and the natural and plausible development of climactic moments. In what was meant as a compliment, a *New York Times* reviewer (September 11, 1900) wrote that not even Boucicault could have done it better. Arthur Hobson Quinn said of the play, "*Arizona* is reality – here is the West painted in primary colors, but with no exaggeration."[3]

As in his other plays, Thomas adroitly employed the anticlimactic ending. When Estrella pleads for forgiveness, Thomas avoids a dramatic embrace. Rather he shows Bonham, as he is about to go to war, picking up a rose that his wife had dropped, thereby symbolizing through the use of a prop the bittersweet possibility of an eventual reconciliation.

Similarly, Thomas once again utilized numerous realistic touches, from the dusty alkali that the soldiers brushed from their uniforms to the Apache pottery and Navajo blankets that adorned Canby's dining room in Acts III and IV. Props such as Bonita's hair combs and an olla for drinking water served the action of the play. Walter Burridge and Charles Ritter painted the scenery from sketches of Arizona and from actual rooms at a ranch and a military post. The set carefully displayed three-foot-thick adobe walls with window recesses deep enough for chairs. The colonel's drawing room included a Mexican loom. The chairs at Canby's ranch had seats and backs of cowhide. The military expressions, movements, uniforms, and bugle calls were also authentic. In this way Thomas conveyed a sense that the environment – whether heat, dust, thirst, or a lonely, barren expanse – genuinely affected the characters.

As reviewers pointed out, there was little new in the plot or characters of *Arizona*. The old man, the young wife, the tempter, the noble young man, and the virtuous heroine were time-tested commodities. The *New York Times* critic (September 11, 1900) noted, "the entire fabric of Mr. Thomas' play belongs to the stock-in-trade of every playwright . . . [and] the situations in which they now figure have done duty over and over again." The *New York Evening Sun* echoed that sentiment, pointing out that "several of the situations are almost as old as melodrama itself," while a third critic labeled the incidents "hackneyed."[4] The villain seemed an especially dastardly caricature. Hodgman, sporting a black moustache, had been involved in previous scandals and almost expelled from the Cadet Corps. He fathered a bastard child whom he neither supports nor acknowledges, and he romances not only Estrella but also her sister, Bonita.

Still, while the basic story and characters were conventional, Thomas' language, realistic details, and contrasting shades within the standard character types provided originality. The same review that called the incidents hackneyed praised the characters as "strong, distinct, and interesting," and the language as "intense, clear, virile, and even stirring." Canby, as portrayed by Theodore Roberts, vibrantly combined authority and tenderness with a sense of humor that recalled Bret Harte's finest creations. Quinn called the character "one of the best drawn figures of the modern drama."[5] Canby spoke of marriage in ranching terms: "A woman that's married to a fellow has a pretty tight cinch on him – that is, if he likes her."[6] Elsewhere he talked of newlyweds' squabbles: "When you first yoke 'em up, they jes' whip-saw that way."[7] In Bonita and Estrella, Thomas extended the stereotype of passionate Hispanic women, though Bonita provided an attractive combination of skill, intelligence, and fiery independence. Lena Keller was another intriguing character, unconventional in that she had had an illegitimate child just prior to Act I and yet gained a respectable marriage proposal in Act IV, echoing Mary Brandon of *My Partner*. Equally appealing is Lena's admirer, Tony, who displays a romantic side in his adoration of Lena, but is also spirited, impulsive, and jealous. Tony employs an entertaining combination of proper and improper English, as he demonstrates when he declares his love to Lena by erupting with "damn-to-hell-my-soul, I love you."[8]

Another fresh element in this frontier drama was Thomas' use of the outside world of the Spanish-American War as a pretext for the movement of the soldiers. After his visit to Arizona, Thomas conceived of the troops moving in response to an Indian uprising, but current events changed his mind.[9] Here as in other arenas – numerous plays about the Spanish-American War emerged and even Buffalo Bill's Wild West incorporated references to it – the larger world began to impinge on the world of the frontier.

Thomas' penchant for props resurfaced in *Arizona*, where he utilized two props especially well to convey very different emotional attitudes. At the end of the play, the rose sentimentally implied the eventual reunion of Estrella and Colonel Bonham. Earlier he employed a set of hair combs for romance and comedy. In the first scene Denton uses one of Bonita's side combs to comb his hair. He asks her if any other fellows have ever used that comb. She shakes her head demurely, but just as Denton registers pleasure at that response, she deflates him by adding, "I haven't had it very long." Shortly afterwards Bonita assents to Denton's request that she will not allow anyone else to use the comb. Then she removes the *other* comb from her hair, coyly observing, "It's pretty hard, though, to tell them apart."[10]

Just as Belasco accentuated the emotional context of *The Girl I Left Behind Me* through music and lighting, so, too, did Thomas in *Arizona*. A sunset bathes Act I, while moonlight glows in Act II. Tony's mandolin music underscores a romantic scene between Bonita and Denton in Act I, and in Act III Tony serenades Lena. The music created both a Spanish aura and a proper romantic mood, and it accompanied Tony and Lena throughout the production. In Act II, dance music from a military band complemented the action but stopped just prior to the aborted elopement to accentuate the tension with a quiet stillness.

Arizona ran for 140 performances and spawned a host of touring companies. It became the most financially rewarding play produced in America up to that time, and within five years it brought Augustus Thomas a quarter of a million dollars in royalties.[11] Thomas eventually wrote nearly seventy plays, many of them regarded as superior to *Arizona*, but none bettered its financial return. In the early twentieth century Thomas wrote a series of farce comedies including *The Earl of Pawtucket* (1903). Then he turned to more serious works about telepathy and the human mind, writing what many critics considered his best and most profound work with *The Witching Hour* (1907) and *As a Man Thinks* (1911). Thomas also authored several more plays about frontier subjects. He wrote *Colorado* (1901) after a visit to the mines in that state, but the implausible plot and the confusion of five pairs of love interests led to a disappointment that closed after only forty-eight performances. *The Ranger*, in 1907, featured United States Rangers on the southern border chasing nefarious miners and warding off attacks by border-crossing Mexicans. Charles Frohman, who missed out on the success of *Arizona*, produced that play to a loss of nearly $30,000 when it closed after just twenty-four performances. In 1916, Thomas' own son, Luke, was a cavalry lieutenant in Texas guarding against raids by Pancho Villa when Thomas wrote *Rio Grande*. Focusing on a young woman married to an older man, the play seemed little more than an adaptation of *Arizona* with a tragic ending and closed after fifty-five performances. Three years later, Thomas wrote *Palmy Days* – also referred to as *Cricket of Palmy Days* – based on Bret Harte's stories. Set in a California mining camp in the 1850s, the play links the mining camp life with a touring dramatic troupe passing through the area. It ran for fifty performances.

Arizona spawned three film adaptations as well as a stage musical. State Rights released the earliest film version in 1913 directed by Augustus Thomas and featuring Robert Broderick as Canby, Cyril Scott as Denton, and Gail Kane as Bonita. Taking advantage of the publicity for the movie, William Brady in the same year produced a stage revival that ran for forty performances. In 1918 Jesse Lasky's Famous Players starred Douglas Fairbanks as Denton with Theodore Roberts reprising his role as Canby and Marjorie Daw playing Bonita in a version filmed on location in Arizona. Columbia released a talking, John Wayne version of the play in 1931 with the title *Men Are Like That*, and Sigmund Romberg wrote a musical version, first called *Bonita* and then *The Love Call*, which recorded eighty-eight performances in 1927.[12]

In addition to securing the reputation and financial security of Augustus Thomas, *Arizona* also established the New York presence of the Shubert brothers, who eventually displaced the Syndicate as the dominant producers of drama in the United States. Lee, Sam, and Jacob Shubert achieved their first important theatrical triumph in 1894 when Sam secured touring rights to Charles Hoyt's popular comedy, *A Texas Steer*. Booking the Herald Square Theatre for *Arizona* provided the brothers with their first foothold in New York, and its success fueled their meteoric rise to theatrical prominence.

Arizona also helped establish the career of at least one of the lead actors, Theodore Roberts, who played Canby. Roberts had previously played the cunning Ladru in *The Girl I Left Behind Me*. Later, he would star again as a chief in another significant frontier play, Edwin Milton Royle's *The Squaw Man*. He would also play crucial roles as an army major in a stage adaptation of Frederic Remington's *John Ermine of the Yellowstone* and as the sheriff in Bret Harte's *Sue*. Roberts eventually turned to film and acted in numerous movies, especially as a member of Lasky's Famous Players group, appearing in *The Girl of the Golden West* (1915), *The Trail of the Lonesome Pine* (1916), and *M'liss* (1918).

The Virginian

Theatre managers competed eagerly to duplicate the success of *Arizona*, and in the next few years the production of frontier plays in top-flight theatres proliferated. The next major success, however, evolved from a story that was not originally written for the stage. Owen Wister symbolized the pure-bred eastern establishment. Born in 1860 to Philadelphia society parents, he graduated from Harvard with honors in music and passed his law exams. Although Wister was a grandson of the noted actress Fanny Kemble, his experience with theatre was limited to writing comedy for Harvard's Hasty Pudding productions. Through his youthful travels abroad Wister was more familiar with the capitals of Europe than the towns of the American West. In 1885, however, he scheduled a trip to Wyoming to restore his failing health, and the journey changed his life. Never comfortable with his law career, Wister adored the freedom from what he perceived as the regimented and stifling society of the East. Over the next decade Wister made seven more trips to the West, and as he recorded his observations he turned increasingly from law to writing.

Wister believed that previous writers had not justly depicted the American West and that easterners held simplistic ideas of the region, and therefore determined to provide a more serious and artistic vision of the land. He also realized that the western frontier was rapidly passing, and he set out to record its history and romance before it was entirely forgotten. Wister wrote popular stories and articles in the 1890s, primarily for *Harper's Weekly* and *Harper's Magazine*. In 1902 he strung his observations together in a loosely knit novel called *The Virginian*, in which a cowhand breaks up a ring of cattle thieves and wins the hand of a lovely schoolmistress. As with Thomas' *Arizona*, the primary attraction of the novel lay not in the story, but in the characters, the language, and the incidental byplay that generated a distinctive western atmosphere.

The novel enchanted eastern audiences, and less than two years after its publication producer Kirke La Shelle helped Wister to turn the novel into a script, which La Shelle produced at the Manhattan Theatre on January 5, 1904, after tryouts in Buffalo, Boston, and other cities. The play begins at a

Figure 19. Final scene from Owen Wister's *The Virginian*.

ranch house along the Bear Creek in Wyoming on the occasion of the christening of the Hughey twins.[13] The scene introduces the impressionable young cowboy, Steve, who is falling under the negative influence of Trampas, Shorty, and Spanish Ed. It also introduces the prim Vermont schoolteacher, Molly Wood, who meets a dashing ranch hand referred to only as the Virginian, but their relationship gets off to a rocky start. Later, at Judge Henry's ranch, several cattlemen plan a raid against cattle thieves. The Virginian tries to warn his friend Steve, but Steve rejects his overtures and rides off with Trampas and his gang, ensuring that his name is added to the list of outlaws. The Virginian also courts Molly, who is teaching him to read, but she is appalled that he intends to lead a vigilance group against the cattle thieves. Act III reveals the cattle thieves encamped at Horse Thief Pass, playing poker and waiting for the dawn to move their ill-gotten herd. When the Virginian and his men surprise the thieves, Trampas escapes, but Steve is caught and hung for his crimes. As the hanging takes place, a shot fells the Virginian, and a short time later Molly discovers him, wounded and delirious, and transports him to her cabin, where she nurses him back to health and finally agrees to marry him. The setting for the final act is a street corner in Medicine Bow, Wyoming, on the day before their wedding. When a drunken Trampas orders the Virginian to leave town by sundown or be shot, Molly pleads with the Virginian to go, but he refuses to kowtow. Finally, Trampas confronts his nemesis and shoots, but the Virginian shoots straighter and kills him, leaving Molly and the Virginian to embrace at the final curtain.

Dramatizing a novel is always difficult in that novels typically contain a large amount of complex narration that must be condensed into a stage performance of only two or three hours. Wister's novel presented a particular problem because the basic story line was so thin. The charm of the novel lay in atmospheric vignettes that had little to do with the plot. Wister and La Shelle altered the novel's first-person style to the requirements of the stage, making Ogden, who appears in the novel as a visitor from the East, the stand-in for the naive "tenderfoot" narrator. They included many of the critical lines and incidents from the novel, but they reworked and reordered the material. The courtship, which in the novel progresses gently over four years, occurs much more rapidly in the play. Steve, the misguided friend of the Virginian in the play, is compounded from a similar "Steve" in the novel and a character named "Shorty," whom Trampas leads into crime. The play retained the novel's strong emphasis on the relationship between Steve and the Virginian – as Burns Mantle wisely commented, "It is the story of the friendship of the Virginian for Steve quite as much as it is the story of the Virginian's love for Molly Wood."[14]

The attempt by Wister and La Shelle to reproduce and rearrange as much of the novel as they could reasonably cram into the play resulted in a certain looseness. Entrances and exits are especially jarring. Characters arrive and leave with little justification. Frequently one set of characters exits and another group enters with no attempt to overlap or integrate the action. "The grim truth is," one critic wrote, "that the romance is made up in large measure of disconnected scenes, most of which have no or little bearing upon the love story."[15] As in the case of *Arizona*, reviewers criticized *The Virginian* for its thin plot and its wobbly dramatic construction while praising its characters and dialogue. The same typical review noted the "smoothness, vivacity and expressiveness" of the dialogue and the "well and fully developed" characters. The *New York Times* (January 6, 1904) called the production "a series of exquisitely real and soundly sentimental pictures of life and character, with little or no bearing on the story, which crops up at irregular intervals." The writer labeled the play a western melodrama amalgamated with the "static theatre" of Belgian playwright Maurice Maeterlinck, in which plot was de-emphasized in order to focus on the symbolic significance of everyday events. "It is probable that neither the western melodrama nor the static drama is a first rate art form, and . . . the blending of the two species does not produce the soundest and most vital drama. Yet something there was about it that caught the attention and . . . held it from curtain to curtain."

Among several notable attributes of the play and the production, the title role probably generated the most enthusiastic response. While the Virginian certainly fell within the mainstream of the noble hero, numerous qualities gave him added dimensions. In the first scene, for instance, he switches the blankets and clothing of several sleeping babies, which leads to consternation among their parents. His practical joke conveys a boyish immaturity, which allows him to grow in the course of the play as he rises from ranch hand to foreman. His impish humor melds with his sense of honor to produce an utterly charming combination. When the parents return to straighten out the jumbled children, for example, the scene establishes a delicate mixture of laughter and anger. After the Virginian confesses his part in the shenanigan, the parents grudgingly forgive him. One mother remarks, "If he only looked ashamed," to which the Virginian, struggling to keep a straight face, responds, "I am trying to ma'am." In Act II, talking about Shakespeare, queens, poker, and religion, the Virginian demonstrates a Will-Rogers-like wit, remarking that there are fifteen different religions, but only one God.[16]

Wister's villains were perhaps even more unconventional than his hero. Steve, of course, represents a good man subjected to evil influences. He confronts winning and losing – in poker and in life – with resignation. "Play the game," he tells Spanish Ed. "If we win – we win. If we lose – we'll take our medicine graceful."[17] And he does, poignantly passing out his personal effects to his friends as they are about to hang him. But Steve was not the only unusual villain. As the cattle thieves sit around the campfire before their capture, they dream of traveling to Paris, Rome, and Monte Carlo with their loot. Spanish Ed's ineptness at poker evokes hilarity. Too eager with his strong hands and too daring with his bluffs, Spanish Ed plays poker as though his eyes reflect his cards, which leads Trampas to tell him his "face don't fit a poker hand."[18] Though a traditional villain, Trampas seems almost as much a jokester as an evil man. In the last scene he regrets issuing his threat to the Virginian, for it is he who feels trapped by his own ultimatum.

Trampas' description of Ed's face, quoted above, indicates the original and appropriate language employed in the play. When Steve and the Virginian first meet, Steve greets him with "Hello you old son of a bitch." The judge informs Ogden, "That's friendship, Mr. Ogden. It's all in the tone, not in the words." As if to prove that point, when Trampas refers to the Virginian a few lines later as "only a son of a bitch," the Virginian responds in a line that became a classic: "When you call me that, smile."[19]

Such casual dialogue and the actors' ability to hurl robust words such as "liar" and "thief" without theatricality impressed the *Times* reviewer.

Like the productions of the Belasco and Thomas plays, *The Virginian* included calculated and arresting production values. The walls of Uncle Hughey's home in Act I were roughly papered with pages from illustrated magazines. At Horse Thief Pass, water trickled down a hillside to create an on-stage pool. Shadowy trees enveloped the nighttime scene, while stark silhouettes among the tree branches marked the hanging of Steve and Spanish Ed. Lighting also enhanced that scene as the campfire and cloud-shrouded moonlight resolved to dawn. The production adroitly exploited music, just as other frontier dramas had. A familiar cattle song denoted Trampas' presence. The dance music at the christening provided lively accompaniment to the good cheer of the first act. Music from the bunk-house as the cowboys celebrated the Virginian's promotion to foreman in the second act counterpointed the serious business of entering names on the list of cattle thieves.

The production followed Thomas in its reliance on anticlimactic moments. When the Virginian and his men trapped Steve and Spanish Ed, no shots were fired. In fact, Steve and Ed did not even bother to draw their guns. Similarly, the climactic gunfight erupted with little contrived buildup.

The play successfully transferred much of the thematic content from the novel, especially in the gap between "Vermont," typified by Molly's prudish ways, and "Wyoming," as exemplified by the cowboys. The contrast between East and West centered on Molly's reactions to the Virginian. When she indicated that he was not the kind of man she wanted, he said, "I *am* the sort of man you want. Only you don't know it – yet."[20] In Molly's world the most important considerations involved whether a man and woman had been properly introduced, but the reality of the West demanded concern for more practical skills.

Most importantly, *The Virginian* justified the idea of fighting violence with violence, even outside the law. Molly is appalled that the Virginian would lead a vigilance raid and hang people without trials, but the Virginian argues that the criminals have usurped the court system and avoided punishment even when they were obviously guilty, leaving the ranchers with no other choice. Interestingly, Wister places the Virginian in the position of foreman. He is not a rich rancher at the top of the economic chain, but he has risen above the status of a mere order-taker at the ranch hand level. He is middle management. He argues against putting Steve's name on the list of thieves, but when other ranchers insist that he is part of the gang, Steve's name is entered. The Virginian does not make the decision to go after the outlaws, but he certainly supports it and leads the operation. The sense of the Virginian between management and workers spoke to the emerging American middle class, as it accentuated his disappointment at seeing his friend go down the wrong path while raising his own sense of responsibility for the consequences of his actions. Structurally, the cloudy moral choice of lynching the cattle thieves occurs near the middle of the play, immediately after which the Virginian receives a torturous wound. Lee Clark Mitchell has observed that the bodies of western heroes typically undergo pain and torment, and that this confirms their manhood, which it certainly does in the case of the Virginian.[21] It also serves as a kind of punishment for his unwavering moral choice, but it does not change his mind, and eventually even Molly, in accepting the hero, inherently accepts his actions and his rationale. At the end of the play his duel with Trampas presents a more obvious moral choice, as Trampas instigates the confrontation.

The Virginian continued the trend toward romantic frontier dramas. The defining moment of the early relationship between Molly and the Virginian – narrated rather than shown – occurs when he rides into a raging river and carries her safely to the bank, which recalls Davy Crockett riding into the wedding and bearing off his beloved Eleanor. The Virginian provided a turn-of-the-century model for masculinity that glorified boyish charm, physical skill, friendliness, and ultimate acceptance of responsibility. One critic raved that Dustin Farnum, who enacted the lead role, was "as splendid a specimen of physical manhood as ever came east of the Mississippi River and as fine an actor as ever went west of it." Amy Leslie said Farnum projected "sympathy, charm and manliness."[22]

Leslie went on enthusiastically, calling *The Virginian* "a triumphantly enjoyable American play ... [that] takes hold of the sensibilities, charms the eyes, thrills the emotions and presents an absolutely truthful picture of its territory." The public agreed. *The Virginian* ran 138 performances before closing for the summer, and it reopened in October for an additional two weeks at the Academy of Music. Wister's story occasioned numerous screen treatments, the first in 1914, in which Cecil B. DeMille directed Dustin Farnum. Shot on location in California, that movie was the first release of a new company called Paramount Pictures. Preferred Pictures released a version in 1923 with Kenneth Harlen in the lead, Florence Vidor as Molly, and Russell Simpson as the villain. Gary Cooper starred as the hero with Walter Huston as Trampas in a 1929 Paramount release, and Paramount issued yet another version in 1946, with Joel McCrea as the Virginian.

A handsome young newcomer, Dustin Farnum, played the Virginian in its 1904 stage debut, and the role of the loveable hero became his springboard to an illustrious career. Farnum, a rugged six-footer, was born in New Hampshire in 1874 to a pair of professional actors. He received his first major opportunity when he followed Vincent Sarrano in the role of Lieutenant Denton in *Arizona*, which led directly to his even greater success in the title role of the Wister play. Farnum enacted several significant frontier roles after *The Virginian*, including Captain Esmond, who vanquishes Mexican marauders to win the mine owner's daughter in Thomas' *The Ranger*. He also played in the 1913 revival of *Arizona* and in a 1910 revival of *The Squaw Man*. His frontier portrayals led to an extensive film career. He reprised his lead role in *The Virginian* (1914), and the same year played the lead in *The Squaw Man*, directed by Cecil B. DeMille. He acted the title role in *Davy Crockett* in 1916, and, with his horse, Dusty, became a well-known star of early westerns. Farnum appeared in over forty films, retiring after his 1926 appearance as George Custer in *The Flaming Frontier*.

With *Arizona* and *The Virginian* blazing the trail, the wagon train of success for frontier drama rolled forward, and authors, producers, and performers clambered to get aboard. Annie Oakley left Cody's Wild West show after a 1901 train accident, and in the fall of 1902 starred in *The Western Girl*, a melodrama by Langdon McCormick. It lasted only until March 1903, however, faring little better than Oakley's earlier attempts at frontier melodrama, *Deadwood Dick; or, The Sunbeam of the Sierras*, which she played in the winter of 1888–89, and *Miss Rora*, which she toured in the United States and in England in the 1894–95 season.[23]

In 1903 Louis Shipman dramatized Frederic Remington's novel *John Ermine of the Yellowstone*, which traces the story of a white youth raised by Indians who is accused of a murder when he reconnects to white society. James K. Hackett, son of the great James H. Hackett, played the title role, and Theodore Roberts portrayed an army major. The following year, Richard Harding Davis adapted his own *Ranson's Folly* for the stage. Both *John Ermine* and *Ranson's Folly* were later turned into movies. Clay Greene's *A Man from the West* (1900) used the typical device of the westerner placed in the East: a shy Montana sheriff visits New York with a Wild West show. The atypical aspect of that production was its casting of heavyweight champion Jim Jeffries as the sheriff. *Across the Trail* by W. H. Collings (1901), like *Ranch 10*, used the artifice of the same actor playing a pair of brothers. *A Montana Outlaw* by Fred S. Gibbs and Herbert H. Winslow in 1902, *Montana* by Harry D. Carey in 1906, and *The Cow Puncher* by Hal Reid in

1906 all featured stories with a ranch setting. Other early-twentieth-century frontier plays included *A Texas Ranger* in 1904 by Jane Maudlin Feigl; *Custer's Last Fight* in 1905 by Hal Reid, which focused more on Buffalo Bill than on Custer; *Sam Houston*, which starred Clay Clement in the title role in 1906; and *The Judge and the Jury* in 1906 by Harry D. Cottrell and Oliver Morosco, a story of a love triangle in a New Mexico mining town. Such mining-camp plays retained their popularity. *Sunset Mines* played New York's Third Avenue Theatre in 1901, and *At Cripple Creek* was offered at the Metropolitan the same year. *Alaska* in 1902 ventured into a further frontier mining outpost, while *Nevada* in 1903 returned to familiar territory, as did *The Goldfields of Nevada* in 1906. *The Missourians* in 1904 was directed by a youthful Cecil B. DeMille, who also played a key role in the production, and in that same year *A Struggle for Gold* played the Third Avenue Theatre.

Interracial love and "the Girl"

A list of the best plays of 1905 would almost certainly include two frontier dramas – *The Girl of the Golden West* by David Belasco, and *The Squaw Man* by Edwin Milton Royle – and one play with an intriguing Native American character – *Strongheart* by William C. deMille. *Strongheart*, which opened at New York's Hudson Theatre on January 30, was anything but the typical western melodrama. Billed as a comedy, it was set entirely in New York City: in a room at Columbia University, a locker room at the Polo Grounds, and an elegant residence.[24] Only the main character, the chief's son Soangataha, who has come east for an education, provides a frontier connection. Athletic, earnest, and intelligent, Soangataha – known as Strongheart – succeeds in the classroom, on the athletic fields, and in the parlors of society. The play presented vivid dramatic evidence for successful assimilation as well as a powerful indictment of society's racism. At the climax, however, it made use of an end run to avoid seriously confronting the issue of interracial marriage.

Football nomenclature is appropriate to this play, for in the first two acts Strongheart helps Columbia win a key football match. At a victory celebration in the home of his best friend, Frank Nelson, Strongheart declares his love for Frank's sister, Dorothy, and asks her to marry him. Troubled by her conflicting emotions, she delays her answer. When Strongheart reveals his love for Dorothy to Frank and another teammate, his supposed friends rebuke him. "You are not one of us," Frank declares, clearly delineating the racial boundary confining the young Indian. Dick Livingston, who also loves Dorothy, brands his pursuit of the girl a treacherous betrayal.[25] In the last act Dorothy pledges her love to Strongheart, but soon a messenger from the tribe arrives – grim-faced and long-haired – informing Soangataha that his father has died and that he must return to his tribe to accept the mantle of leadership. The messenger treats Strongheart's white fiancee with disdain, insisting that she stay behind. Dorothy remains determined to go, but after an inner struggle Soangataha tells her it would not be fair to force her into the deprived conditions that plague his people, and, despite his feelings of despair and desolation, he renounces his love for the girl.

Strongheart did not invent the educated Indian trapped between two cultures. Credit for that goes to *Northern Lights*, performed a decade earlier. *Strongheart* did, however, use the character effectively to illumine racial prejudice. The structural problem with the play was that for two and a half acts the piece fostered the gay, pennant-waving jollity of an afternoon college football game, with innocuous problems involving the theft of a play list and two students courting the same young lady, and then, midway through Act III, the tone shifted rather awkwardly to that of a social problem play.[26] Thematically the end is rather an avoidance of issues than an examination of them. The tribal messenger exhibits the same racial bias toward Dorothy that Frank and Dick display toward Strongheart, and Strongheart's unilateral decision to end his relationship with Dorothy – a show of chauvinistic righteousness that completely devalues her carefully considered opinion – is more theatrical sentimentalism than dramatic necessity.

The production was a modest success, but not of the magnitude of some of the more traditional frontier dramas. *Strongheart* ran for sixty-six performances before moving to the Savoy Theatre, where it played an additional thirty-two performances. *Strongheart* was the first produced play written by William deMille, the son of Belasco collaborator Henry C. DeMille, and the collegiate scenes reflected the fact that William, like his father, had attended Columbia. William wrote several other plays, his greatest success coming with the 1907 Civil War drama *The Warrens of Virginia*. He also collaborated with his brother, Cecil, on several mostly unsuccessful works, including *The Royal Mounted* in 1908. Not long after the failure of the brothers' *After Five* in 1913, William followed Cecil to the west coast and prominence in the burgeoning movie business.

While *Strongheart* examined the love between an Indian boy and a white girl, another even more prominent play of 1905 focused on a love affair between a native maiden and a white man. The opening of Edwin Milton

Royle's *The Squaw Man* at Wallack's Theatre on October 23 must have surprised audiences expecting a border drama, for the first act did not take
place in the West, but at Maudsley Towers, the English estate of the Earl
of Kerhill.[27] There James Wynnegate, to spare his beloved sister-in-law,
Diana, from disgrace and scandal, accepts the blame for his older brother's
embezzlement and leaves England. Act II is set in the Long Horn Saloon
in Maverick, a cow town on the Union Pacific rail line, two years later.
Wynnegate is now Jim Carston, a rancher, and when a trainload of English
tourists including his brother Henry and his wife Diana enter the bar, Jim
conceals his identity. Jim also stifles the villainous schemes of Cash
Hawkins to ply the Ute chief Tabywana with alcohol, swindle him out of
his cattle, and take his daughter, Nat-u-ritch. When the enraged Hawkins
tries to ambush Jim, Nat-u-ritch shoots him. Act III takes place seven years
later, in front of Jim's dilapidated ranch house in Green River, Utah. In the
intervening years Nat-u-ritch has nursed Jim through a dangerous fever and
refused to leave him. "The inevitable" has happened, they have had a son,
and Jim has become a socially ostracized "squaw man." The circumstances
shift, however, when Diana arrives with the news that Henry is dead, having
confessed to the embezzlement, and that Jim is now the Earl of Kerhill. Jim
refuses to leave Nat-u-ritch, but agrees to send his son, Hal, to be educated
in England as the next Earl. Nat-u-ritch, however, is devastated, and as the
wagon leaves with young Hal, a shot rings out, and Tabywana enters with
the body of his daughter, who has killed herself, draped over his out-
stretched arms for the final tableau.

Despite criticism of the awkward first act, *The Squaw Man* startled and
impressed its audiences. The *New York Morning Telegraph* declared it "one
of the best plays of the season." The *New York Tribune* called the play "sentimental without mawkishness and vivid without sensationalism." The *New
York Times* agreed: "The things that were done were lively, picturesque
things – things with contrast – things to induce both laughter and that
swelling of the heart which follows brave deeds or noble sentiments."[28]
Critics especially praised the emotional moments of the piece, such as
Diana's discovery of Jim's son, the farewell between Jim and his boy, and the
final tableau. The conception of Nat-u-ritch, a role performed completely
in pantomime, was also distinctive. Strains of native music underscored and
reinforced dramatic points. "It is," gushed the *Times* (October 29, 1905), "a
kind of symphony played upon the heart strings."

The symphony played well. *The Squaw Man* ran for 222 performances followed by another week at the New York Theatre in 1907 and an additional

Figure 20. Tabywana cradles Nat-u-ritch in Act IV of Edwin Milton Royle's *The Squaw Man*.

thirty-two performances at the Academy of Music in 1908. At the end of March 1910, in Rochester, it recorded its two-thousandth performance.[29]

The evident sincerity of the script and the acting engendered positive reactions. Reviewers especially credited the play with an innovative depar-ture in its use of actual Ute words with an interpreter for Tabywana.[30] "Hitherto," intoned the *Times*, "our stage Indians have had a most excellent understanding of English." In an interview with the *Times* (March 4, 1906),

Theodore Roberts, who played Tabywana, declared that the use of an Indian character speaking his native language through an interpreter was a first. Roberts, who had appeared in Indian roles in both *The Girl I Left Behind Me* and *Arizona*, said that actors in those plays had simply used "picturesque gibberish," whereas, for *The Squaw Man* Baco White – the Native American who played the interpreter in the production – had supplied Indian words that Roberts then wrote out phonetically and memorized. The attempt to make the white actors look authentically native received similar praise. Roberts selected a photograph of a Sioux chief, which he used as a guide. Each night, in a makeup process that took almost an hour, he molded brown putty to form high cheekbones and an arched nose.

Looking back from the perspective of the twenty-first century, the self-congratulatory tone of the *Times* article in praising the use of Indian speech and the attempt to duplicate native appearances seems ironic. The writer says that earlier plays had given unsophisticated depictions of evil, painted savages or noble warriors, "gentle, fawnlike" maidens who rescued the heroes, and aging chiefs who sat before a lonely wigwam "eyeing the landscape with primitive north American gloom." Yet Nat-u-ritch could hardly be more gentle and fawnlike. Not only does she save the hero from death on at least two occasions, but she sacrifices herself at the end of the play to clear the way for his happiness. Furthermore, the critic's sense of the genuine depiction of Indians extends only to whites playing Native Americans. The writer makes no mention of actual Indian performers such as Gowongo Mohawk nor of the many Indians who traveled and appeared with the earlier border melodramas, who, one presumes, both looked genuine and spoke some native phrases.

A few critics rejected the emotion of *The Squaw Man*. Alan Dale, writing in the *New York American* (October 26, 1905), found the situations "preposterous" and called the play "laughably dreadful . . . an orgy of heroism." Burns Mantle, reviewing a performance in Chicago prior to the New York debut, expressed his dissatisfaction with the death of Nat-u-ritch, an ending that he found "unnecessarily uncomfortable."[31]

Mantle's discomfort is understandable, for rather than confront the cultural clash of the interracial marriage, Royle, like deMille in *Strongheart*, opts for a sentimental twist that dodges real issues and that clears the path to a happy ending for Jim and Diana. The final image of Tabywana cradling his dead daughter explodes with allusions to America's frontier past. Like *Metamora*, the picture presents the last of a race. Nat-u-ritch is dead, and her son will be educated not only in America but in England. The scene

echoes the myth of Pocahontas, willing to sacrifice herself for the convenience of a white man. It shows us the Indian who has been a savior, a protector, a nurse, and a lover to the white man, but who has outlived her
usefulness and must step aside so that he may be happy. Finally, it portrays
a female Indian futilely in love with an aristocratic white male who can
respond to her womanly advances, have sex with her, and even care for her,
but who cannot ultimately really love her. Thus *The Squaw Man* fell in line
with a tradition of American drama that regularly killed off inconvenient
minorities in order to avoid tackling the uncomfortable reality of interracial
sexuality.

Audiences, however, accepted the sentimental elimination of Nat-u-
ritch as a necessary precondition for bringing the lovers together, and the
resulting popularity of *The Squaw Man* created a matinee idol of the
British-born lead actor, William Faversham. Known as "Favey" to his
adoring public, Faversham reigned as the Clark Gable of the early-
twentieth-century New York stage.[32] Born in London in 1868, Faversham
worked briefly in theatre there before emigrating to America in 1886, where
his handsome looks and European charm won him roles with Daniel and
Charles Frohman. His greatest success prior to *The Squaw Man* came as
Lord Algernon in *Lord and Lady Algy* in 1899. The lead role in the Royle
play perfectly suited the buoyant, dashing Englishman, and he played Jim
Carston for three years. While reviews generally gave his acting in *The
Squaw Man* high marks, not everyone agreed. The *New York Times* (October
29, 1905) liked the character of the "splendidly vigorous" hero, but objected
to its "presentation by an actor whose whole method is artificial, strained,
and beset with affectation."

Faversham's portrayal of the Royle hero proved to be the zenith of his
career. He returned to more traditional and classical roles, such as Iago,
Othello, Romeo, and Antony, and appeared in a few movies, though
without ever really making an impact in the new medium. When *The Squaw
Man* was filmed, Dustin Farnum, who succeeded Faversham in the title
role, played the lead. Faversham's personal life also ran into difficulties. He
divorced Merion Merwin to marry actress Julie Opp in 1902, but she died
in 1921. After her death Faversham's personal finances crumbled, leading
him to declare bankruptcy in 1927 and again in 1935. His last role came in
1933 as Jeeter Lester in a touring production of *Tobacco Road*. He died in
1940, destitute and forgotten.

While *The Squaw Man* marked the high point of Faversham's professional life, for another actor in the cast it represented just one significant

step toward a spectacular career. William S. Hart played the villain, Cash Hawkins, and the portrayal was almost universally praised.[33] Cash Hawkins represented a departure from the usual stage villain not only through Hart's self-confident portrayal but also because the villain dies before the play is half over. Hart, born in Newburgh, New York, in 1870, fell in love with the West when he traveled there as a child. He began his stage career in 1889 and quickly gained a reputation as a competent stock actor – the *New York Dramatic Mirror* featured him on its cover of January 30, 1892. For Lawrence Barrett's company he played young romantic leads including Romeo and Orlando, but his breakthrough role was the antagonist Messala in the elaborate 1899 production of *Ben-Hur*. Royle's border drama provided a special opportunity, for Hart seemed particularly comfortable with the frontier atmosphere. After his success with *The Squaw Man*, Hart played the title role in *The Virginian* in touring productions from 1907 to 1910. In 1914 at the age of forty-four he transposed his western character into movies, where it proved exceptionally popular and enduring. Over the next eleven years, up to his last movie, *Tumbleweeds*, of 1925, Hart played a pivotal role in the development of the frontier film. He virtually invented the adult western by bringing to the screen the concept of the "good bad guy." While other movie makers emphasized pure action, Hart insisted on complex characters and realistic stories. In all, Hart made over fifty films, many of which he directed and some of which he wrote.

While *The Squaw Man* provided merely a springboard for Hart, for author Edwin Milton Royle, as for William Faversham, it proved to be the pinnacle of his career. Ironically, the play was utterly different from anything Royle had previously written. Like Owen Wister, Royle was a prominent member of society. Born in Missouri in 1862, he studied at Princeton, Edinburgh, and Columbia Law School. Also like Wister, Royle disdained the legal profession and instead wrote material for himself and his wife, Selena Fetter Royle, which launched their careers as a comic acting team. He achieved success as a comic playwright, starring with his wife in *Friends* (1892) and *Captain Impudence* (1897). The latter play, which used the Mexican War as its setting, evidenced Royle's interest in a frontier locale. More typical of Royle, however, was his third success, the playful *My Wife's Husbands* (1903), which was adapted into the musical *Marrying Mary* in 1906. Royle originally presented *The Squaw Man* as a one-act sketch at the Lambs Club, a New York gathering place for theatrical luminaries. Response was so positive that he quickly extended the piece. Both the setting and the serious elements of *The Squaw Man* represented a departure from Royle's other work, and although he wrote more than a dozen other plays before his death in 1942 he did not produce anything approaching the popularity of his foray into border drama.

The Squaw Man proved as popular on film as it was in the theatres, especially with Royle's nephew, Cecil B. DeMille. In 1914 DeMille directed Dustin Farnum as James Wynnegate in Hollywood's first feature-length film. That was also the first film made by DeMille in collaboration with Samuel Goldwyn and Jesse Lasky. In 1918 DeMille directed a second version with Elliott Dester as Jim, Noah Beery as Tabywana, and Theodore Roberts moving over to the role of Jim's faithful ranch hand, Bill. In 1931 DeMille made a third version of the play, this time for Metro-Goldwyn-Mayer starring Warner Baxter and Lupe Velez. So popular was the story of *The Squaw Man* that in 1917 Paramount even released a sequel to it called *The Squaw Man's Son*, which was based on Royle's own sequel, *The Silent Call*, and followed the fully grown Hal as he leaves England to seek his roots in his mother's land.

In addition to its cinematic incarnations, *The Squaw Man* was accorded a major New York revival in 1921, again with Faversham, which ran fifty performances; it also played in London in 1908 as *The White Man*. Composer Rudolph Friml produced a musical treatment of the play in 1927, *The White Eagle*, which recorded forty-eight performances.

An even more popular and influential frontier play opened in New York only three weeks after *The Squaw Man* began its run. That play was David Belasco's *The Girl of the Golden West*, which opened at the Belasco Theatre on November 11, 1905. It ran for 224 performances with twenty-two more at the Belasco in 1907 and another twenty-four at the Academy of Music in 1908. The production starred Blanche Bates as Minnie, the proprietor of the Polka Saloon in the 1850s mining camp of Cloudy Mountain, California. The sign above the saloon bar, which is the setting for Act I, reads "A Real Home for the Boys," and that is what Minnie tries to provide.[34] She is the darling of the camp and the particular quarry of sheriff Jack Rance, who has taken a liking to Minnie despite the fact that he has a wife in New Orleans. Into this environment strides Dick Johnson, a handsome stranger. When almost all the men form a posse to track the dangerous outlaw Ramerrez, their departure leaves Minnie and Johnson alone to establish an instant rapport. Johnson is actually Ramerrez and has planned to rob the saloon, but his burgeoning feelings for Minnie dissuade him. The romance progresses rapidly, and Minnie invites Johnson to her cabin, where they pledge their love to each other. Johnson eventually leaves in the middle of a raging snowstorm, but he soon returns, wounded. Minnie hides him in her loft, and when Rance arrives she convinces him that Johnson is not there. The sheriff is about to leave when a drop of blood falls from the loft, revealing Johnson's presence. To save her lover, Minnie challenges Rance to a card game: if he wins, he gets Johnson and Minnie; but if he loses, he leaves without the wanted man. Minnie pulls a card from her garter to win the deciding third hand, after which Rance, true to his word, departs. In Act III the posse captures Johnson and prepares to hang him, but the miners are so touched by Minnie's desperate love for the outlaw that they allow Johnson to go free to begin a new life with Minnie.

The *New York Times* (November 15, 1905) initially responded enthusiastically, pointing out that Belasco had taken a simple love story and familiar characters and reworked them into a fresh new creation. By the weekend, however, when the *Times* analyzed the play anew (November 19), its opinion had turned decidedly cooler. It praised Belasco for his "highly inventive and ingenious" staging techniques, and it acknowledged the appealing drama of the discovery of the robber in the girl's loft, the card game, the love scenes, and the final decision of the miners to let Minnie have her man, but its compliments turned ironic, as though the playwright had hoodwinked the audience into liking the play. "So skillful is [Belasco]," the critic wrote, "in glossing over inconsistency of character and situation that the average spectator is blinded to the falsities in the one and the impossibilities of the other." The writer – naturally more astute than the "average spectator" – discerned such inconsistencies as the dramatic reversal that overcame the robber at the sight of the girl.

Yet even with these reservations the same critic noted that Belasco had developed the production "with touches of something very like poetic inspiration." The reviewer praised the dialogue: "The talk in the Polka Saloon is not literary, but it is natural." According to the *Boston Daily Globe*, the audience did not flinch at the "hells" and "damns" sprinkled through the lines, although the ever-vigilant William Winter, writing for the *New York Tribune*, objected to what he labeled vulgar and offensive language, declaring, "The fact that some people swear in actual life is no good reason why anybody should swear in a work of art."[35] The character of the sheriff, with his Louisiana-bred southern chivalry and his penchant for keeping his word, proved especially arresting. Rance combined a philosophical outlook toward the world with a cynical sympathy that made him a highly unusual antagonist, a far cry from the mustachioed lothario of *Arizona*. The *Times* (November 15, 1905) declared Rance a "splendidly, picturesquely, forcefully drawn" character. The character who came to be known simply as "the Girl" was equally intriguing. On the one hand she was the exact opposite of the refined schoolteacher from the East exemplified by Molly Wood. Minnie was independent and feisty, a businesswoman and a western female who could stand up to the advances of Sheriff Rance and the demands of the miners. Yet she could also be dreamily romantic. Her naivete and innocence recalled M'liss, but she was more experienced and had a clearer idea of what she wanted. When it appeared in the person of Johnson she instinctively grabbed it.

The character of Ramerrez provides a complex set of associations. At first his outlaw status confirms the tradition of negative portrayals of Hispanic characters. As with Vasquez in *Si Slocum* and the other Hispanic characters that had preceded him, Ramerrez lacks any specific Mexican or Spanish cultural identity. Like Rahl Mendoza passing himself off under the Anglo alias Dell McWade in *Nobody's Claim*, Ramerrez assumes the Anglo identity of Dick Johnson. In this play, however, the apparently treacherous outlaw reforms, escapes hanging, and gets the girl. In order to achieve that, however, he drops his Hispanic name and his Mexican lover and becomes, in effect, a converted Anglo-Saxon. Hollywood eventually completed the Anglicization of Ramerrez, for in none of the several movie versions of the play was Ramerrez played by a Hispanic actor.

Belasco wove several thematic images through his play. Gambling provides one powerful motif. The miners gamble with their lives to make their strike. Rance is the sheriff, but he is also known for his poker skills. Johnson, knowing he should leave the town, gambles his fate for an hour with Minnie. In the play's most dramatic moment, Minnie gambles her sexual virtue on a deal of the cards. "We're gamblers," Minnie states, "we're all gamblers!"[36] Deception, too, plays a thematic role, for all the characters have mysterious pasts. The gallant Johnson is also the robber Ramerrez, and Rance has his shadowy wife in New Orleans. As Minnie observes, echoing Bret Harte, all the miners go by invented names, having previously discarded some other reality.

Belasco included literary allusion with his imagery. In *Davy Crockett*, when the violent storm strands Davy and Eleanor in his cabin, Eleanor reads Scott's *Lochinvar* to establish the literary motif of the play. In *The Girl of the Golden West*, when a similar violent snowstorm strands Minnie and Johnson, they relate their situation to that of Dante and his beloved Beatrice. In the *Vita nuova*, Dante declares that he would give anything for one hour with the wondrous Beatrice. Minnie and Johnson not only describe Dante's vow, they enact it. Johnson arrives at Minnie's cabin at one in the morning, and, after their conversation, Belasco uses a darkening of the stage to represent Johnson's one hour with Minnie. The hour they spend together transforms Johnson, and that, combined with the snowstorm, created another image: evil is washed away to provide a new, clean beginning. Johnson sees the snow as an omen for his life, declaring that "the old trail is blotted out and there's a fresh road."[37] In one sense the power of their love cleanses all past wrongs. In another sense the near lynching of Johnson represents a kind of purgatory through which the couple must pass to purify their love. Johnson articulates both of these ideas when, just before he leaves for what he thinks will be his hanging, he tells Minnie, "We both came out of nothin' an' we met, but, through loving, we're goin' to reach things now – that's us! We had to be lifted up like this, to be saved."[38]

The landscape, too, plays a part in Belasco's imagery. For Minnie, as for Sandy in *The Danites*, the mountains are the closest man can get to God. Minnie cries out, "Oh, my mountains! My beautiful peaks! My Sierras! God's in the air here, sure. You can see Him layin' peaceful hands on the mountain tops. He seems so near, you want to let your soul go right on up."[39] Even though Johnson repents his evil ways and is freed by the miners, and even though he and Minnie are together at the end, the play implies that their new beginning, their "fresh road," must take them *away* from this land close to God. Like Adam and Eve expelled from the Garden of Eden, Minnie and Johnson must leave their treasured western peaks to make their new life in the East. Minnie refers to the mountains they are leaving behind as "The Promised Land," to which Johnson replies, "We must look ahead, Girl, not backwards. The promised land is always ahead." Minnie's last line echoes her earlier declaration. On the trail to the East she cries out, "Oh, my mountains – I'm leaving you – Oh, my California, I'm leaving you – Oh, my lovely West – my Sierras! – I'm leaving you!" Then, as she embraces Johnson, she finishes, "Oh, my – my home."[40]

Naturally, as was the case with almost any Belasco production, viewers were impressed by the scenic elements. "Nothing more beautifully picturesque has been seen upon our stage," the *Times* declared (November 15, 1905). At the outset of the play Belasco used an ingenious vertical panorama – similar to a modern camera tracking shot – to follow Minnie from her cabin to the saloon. For the storm that engulfed the cabin, Belasco engaged thirty-two stagehands to create a howling wind, snow enveloping the cabin, ice forming on the window panes, and sleet hitting the glass. As for the interior of the cabin itself, that was "a masterpiece of scenic realism, full of correct minutiae."

Just as he had in *The Girl I Left Behind Me*, Belasco skillfully employed music to underscore the emotional impact of scenes. Instead of the normal theatrical pit orchestra, Belasco hired a banjo, concertina, and percussion to play popular airs, including "Dooda Day" ("Camptown Races"), which he had also used in *The Girl I Left Behind Me*. To set the mood for the saloon, a wandering minstrel with a banjo sang lively and then lachrymose songs for the miners. A piano played various tunes in Act I, including a polka that Minnie and Johnson danced to.

And Belasco had lost none of his skill in building the tension of a scene. He played on a variety of emotions as Minnie hid Johnson not once but twice in Act II. Equally effective was Minnie's emotional farewell to Johnson in Act III, with Minnie unaware that the miners stood just beyond the door, eavesdropping on her teary goodbye, waiting to hang her lover.

By this time David Belasco had already become a household name where the theatre was concerned, but *The Girl of the Golden West* spurred the career of lead actress Blanche Bates. Born in 1873 in Portland, Oregon, Bates worked in San Francisco before making her New York debut as Bianca in *The Taming of the Shrew* at Augustin Daly's Theatre in 1897.[41] Under Belasco's tutelage she quickly developed into a star. Her first major success came as Cho-Cho-San in *Madame Butterfly* in 1900, and she followed that with performances as Cigarette in *Under Two Flags* in 1901 and Yo-San in *The Darling of the Gods* in 1902. Yet despite the success of these other plays – she performed Yo-San over one thousand times – it was her portrayal of "the Girl" that remained her most famous. William Winter noted that although she carried the major load of the play and had to express a wide range of taxing emotions she "met and satisfied" every challenge.[42] Bates' last role for Belasco was Roxanna Clayton, a woman saddled with a wandering husband in *Nobody's Widow* in 1910. She continued to act in plays that displayed her vigorous and impulsive acting, including *The Famous Mrs. Fair* (1910), where she performed the free-thinking title role, and *The Changelings* (1923), a play about spouse swapping. She retired from the stage in 1926 and returned to San Francisco, but in 1933 she abandoned her retirement for a short tour of *Dangerous Corner* and a performance with Katharine Hepburn in *The Lake*. She acted in only one movie, a western thriller called *The Border Legion* of 1918. She died in 1941.

The play did not have the same impact on the careers of the male leads – Frank Keenan, who played sheriff Jack Rance, and Robert Hilliard, who enacted the outlaw – despite critical acclaim for their work. A reviewer in the *New York Times* (November 19, 1905) hailed Keenan's depiction of the gentlemanly villain as "a veritable masterpiece of character delineation." Still, the role did little to elevate Keenan into the "star" category, and he remained a capable supporting actor. Hilliard was a handsome young man who had played opposite Lillie Langtry and starred in an early production of Henrik Ibsen's *The Pillars of Society* in 1891. Although he appeared in other roles after his portrayal of Johnson, including a man whose life is ruined by a tantalizing woman in *A Fool There Was* (1909) and a cool-headed detective in *The Argyle Case* (1912), *The Girl of the Golden West* was the highlight of his career.

The Girl of the Golden West was adapted to the screen several times. Cecil B. DeMille directed the first version, a 1915 Paramount release with Theodore Roberts as Rance, Mabel Van Buren as Minnie, and noted silent western star House Peters as Ramerrez. In 1923 First National produced a version generally regarded as one of the most outstanding silent films ever made with J. Warren Kerrigan as Ramerrez, Sylvia Breamer as Minnie, and Russell Simpson as the sheriff. First National remade the film with sound in 1930 with Ann Harding, James Rennie, and Harry Bannister, and Metro-Goldwyn-Mayer provided a musical interpretation starring Jeanette MacDonald, Nelson Eddy, Walter Pidgeon, and Buddy Ebsen in 1938.

Undoubtedly, however, the most notable adaptation of *The Girl of the Golden West* is Giacomo Puccini's operatic treatment. Puccini was enchanted when he saw the play in January 1907, and in March he asked Belasco for permission to create an opera. The finished opera, *La fanciulla del West*, first played at the Metropolitan Opera House in New York on December 10, 1910, with Emmy Destinn as Minnie, Pasquale Amato as the sheriff, and Enrico Caruso as the robber. Arturo Toscanini conducted. The reception at the time was prodigious, but although the work is still occasionally performed it did not achieve the stature accorded to the composer's *Madama Butterfly*, *Tosca*, or *La bohème*. Still, *La fanciulla del West* was the first grand opera on a specifically American theme, and as such it cemented the frontier as a proper subject for highbrow artistic expression.

Additional frontier plays followed in 1906. William A. Brady's production of Donald MacLaren's *The Redskin* was unique in that the play focused entirely on a native tribe, with no white characters. One-dimensional characterizations and stilted dialogue, however, resulted in a less than successful production. A future winner of the Pulitzer Prize, Harvard-educated Owen Davis, tried his wings with frontier melodrama in *The Gambler of the West*. Al Woods, who was just emerging as a producer of popular melodrama, backed the production, in which an honest gambler befriends and eventually marries a rich heiress from the East who is seeking her long-lost father and brother. The most successful border plays of 1906, however, involved a rose, a mine, and the continental divide.

The rose, the mine, and the great divide

As for 1905, a list of the best plays of 1906 would almost surely include a trio of striking frontier dramas, including another Belasco offering, *The Rose of the Rancho*, and two distinctive works by new authors, *The Three of Us* by Rachel Crothers and *The Great Divide* by William Vaughn Moody. Belasco tried to repeat the success of *The Girl of the Golden West* with *The Rose of the Rancho*, which he adapted with Richard Walton Tully from an earlier Tully script called *Juanita*. Tully was a native Californian, born there in 1877 and educated at the University of California, and the play reflects his under-standing of the state's heritage. Set in California in 1850, greedy Americans are jumping old Spanish title claims and evicting the original Spanish owners from their lands.[43] The villain, Ezra Kincaid, has his eye on the rancho of old Dona Petrona Castro and on Juanita Kenton, her impetuous granddaughter, whose mother is Spanish but whose father – never seen in the play – was American. Belasco's Spanish rancho and the fiery daughter hark back to Harte's unsuccessful *Two Men of Sandy Bar* thirty years earlier, which was set at the California ranch of Don Jose Castro and featured his emotional daughter, Jovita. Belasco's plot, however, differed markedly from Harte's effort.

In Belasco's play, which opened at his own theatre on November 27, Robert Kearney is sent by the government to straighten out the problems of old Spanish land titles, and he and Juanita immediately fall in love. Juanita's mother, however, wants her to marry Don Luis de la Torre, a wealthy but indolent Spaniard, and disowns her daughter when Juanita declares her love for Kearney. Kearney, meanwhile, files documents to protect the Castro lands and calls for troops to defend the rancho. In the last act, in a scene reminiscent of *The Girl I Left Behind Me*, the women huddle behind a barricade on the roof of the casa while Kearney and the Spanish men await Kincaid's attack. As he had in *The Girl I Left Behind Me*, Belasco accentuated the contrast and tension with music and solemn words, for, as the Spaniards await the dawn, the old Franciscan padre leads prayers and hymns. At the climactic moment, Kearney's aide arrives with the troops from Monterey, thus defeating Kincaid, saving the rancho, and uniting Juanita and Kearney.

When his protégée, Mrs. Leslie Carter, eloped and deserted him, Belasco cast about for a new actress to play the role of Juanita, and he settled on Frances Starr. Born in Oneonta, New York, in 1881, Starr performed for several years in regional stock companies before she replaced Minnie Dupree in Belasco's *The Music Master*. Still, she was a relative unknown when Belasco tapped her for the "rose" of the title. The part required her to sing, dance, laugh, flirt, and rage, and the young actress met every challenge. The *New York Times* (November 28, 1906), praising her "charming blend of ingenuousness, coquetry, grace, and sudden girlish passion," bubbled that "her accomplishment is one of uncommon beauty and attractiveness." With her portrayal of the title role, Frances Starr achieved almost instantaneous stardom. Nor was she merely a one-hit wonder. Two years later she created the memorable role of Laura Murdock, the sensitive, desperate woman unable to resist the temptations of the good life in Eugene Walter's *The Easiest Way*, also staged by Belasco. She continued to act for Belasco, playing a girl with a dual personality in *The Case of Becky* (1911) and a seamstress in love with a sailor in *Shore Leave* (1922), among other roles. Although her career declined after she and Belasco parted, Starr acted sporadically into the 1950s. She died in 1973.

As always, critics awarded high marks to the production values of the Belasco piece. Belasco interpreted the play as a western *Romeo and Juliet*, and at one point he replicated Shakespeare's balcony scene, with Kearney in the courtyard wooing Juanita as she leaned over the second-story veranda. Guitars and castanets contributed a distinctively Spanish sound. Dances and gaiety contrasted starkly with Kincaid's dark threats, especially in the Act II engagement party for Juanita and Don Luis. The combination of music, soft light, and elaborate costuming produced scenes that were, in the words of the *Times*, "bewilderingly lovely to the minutest detail." Yet again, the reviewer paid compliments to Belasco's work somewhat grudgingly, concluding that "this 'pretty Spanish dream' ought not to be judged according to the standards of criticism which apply to thoughtful drama."

Belasco's *Rose* represents perhaps the most sympathetic treatment of Hispanic characters in any frontier drama. Yet, while it presented a generally compassionate perspective on the Spanish in California and a negative view of greedy Americans, it was, after all, focusing on a problem that had existed fifty years earlier. What is more, rather than acknowledging the losses suffered by the Spanish inhabitants, the play pretended that virtuous Americans had prevailed and the United States government had fixed the problem. That, of course, was false. Moreover, given the assimilation evident

Figure 21. Robert Kearney (Charles Richman) courts Juanita (Frances Starr) in David Belasco's *The Rose of the Rancho*.

in the play, the Spanish lands would ultimately become American lands one way or another. If Kincaid prevailed, they would fall into American hands immediately, and if the half-American Juanita married Kearney instead of Don Luis, the Castro lands would devolve to children who would be only one quarter Spanish anyway.

Sugarcoating notwithstanding, the public judged the production a success. It ran 240 performances, closed for the summer, and then reopened for an additional eighty-seven performances. The following year it recorded another thirty-two performances at the Academy of Music. Lasky–Paramount produced a film version in 1914 with Bessie Barriscale and J. W. Johnston as the young lovers, and Paramount released a second adaptation in 1936, which included numerous songs and starred John Boles with Metropolitan Opera star Gladys Swarthout in her film debut.

While *The Rose of the Rancho* was a notable success, the champion frontier drama of 1906 was William Vaughn Moody's *The Great Divide*. The story of the emergence of this play is reasonably well known. Moody was a professor of English at the University of Chicago, where his specialty was the translation of Greek verse. Born in Spencer, Indiana, in 1869, he had taken both a bachelor's and a master's degree from Harvard, where he taught before moving on to Chicago.[44] Moody was not a particularly popular instructor, apparently caring more about his research than his teaching, and he relished his travels away from the campus, especially to Europe. He also journeyed, however, to the American Southwest, and when his girlfriend, Harriet Brainard, sent him an account from that area of a woman who had promised herself to one man in order to protect herself from another, Moody derived from it the play that he entitled *A Sabine Woman*, referring to the myth of early Romans abducting women for their wives. Margaret Anglin, a popular emotional actress, read a copy of the script and was so impressed that she interrupted her production schedule and arranged an immediate trial of Moody's play at Chicago's Garrick Theatre. The audience response was electric, and by the intermission after Act II, it was clear that the piece would be a valuable commodity. Moody had not yet signed an option for the play, so, while the audience endured an hour's delay, managers for Anglin and Moody hashed out a contract for the rights to the drama before the curtain rose on the final act. Moody won enormous acclaim for the play, which was eventually renamed *The Great Divide*, but, although he also wrote *The Faith Healer* (1909) and two of a planned trilogy of verse plays about God and humans, he died prematurely of a brain tumor in 1910 without realizing the potential he demonstrated in his seminal work.

After Anglin performed *The Great Divide* in Chicago, she arranged to produce the piece with Henry Miller, an actor and manager with whom she had performed several plays in San Francisco and New York. Although Miller publicly denied that he had rewritten the play, at some point the title was changed and characters' names were altered.[45] The heroine went from being Zona Murchee to having the Biblically-inspired name of Ruth Jordan, while the hero changed from Frank Stephens to Stephen Ghent. Newly rechristened, *The Great Divide* opened at the Princess Theatre in New York on October 3.

Henry Miller and Margaret Anglin made a natural match. Miller was born in Islington, a suburb of London, in 1859.[46] His parents emigrated to Canada, where he began his theatrical career. After an apprenticeship of juvenile roles he moved to Augustin Daly's company in New York in 1882, and by 1893 he was playing leads for Charles Frohman in his Empire Theatre company. In 1901 he teamed with Anglin in a series of productions, including *Camille* and *The Devil's Disciple*, which led ultimately to their collaboration on *The Great Divide*. Miller turned increasingly to producing, and eventually opened his own theatre on Forty-third Street, which he operated until his death in 1925.

Anglin, like Miller, was born a British subject in Ottawa in 1876, where her father was Speaker of the Canadian House of Commons.[47] She was educated at a convent school, and at seventeen, with her mother's acquiescence and her father's disapproval, she moved to New York to study elocution. Within a year Anglin made her New York debut as an extra in Belasco's *The Girl I Left Behind Me* and won a small role in Charles Frohman's production of *Shenandoah*. She worked with James O'Neill and E. H. Sothern prior to gaining her first major triumph in 1898 as Roxanne in Richard Mansfield's production of *Cyrano de Bergerac*. She recorded another remarkable success as the adulterous Felicia Dane in Henry Arthur Jones' *Mrs. Dane's Defense* (1900) before joining Henry Miller in a series of productions. Despite her unparalleled success in *The Great Divide*, Anglin's forte was the classics. She played the full range of Shakespeare's women and also starred as Antigone, Iphigenia, Clytemnestra, Electra, and Medea in productions that helped popularize the Greek tragedies, many of which she produced herself. Her last performances occurred in a touring production of Lillian Hellman's *A Watch on the Rhine* and a west-coast tour of *The Rivals* in 1943. A tall, statuesque woman, Anglin was famous for her emotional outbursts, which led one writer to label her "America's teariest actress."[48] At her death in 1958, the *New York Times* (January 8) wrote, "If she had not become the first lady of the American stage, she had at least become its unchallenged first practitioner of anguish. There was ever in Miss Anglin's professional hands a piece of damp lace, come to its moist estate, matinees and evenings, through the shedding of genuine tears."

The Great Divide provided opportunity aplenty for Anglin's anguish. The first act is set at Philip Jordon's ranch in the Gila Desert in Arizona, where Ruth Jordan, Philip's sister, has journeyed from Massachusetts to visit her brother.[49] At the opening of the play Philip escorts his wife to the train station, leaving Ruth alone in the cabin. When three desperados burst in, she becomes a captive in her brother's home. The men are about to cast dice for possession of her when she appeals to the least undesirable of the trio to protect her, promising that she will willingly be his if he saves her from his companions. Stephen Ghent accepts her offer. After he buys off one of his accomplices with a string of gold nuggets and kills the other, Ruth rides off with him. Although Ghent's gold mines in the Catalina Mountains eventually make him a wealthy man, Ruth resists happiness. When Philip tracks Ruth to Ghent's house, Ruth tries to repurchase her freedom with a necklace of gold nuggets she has saved, but Ghent refuses and Ruth returns to her home in Massachusetts. Six months later Ruth has delivered a child she conceived with Ghent, but she refuses to nurture the baby, which to her represents her victimization. When Ghent visits her, Ruth's old resentment flares, but, as he expresses his love and speaks tenderly of their child, Ruth's bitterness ebbs. Finally she places the necklace of nuggets about her neck as a kind of token of acceptance and falls into his arms.

When the production tried out in Pittsburgh and Washington reviewers found it bawdy and obscene, tempting Lee Shubert to close the show.[50] But when *The Great Divide* opened in New York the response was overwhelmingly positive, with some critics proclaiming a new epoch in American drama. Lewis V. Defoe called it "[t]he best native product of the last five years." The *Philadelphia Evening Telegraph* (December 7, 1907) went even further, declaring it "the best play yet written by a native dramatist."[51]

The public also responded encomiastically to the riveting new play. It ran 238 performances. After a summer break and a transfer to Daly's Theatre, it recorded 103 further performances and then played at the Academy of Music for another two weeks. In September 1909, the play opened at the Adelphi Theatre in London with Miller reprising his role as Ghent, which he had already played over a thousand times. Although the *Morning Post* called it "except for the first act, rather poorly and pretentiously written," most British dailies responded positively, like the *Daily Chronicle*, which declared it "the most wholly delightful and genuine American play that London has seen since *Arizona*."[52] In April 1913, *The Great Divide* even played at the Théâtre des Arts in Paris. Various touring productions continued the play up to and through the First World War,

Figure 22. Stephen Ghent (Henry Miller), Shorty (H. B. Walthall), and Dutch (Robert Cummings) surround Ruth Jordan (Margaret Anglin) in Act I of *The Great Divide*.

and Miller produced a revival with himself as Ghent in February 1917, which ran fifty-three performances.

The Great Divide not only generated popular acclaim, but, even more significantly, it provoked heated debate. Should Ruth have shot Ghent in Act I when she had a chance to grab his gun? Should she have shot herself? Did she act properly in living up to the bargain she made? Or should she have abrogated the bargain since it was, in effect, forced on her? Should she have made the bargain in the first place? And, having once made the choice to go off with Ghent, should Ruth have tried to make the best of her situation rather than resisting his attentions and wallowing in her despair?[53]

Such questions were complicated by Ruth's obvious attraction to the handsome, rugged Ghent. One of the finest accomplishments of the production was that Moody and Anglin made the tension of that attraction palpable. One writer pointed out that, despite her aversion to the brutal way in which she was taken, Ruth "found in [Ghent] the man who suited her ideals."[54] Still, by accepting her attraction to him, Ruth would have violated her Puritan sense of decency and decorum.

Moody's drama played a sophisticated variation on the old frontier capture motif. In Act I Ruth is the unwilling captive, but her abductor is not the villain, but the hero. In Act II she is not so much rescued by her brother as simply released by her captor to exercise her own will. But Ruth cannot enjoy her freedom, for she is a hostage not to Ghent, but to her upbringing. So, at the conclusion, Ghent, her one-time abductor, becomes her rescuer, freeing her from bonds that hold her far more tightly than the necklace of gold.

The Great Divide created a complex set of characters and issues. Here was no pristine heroine, no terrible villain. Rather, Ghent displayed a mixture of his good actions redeeming his bad, while Ruth roiled in an enigmatic set of desires and revulsions. Furthermore, Moody set the characters within thematic motifs. In the opening scene, Ruth glorified the West, where every day is "radiantly exciting." She rhapsodized about "this moonlit ocean of flowers . . . [where] millions of cactus blooms have opened since yesterday." She compared the territory to her ideal man: "I am talking of a sublime abstraction – of the glorious unfulfilled – of the West – the Desert."[55] The East, on the other hand, represented a failed, constricting establishment. The "great divide" meant not only the Continental Divide that physically demarcated the West, but also the metaphoric chasm that separated prim eastern attitudes from the honest and robust attitudes of the frontier.

In 1915 *The Great Divide* was the subject of a lavish screen adaptation.

With exteriors shot at the Grand Canyon, the Lubin production starring Ethel Clayton and House Peters was regarded as the first big-budget western. First National presented a second film version in 1929, and issued a third variation of the story two years later under the title *Woman Hungry*.

One phenomenon that proved the mainstream popularity of frontier plays was the series of burlesques that *The Great Divide* and other productions inspired. With *Po-ca-hon-tas* in 1855, John Brougham had managed not only to satirize the Pocahontas story, but also to lampoon Edwin Forrest's production of *Metamora*. Billy Rice and his minstrel troupe at Hooley's Opera House burlesqued *Across the Continent* in December 1870, and Buffalo Bill's plays occasioned numerous parodies. The immense popularity of the frontier plays at the turn of the century inspired similar mockeries, especially by Lew Fields and his talented comic troupe. In 1900 Joe Weber and Lew Fields burlesqued *Arizona* with Fay Templeton and Lillian Russell, and in November 1906 Weber and Fields presented *The Great Decide*. In this piece, "Steve the gent," with two fellow escapees from an Arizona jail, enters a cabin, where the aggressively assertive Ruth Jordanmarsh holds a gun on them and demands that one of the three marry her. One man buys his freedom with a chain of gold nuggets, while the other two fight a duel. They exchange numerous volleys, each man missing intentionally in the hope that the other will shoot him and thereby spare him from having to marry the harridan. Finally, Ruth buys Steve for thirty cents, lassoes him, and leads him away. By the end of the evening, Steve is embroidering doilies to buy back his freedom. When he fails to appreciate Ruth's plans for their new house, Ruth threatens to jump off a nearby cliff. In a line that typifies the humor of the piece, Steve tells her, "No, you won't; that's only a bluff."[56] Moody himself attended the satire and wrote that the piece was "excruciatingly funny" and contained "lots of sound criticism in the guise of travesty."[57]

With *The Great Divide* of 1906, frontier drama reached a pinnacle of thought and characterization. There were, of course, other frontier plays that appeared at about the same time. *Billy the Kid* by Walter Woods opened at the Star Theatre in New York in August 1906, and proved to be an enduring melodrama.[58] The *New York Dramatic Mirror* (August 25, 1906) found it "full of heroics and superpuerile bravado," but despite that – or perhaps because of it – the play toured for twelve seasons. In this play, the villain, Boyd Denvers, discovers that his wife, Mary, whom he had deserted years before, has remarried. He tries to blackmail her, but winds up killing both Mary and her husband. Mary's son Will becomes an outlaw – Billy the Kid

– and pursues Denvers. At one point Denvers' men ambush Billy, but he blasts five of them in a tense shootout in the dark. Later, Billy's girlfriend, Nellie, helps him escape Denvers' henchmen by disguising him as a woman. When Billy finally captures Denvers, the villain not only confesses to the murders but also reveals that he is Billy's father. Billy cannot bring himself to shoot his own father, so he gives the broken man his hat and coat and sends him away. As Denvers leaves, however, he is ambushed by his gang, who mistake him for Billy. Since everyone now believes that Billy is dead, he conveniently adopts a new identity and marries Nellie. While *Billy the Kid* included several exciting scenes, such as the shootout in the dark, the cross-dressed Billy tricking the gang, and the final, clever denouement, it seemed almost a throwback to the plot-driven frontier melodramas of an earlier day, and, like them, it had little relation to the real-life outlaw named in the title.

1906 also saw a very different sort of frontier extravaganza when the Shuberts produced *Pioneer Days* on New York's mammoth Hippodrome stage in November, with fifty Sioux Indians, numerous scouts, and a small herd of ponies.[59] The show, in conjunction with a separate aquatic presentation, *Neptune's Daughter*, ran 307 performances. It closed for the summer and then recorded an additional 145 performances in the fall. A year later, the Hippodrome presented another extravaganza, *The Ballet of Niagara*, with an Indian theme and elaborately costumed warriors, which ran 433 performances.

Another significant frontier drama produced in 1906 was the mining-camp play *The Three of Us*. Author Rachel Crothers eventually emerged as one of America's leading playwrights and directors, writing and staging over two dozen Broadway plays. Crothers specialized in stylish comedies that focused on the conflicts between women's independence and their traditional roles, and her first success came in a frontier play that raised those issues. The title referred to Rhy MacChesney and her two brothers, Clem, aged nineteen, and Sonnie, aged thirteen, whom she tries to raise properly in a Nevada mining town.[60] The title is also the name of an abandoned gold mine left to the trio by their father, who died seven years earlier. Crothers' play combines conventional and unconventional elements. On the conventional side, Rhy is courted by the rich but manipulative Louis Berresford and the poor but noble Steve Townley. She and her restless brother Clem become entangled in a competition between Berresford and Townley to buy the mining claim of Rhy's best friend, Mrs. Bix. When Berresford purchases the mine on the basis of a tip he finagles from Clem, who has overheard a private conversation between Townley and Rhy, Townley thinks Rhy has betrayed him. In addition to the basically conventional situation, Crothers employs numerous stock characters. At first Berresford seems a rather sophisticated villain, but he reveals his true colors when he asks for Rhy's love but not her hand in marriage, which, he assures her, will come later. Crothers also plays with variations on such well-known types as an Irish domestic who assists Rhy; an English fop married to Rhy's best friend; and Hop Wing, Berresford's taciturn Chinese servant.

Less conventional is Crothers' reliance on an active and forceful woman as her central figure, as well as her resolution of the complications of the plot. Attempting to settle problems, Rhy visits Berresford alone at night, which only aggravates tensions when Steve discovers her there. Rhy's response is to storm out, declaring her independence and insisting that her honor does not depend on their opinion. "It's in my own [hands], and I'll take care of it," she exclaims.[61] Similarly, when she sees Steve in the final act, she forthrightly declares her love for him in a touching speech in which she tells him to ask her to marry him. She also initiates the kiss that brings them together. Furthermore, although Steve and Rhy are united and Clem demonstrates new signs of maturity, Crothers eschews a neatly packaged ending, for nothing comes of MacChesney's gold mine nor of Townley's business dealings.

In his writings on American drama, Gary Richardson rightly observes that the play forces the audience "to confront the different ways in which society views the similar actions of men and women," but he also insists that in the end Rhy settles for mere conventional domestic happiness and "accepts the idea that she must put [Clem's] moral well-being ahead of her own personal happiness," which seems a rather uncharitable reading.[62] Of course Rhy cares about her brother. Why shouldn't she? If, in the end, she accepts a domestic role, at least she achieves it on her terms and through her own determined actions.

Reviews generally praised the play as a small-scale triumph, although some expressed disappointment that the end failed to live up to the promise of the beginning. One astute critic of the Madison Square Theatre production saw *The Three of Us* as "a strong and sympathetic play . . . of poverty, the heart-sickening of deferred hope, [and] of misunderstanding."[63] Another New York reviewer wrote that "it was a very human little play, with a heart beating steadily through its four acts." Audiences responded to that humanity, and the production registered 227 performances, more than either *The Girl of the Golden West* or *The Squaw Man*. Crothers' play seemed to please New Yorkers more than audiences in other cities, however. A London writer asked the obvious question: why would Rhy not inform her best friend, Mrs.

Bix, that her mine contains a rich vein of gold? Another London critic wrote that the story, after a solid start, "was gradually submerged under a perfect flood of sentimentality and theatrical mock heroics . . . the third act gave the impression that all concerned had temporarily lost their senses." On seeing a road production a reviewer stated that Crothers' characters "begin as vividly truthful beings of life; then they turn puppets of a theatrical game."

In *The Three of Us* Crothers depicts a mining town significantly altered from those rugged days of *The Danites*, *M'liss*, and *My Partner*, or even from *The Girl of the Golden West*. The rough mining camp has matured. Houses with pianos and carpet sweepers cluster together. Residents pop down to the grocery store to buy fixings for the evening meal. Production photographs show well-dressed characters in a well-appointed room. Furthermore, no one in Crother's town actually works a mine. Rather, they all want to sell their marginal claims to large corporations that can mine them profitably. These material changes mirror the innovations in plot, character, theme, and attitude of the turn-of-the-century frontier play and exemplify the distance traveled by the late-nineteenth-century frontier drama from the days of the Buffalo Bill melodramas or the fireworks of *Across the Continent*.

Although this study ends with productions from 1906, the theatre did not simply stop producing plays based on frontier subjects after that date. Some productions that opened after 1906 have already been mentioned, such as *Rio Grande* by Augustus Thomas. David Belasco wrote another frontier play, *The Heart of Wetona*, with George Scarborough. Rex Beach, known primarily as a novelist, dramatized *The Spoilers* with James MacArthur in 1907 and *Going Some* with Paul Armstrong in 1909. Armstrong also adapted Bret Harte material for his *Salomy Jane*, which starred Eleanor Robson in 1907 and ran more than a hundred performances. That same year, *The Round-Up* by Edmund Day recorded 155 performances at the New Amsterdam Theatre in New York. Edward Childs Carpenter set his comedy melodrama *The Challenge*, produced in 1911, on the Green River Basin Ranch in Arizona. Owen Davis opened *Big Jim Garrity* in 1914. *The Claim*, by Charles Kenyon and Frank Dare, played in 1917. *Lightnin'*, by Winchell Smith and Frank Bacon, proved a remarkable hit in 1918 with Bacon playing the slow-talking, slow-moving, ironically named "Lightnin'" Bill Jones, a boozy prevaricator who operates a run-down hotel on the California–Nevada line and foils the machinations of land sharks. This folksy comedy established a record at the time with 1,291 consecutive performances.

Figure 23. Rhy MacChesney (Carlotta Nillson) comforts her brothers Clem (John Westley) and "Sonnie" (Master George Clarke) in Rachel Crothers' *The Three of Us*.

By 1906 frontier plays had become a part of the cultural mainstream, a dominant force in American theatre, but more and more the frontier drama became the province of the movies, especially with the relocation of the film studios to California. Filmmakers turned all the plays listed in the preceding paragraph into movies, but, while movies rapidly eclipsed the stage as a means to depict the frontier, the evolution of the dramatic representation of the frontier did not end. Rather, from the seminal production of Edwin S. Porter's *The Great Train Robbery*, the drama of the frontier was further transformed into silent films and talking movies both in black and white and in Technicolor, as well as into musicals, radio dramas, and television shows throughout the twentieth century. Horses and dogs continued their tricks on celluloid. Shooting stunts were performed easily and safely with the help of film editing. The fast-paced action of galloping steeds, careening stagecoaches, and lumbering locomotives lent itself to the film medium, as did the vast and picturesque landscape of the West. Indians and other assorted villains continued to serve as targets for rifles and revolvers. Refined young ladies from the East and rugged heroes from the West continued to fall in love. And, eventually, cowboys even learned to sing.

Summary

The Squaw Man, The Girl of the Golden West, The Great Divide, The Three of Us, The Rose of the Rancho.
The only dramas by American-born authors to enjoy runs of more than two hundred performances in 1905 and 1906

ONE OF THE GOALS OF THIS BOOK HAS BEEN TO DOCUMENT the range of plays written about the American frontier in terms of subject matter, style, and thematic content. The one hundred and fifty or so plays mentioned in these pages certainly cover a vast geographical area, set on frontiers that span the entire union, from Virginia, Massachusetts, New York, and Connecticut through Kentucky, Tennessee, and Michigan, past Missouri, Arkansas, the Dakotas, and Texas to Nevada, Utah, Wyoming, Montana, Colorado, New Mexico, Alaska, California, and Arizona. Specific locations include Death Valley, Cripple Creek, the Sierra Nevada, the Cordilleras range, Mt. Shasta, Salt Lake City, Tule Lake, and the Missouri, Rio Grande and Little Bighorn rivers. As Hyde indicated, the plays are peopled by an array of characters that include backwoodsmen, trappers, wagon masters, stagecoach drivers, soldiers, ranchers, cowboys, telegraph operators, newspaper writers and editors, prospectors, saloon keepers, religious leaders, teachers, railroad workers, scouts, rustlers, and robbers.[1] While most of each cast consisted of males of northern European descent, females played a prominent role – nearly a quarter of all the performers mentioned in these pages are female. Representatives of ethnic, national, and religious groups also appeared with regularity. Black, Irish, and Chinese characters were employed mainly for humor, although Parsloe's caricatures frequently figured conspicuously in the plots of plays. English dandies appeared as fools or villains. Hispanic characters were often identified only by a Spanish-sounding name with no other distinguishing cultural identity, although a few plays such as *Two Men of Sandy Bar, Arizona*, and *The Rose of the Rancho* gave a greater dimension to the Spanish Southwest. Mormons represented a threat to society's moral norms and were consistently presented as lecherous and vengeful conspirators involved in dark and murderous schemes. About a third of the frontier plays included Indians, and their presentation varied widely. They are ridiculous buffoons in the early Buffalo Bill plays, victims of white incitement in *Across the Continent* and other works, angry rebels in plays such as *The Girl I Left Behind Me*, and warriors on the wrong side of historic inevitability in the Modoc plays. Natives are drunken parasites to white society in *Horizon*, integral components of the western economy in *The Indian Mail Carrier*, noble unfortunates in *The Squaw Man*, and assimilated loners torn between cultures in *Northern Lights* and *Strongheart*.

While most of the plays were melodramas, the forms varied from the bellicose to the poetic, from action-packed thrillers to lachrymose love stories. Other styles were also prominent: comedies, satires, burlesques, extravaganzas, exhibitions, and musicals all featured frontier subjects. The plays also exhibit a range of writing skills and devices. There's the Harte-like use of ironic language in the fact that "The Parson" acquires his incongruous nickname because he swears so much. Wister provides the insight that "son of a bitch" can vary from a friendly greeting to an insult, depending on the delivery. Literary allusions run from Roman legend and Dante to Walter Scott. Especially at the turn of the century the moral issues assumed greater complexity – how *should* Ruth Jordan deal with Stephen Ghent? – and themes of gambling and deception reinforce moral dilemmas. Taken as a group, the frontier plays and Wild West exhibitions presented the march of European civilization across the land, defeating and removing primitive cultures, exploiting the resources of the earth, and bringing social institutions including railroads, the mail service, newspapers, law, the telegraph, and education to every part of the country. They also embodied the perpetuation of European culture through the coupling of heroes and heroines who confront and overcome the anomalous challenges of the frontier.

One reason for the popularity of frontier plays lay in their connections with individuals involved in contemporaneous events. Some productions boasted real-life scouts. Buffalo Bill, of course, stands as the prime example, as he starred in melodramas and his own Wild West shows for forty-five years. But others including "Texas Jack" Omohundro, "Dashing Charlie" Emmett, "Wild Bill" Hickok, Donald MacKay, and "Captain Jack"

Crawford parlayed their western experiences into vicarious excitement for eastern audiences. Even if the actors were not actual western figures, the plays sought to associate themselves with frontier legends. Pocahontas, Davy Crockett, Daniel Boone, George Custer, Kit Carson, Calamity Jane, Sitting Bull, Sam Houston, and Jesse James were all represented by professional performers in frontier plays. Actors impersonated Buffalo Bill and Donald MacKay at the same time that they themselves were appearing on stage. The plays about the James boys assured audiences of a direct connection with frontier events through the use of concrete objects belonging to the outlaws – horses and guns – and through direct reference to robberies linked with the gang. Frontier plays casually dropped references to well-known historical incidents and personages – for example, using the names McKandlass and Tutt in the early Buffalo Bill plays and Hickman in *The Danites*, and mentioning the explosion at the farmhouse of Jesse James' stepfather – even when, as in the Buffalo Bill plays, the plot bore little if any real relation to those incidents or people. Sometimes the connections were implied rather than stated, as in *The Cowboy and the Lady*, where Teddy North substitutes for Teddy Roosevelt. The plays did not present accurate accounts of historical events, but audiences saw actual participants, heard the names of people and events they recognized, and witnessed presentations put forth in a live, convincing fashion, even though that fashion was orchestrated to please the audience and to reinforce their own sense of righteousness and destiny.

David Radavich in a recent article viewed the narrative of the West as a one-dimensional tale of "colonizing, taming, and settling" with no connection to serious issues, and he concluded that "the Myth of the Frontier can be regarded as inherently and insistently undramatic."[2] Just as they frequently employed historical material as a springboard, so, too, the plays reflected society's concerns, its discussions, and its prejudices. *Across the Continent* played on the country's celebration of the completion of the first transcontinental railroad less than a year earlier, and numerous subsequent melodramas implicitly recognized the crucial role of the railroads in western expansion. Mormon plays mirrored the almost universal hostility to the new religious sect that deviated from established moral rules. They latched on to actual events such as the Utah War and the Mountain Meadows Massacre. *The Danites* and *Fonda* appeared just as the government indicted Orin Porter Rockwell for his part in the Aiken Massacre, and the practice of polygamy was banned within five years of the opening of *The Danites*. Even factors such as the Spanish-American War and the western adventures of Teddy Roosevelt found their way directly or indirectly into border plays.

In the literary field, numerous plays reflected the popular acclaim achieved by the publication of the western stories of Bret Harte, Mark Twain, and Joaquin Miller. Although the theatrical forays of Harte, Twain, and Miller occasioned more controversy than success, their writings supplied material for numerous adaptations including *M'liss*, *Gabriel Conroy*, *The Luck of Roaring Camp*, *The Danites*, and *Tennessee's Partner*. More important even than the direct adaptations was the way Harte, Twain, and Miller used local color and distinctive language to achieve detail and meaning, and these skills were advanced through the dramatic abilities of playwrights such as David Belasco and Augustus Thomas.

The Chinese representations in the frontier plays presented a special case. As early as *Horizon*, Daly had presaged the Asian problem by dramatizing the vigilance committee evicting the Chinese laborer for undermining the wage scale. Even as audiences howled at the antics of Hop Sing, Ah Sin, Washee-Washee, Wing Lee, and other Chinese caricatures, legislators debated limits on Chinese immigration. The Exclusion Act of 1882 was passed only three years after the opening of *My Partner*, when Campbell's play was still a prominent touring attraction.

The representation of Native Americans on the stage reflected the changing concerns of society. In the 1870s Indian warfare accentuated the public's interest in the chauvinistic Byron plays and the bloodthirsty Buffalo Bill melodramas, especially ones such as *The Red Right Hand; or, The First Scalp for Custer*. As the potential for armed conflict diminished, society confronted issues of education, assimilation, and regulation. *The Girl I Left Behind Me* springs directly from the ban on native dancing enacted by the Bureau of Indian Affairs, and the whites dancing at the fort offers an ironic comment on that intrusive action. *Northern Lights* and *Strongheart* both entered contemporary debates over education and assimilation with rather discouraging messages. Gowongo Mohawk, on the other hand, not only illustrated economic interaction between whites and natives in her play, but through her own writing and acting she personified a story of cultural assimilation. The Wild West shows fueled society's disputes over the proper role for Native Americans, and the issues raised in those debates, such as whether reservation Indians who appeared in shows were exploited or whether they were provided with education and opportunity, continue to this day.

Although almost all the frontier plays were ultimately resolved by conclusions that were easily acceptable to white audiences, at their thematic best they at least revealed contradictions and raised exactly those questions of unresolved tension that trouble Jeffrey Mason but that are, in fact, as Rosemarie Bank suggests, at the very heart of any interpretation of frontier drama.[3] While Buffalo Bill was "advancing morality through bloodshed," to paraphrase one nineteenth-century critic, and mocking Indians as laughable buffoons, Fanny Herring's *Hazel Eye* presented friendly, respected natives who help the heroine fend off the deceitful villain. What makes these two plays especially contradictory is that they were both written by Fred Maeder on the basis of Ned Buntline stories and were both presented at virtually the same time at the same theatres for the same audiences. Furthermore, as stated above, American natives were also shown in an array of roles, including hostile villains, noble defenders, drunken parasites, upstanding members of the economic community, and uneasy specimens of assimilation.

While most heroines accepted a conventional marital situation at the conclusion of the play, frontier drama regularly presented women in strong and independent roles that harked back to Christine in *She Would Be a Soldier*. Nancy Williams, Annie from Massachusetts, and other ingenues disguised themselves as men, took on masculine work, and proceeded with a determined self-sufficiency. Numerous females demonstrated masculine skills with weapons, lassos, and horses. Annie Oakley, May Lillie, and Lucille Mulhall displayed just such skills in Wild West shows, and in plays Fanny Herring, Kate Purssell, and Gowongo Mohawk exhibited frontier skills while frequently playing male roles. Many of the border heroines defied social conventions and revealed forthright sexuality. Fallen women Mary Brandon and Lena Keller became pregnant, yet still emerged with respectable marriages at the final curtain. Calamity Jane from Belmer's Jesse James play, Belasco's saloon girl, and Crothers' Rhy MacChesney overtly pursued the men they loved. Minnie and Kate Vernon hid their outlaw lovers, and Juanita Kenton defied her family's dictates to love Robert Kearney.

Frontier heroes also presented contradictory messages, from the bellicose Buffalo Bill to the poetic Davy Crockett, and from the stirring Joe Ferris to the retiring Joe Saunders – all of whom were delighting audiences simultaneously. Such heroes demonstrate the range of innocence and ruthlessness that Richard Nelson defines as unique to the American character.[4] With courage, daring, aggression, and physical skill on the one hand and humility, humor, earnestness, and boyish charm on the other, these heroes defined late-nineteenth-century manhood. Although both Buffalo Bill and

James H. Wallick de-emphasized or reduced the violence in their plays to heighten their appeal to wider audiences, still, as Gary Richardson notes, the potential for violence was ever present, symbolized by the "pistols that hang in every man's girdle and are thrust in every man's face."[5]

Frontier plays also began to examine the nature of good and evil as represented by traditional heroes and villains. Jesse and Frank James are outlaws, but they turn to lives of crime in response to persecution. Jesse dies for his sins, while Frank receives an almost heavenly pardon. The train robber Travers in *In Mizzoura* writes letters to exonerate an innocent party and delays his escape to court the woman he adores. Like Jesse James, Travers dies for his misdeeds, but Ramerrez in *The Girl of the Golden West* is utterly transformed by Minnie's love, and, after passing through a purgatorial cleansing of fire and ice – his wound and the snowstorm – he escapes the noose and walks off into the sunset with the girl. Billy the Kid becomes an outlaw through the confusions of Fate, and at the end he wins the hand of his love and assumes a new, guilt-free identity. The Virginian's pal, Steve, seems a misguided innocent and provides a touching farewell before his hanging. Stephen Ghent, the would-be rapist of *The Great Divide*, emerges as a sensitive hero.

The law itself, which represents one of society's primary civilizing influences, is called into question in numerous border plays. Trials occupy a central position in *M'liss* and *My Partner*, but courtroom procedures are often mocked, as in *Ranch 10*, where the judge appoints one man as defense attorney, court clerk, and defendant. Vigilante justice trumps the rule of law and courts in *The Virginian* and *Horizon*. Law officers, in Rosemarie Bank's words, "are at best incompetent and at worst venal."[6] Jack Rance keeps his word, but he pursues an adulterous flirtation and lets an outlaw go free. Sheriff Radburn makes a personal decision to act outside the law when he sends Travers on his way in *In Mizzoura*. The miners' collective vote has the same effect when they permit Minnie and Ramerrez to go off together in *The Girl of the Golden West*.

Strongheart, *The Squaw Man*, *John Logan* and other plays addressed the subject of interracial love and marriage. DeMille and Royle both concocted endings that allowed them to dodge the ultimate question, however, and, in that sense, they fell into line with the authors cited by Forrest Robinson who insisted on "having things both ways" by calling up serious concerns and then avoiding the implications of those concerns.[7]

The western landscape also provided contradictory messages. The land was significant in its beauty and majesty whether represented by words as in *The Danites* and *The Girl of the Golden West* or by arresting panoramas and scenic illustrations of waterfalls, pools, forests, rivers, and mountains. The land was also important in that it represented the often conflicting claims of possession and ownership of resources. The plots of many frontier plays revolve around the acquisition of land (*Si Slocum*, *The Rose of the Rancho*), cattle (*The Virginian*), or gold (*M'liss*) or around native attempts to retain tribal land. While the landscape provided beauty and opportunities for economic enrichment, it also contained danger, like Death Valley in *Fonda*. Forts and train stations were lonely, vulnerable outposts in *Across the Continent*, *The Girl I Left Behind Me*, and *The Limited Mail*. The isolation of the West also provided peril as in *The Great Divide* and psychological pressure as in *Arizona*.

Whether the plays were serious or comic, whether they addressed significant concerns of society or merely sought to entertain an audience for a few hours, the frontier productions created a scrapbook of memorable characters enacted by a gallery of enormously popular performers. When audience members bought tickets to a border drama, they were in many cases purchasing the story of a particular performer along with the story of the play. In the case of Buffalo Bill and the other authentic western personalities, audiences purchased a nugget of history along with their entertainment. New York audiences patronized hometown icons such as Fanny Herring and Francis S. Chanfrau. The public bought unusual combinations such as John Omohundro and Giuseppina Morlacchi or Charlie Emmett and Alice Placide. With their ticket purchases they selected charming Annie Pixley to impersonate M'liss despite Kate Mayhew's legal claims to the material. Audiences bought dashing good looks with O. D. Byron and William Faversham, earnest humility with Louis Aldrich and Frank Mayo, and roguish fellowship with McKee Rankin, and they supported Dustin Farnum's youthful exuberance on both the stage and the screen.

While audiences applauded their favorite frontier performers, critics, on the whole, did not. Illustrating Lawrence Levine's "highbrow–lowbrow" dichotomy in action, they castigated the unworthy border plays and those who labored in them for luring patrons away from proper drama.[8] They ridiculed Byron and Buntline, marginalizing their deviation from approved models in precisely the manner Susan Harris Smith identified.[9] The few plays deemed acceptable were accorded only a qualified status by being relegated to subcategories of artistic achievement. Critics repeatedly expressed the opinion – perhaps wishful thinking – that frontier drama had achieved all it was capable of, only to watch helplessly as the genre changed direction and continued to attract audiences. Finally, however, in a real-life variation of the "republican revolution" that Bruce McConachie identifies in melodrama, the "unwashed" triumphed.[10] The mobs did not convert the critics, but contact with the West converted the social elite, and, from Augustus Thomas on, writers and producers with Ivy League credentials led border drama toward more aristocratic concerns and converted the critics to supporters.

By 1906 drama of the frontier had not only won acceptance by mainstream New York theatres. It had become the dominant subject of American drama. In 1905 and 1906 only five dramas by American-born authors enjoyed runs of more than two hundred performances, and all of them were frontier plays: *The Squaw Man* (222), *The Girl of the Golden West* (224), *The Great Divide* (238), *The Three of Us* (227), and *The Rose of the Rancho* (240). Puccini's use of *The Girl of the Golden West* as the subject of the first grand opera on an American theme testified to the arrival of frontier drama at the pinnacle of high art. Little wonder, then, that as movies emerged as the dominant purveyor of drama they turned immediately to the frontier for material. Not only had the subject matter become artistically respectable, but it was well known to the public. Furthermore, the individuals who were producing and directing the early movies had an intimate knowledge of the frontier plays. The first movie of Cecil B. DeMille – whose father wrote the frontier melodrama *The Main Line* and whose brother wrote *Strongheart* – was *The Squaw Man* in 1914. That was the first release of Jesse Lasky's Feature Play Company as well as the first Hollywood-made feature-length production. Lasky and DeMille quickly followed that with *The Virginian*, *The Rose of the Rancho*, and *The Girl of the Golden West*, all shot in 1914. Lasky also distributed Douglas Fairbanks' *Arizona* and Mary Pickford's *M'liss* in 1918, as well as other frontier-related features.

The characters, stories, devices, and ideas of frontier drama became grist for western movies. To watch western classics such as John Ford's *Stagecoach* (1939), for example, is to behold the descendants of frontier drama. A vigilance committee tosses out the undesirables, as in *Horizon*. A baby is born in the wilderness, just as in *The Danites*. Warriors chase the stagecoach, as they did in Buffalo Bill's Wild West. When the passengers run out of ammunition, Hatfield is about to shoot Lucy Mallory to save her from the fate worse than death, exactly as in *The Girl I Left Behind Me*. Then she hears the sound of the approaching cavalry, as Kate Kennion does in the Belasco play and as Joe Ferris does in *Across the Continent*, and, as in numerous border dramatizations, the cavalry arrives at the optimal moment. The

Ringo Kid is a reformed outlaw, reminiscent of Stephen Ghent and Ramerrez, who falls for Dallas, a fallen woman not unlike Mary Brandon or Lena Keller. In the end Curly the lawman assists their escape as Sheriff Radburn does in *In Mizzoura*, and they ride off into the glorious landscape like Minnie and Ramerrez in *The Girl of the Golden West*. Of course many of the characters and incidents can also be located in nineteenth-century fiction, but that hardly diminishes the correspondence between nineteenth-century border drama and the movies that emerged in the twentieth century. A later John Ford epic, *The Searchers*, of 1956, features cold-hearted Indians killing settlers and kidnapping a girl, and the remainder of the movie involves an extended chase and rescue, as in the old Buffalo Bill melodramas. One could trace similar influences from nineteenth-century frontier plays in almost any twentieth-century movie or television western, so broadly disseminated and pervasive were the characters, plots, and ideas of the theatrical representations, for those nineteenth-century frontier dramas opened the stage door to the characters and the plots, to the paradoxes and the contradictions that kept frontier drama alive through three-quarters of the twentieth century.

Notes

Introduction: conditions and contradictions

1. Stuart Wallace Hyde, "The Representation of the West in American Drama from 1849 to 1917," unpublished Ph.D. dissertation, Stanford University, 1953.
2. Henry Nash Smith in *Virgin Land: The American West As Symbol and Myth* (Cambridge, Mass.: Harvard University Press, 1950, pp. 174–183) explains how the myth of the garden confronted the myth of the barren land.
3. In *The Fatal Environment: The Myth of the Frontier in the Age of Industrialization 1800–1890* (New York: Atheneum, 1985), Richard Slotkin examines in some detail the lowered status of mixed breeds in the nineteenth-century racial hierarchy, pp. 173–190 and throughout.
4. Jeffrey D. Mason, *Melodrama and the Myth of America* (Bloomington, Ind.: Indiana University Press, 1993), p. 153.
5. Forrest G. Robinson, *Having It Both Ways: Self-Subversion in Western Popular Classics* (Albuquerque, N. Mex.: University of New Mexico Press, 1993), pp. 3, 4, 39.
6. Rosemarie K. Bank, *Theatre Culture in America, 1825–1860* (Cambridge: Cambridge University Press, 1997), pp. 60, 69.
7. Slotkin, *Fatal Environment*, p. 502.
8. Gary A. Richardson, *American Drama from the Colonial Period through World War I: A Critical History* (New York: Twayne Publishers, 1993), pp. 146–147, 145, and 144.
9. Ibid., p. 144.
10. Bank, *Theatre Culture in America*, pp. 60, 70.
11. Rosemarie K. Bank, "Frontier Melodrama," in *Theatre West: Image and Impact*, ed. Dunbar H. Ogden with Douglas McDermott and Robert K. Sarlos (Amsterdam: Rodopi, 1990), p. 158.
12. Compare Richardson's comments (*American Drama*) on the Belasco and Moody plays, pp. 148–150 and 235–238.
13. *"Strictly Dishonorable" and Other Lost American Plays*, ed. Richard Nelson (New York: Theatre Communications Groups, 1986), p. vii.
14. Michael Kimmel (*Manhood in America: A Cultural History*, New York: Free Press, 1996) emphasizes the conflict between autonomy and responsibility. He identifies

the cowboy as a prime "exemplar of rugged outdoor masculinity," (p. 148), but the same could be said of almost any of the frontier heroes. E. Anthony Rotundo (*American Manhood: Transformations in Masculinity from the Revolution to the Modern Era*, New York: Basic Books, 1993) examines the changes that occurred in the concepts of manhood after the Civil War, especially ideas about animal instincts, physical prowess, and boyish vices.

15. Slotkin (*Fatal Environment*, p. 32) focuses exclusively on literary elements and dismisses non-literary media without even mentioning dramatic presentations, and, as Marvin Felheim points out (*The Theater of Augustin Daly*, Cambridge, Mass.: Harvard University Press, 1956, p. 70), Lucy Hazard in her seminal *The Frontier in American Literature* (New York: Barnes & Noble, 1941) does not refer to even a single play.

16. Lawrence W. Levine, *Highbrow/Lowbrow: The Emergence of Cultural Hierarchy in America* (Cambridge, Mass.: Harvard University Press, 1988), p. 76.

17. Gerald Bordman, *American Theatre: A Chronicle of Comedy and Drama, 1869–1914* (New York: Oxford University Press, 1994), p. 81.

18. Bruce McConachie, *Melodramatic Formations: American Theatre and Society, 1820–1870* (Iowa City, Iowa: University of Iowa Press, 1992), p. 124.

19. Susan Harris Smith, *American Drama: The Bastard Art* (Cambridge: Cambridge University Press, 1997), p. 62.

20. *The Eleventh Census of the United States*, vol. 1, pt. 1 (Washington: Government Printing Office, 1894), p. xi. Foster Rhea Dulles in *America Learns to Play: A History of Popular Recreation, 1607–1940* (New York: D. Appleton-Century Company, 1940) also notes that increases in the size of cities accelerated opportunities for entertainment (p. 211 *et passim*). Russel Nye, *The Unembarrassed Muse: The Popular Arts in America* (New York: Dial Press, 1970), examines the ways in which technological advances and increases in population affected the development of popular culture.

21. *Preliminary Report of the Eighth Census, 1860* (Washington: Government Printing Office, 1862), table 38, pp. 234–235. Also *Compendium of the Tenth Census (June 1, 1880)* (Washington: Government Printing Office, 1883), table LXIII, p. 1257. See also Jack Poggi, *Theatre in America: The Impact of Economic Forces, 1870–1967* (Ithaca, N.Y.: Cornell University Press, 1968). Smith, in *Virgin Land* (pp. 46–47), stresses the metaphoric significance of the railroad.

22. Alan Nevins, *The Emergence of Modern America, 1865–1878*, vol. VIII of *A History of American Life*, eds. Arthur M. Schlesinger and Dixon Ryan Fox (New York: Macmillan Company, 1944), p. 47.

23. See, for instance, Lewis O. Saum, *The Popular Mood of America, 1860–1890* (Lincoln, Nebr., and London: University of Nebraska Press, 1990), pp. 69–103, and Constance Rourke, *"The Roots of American Culture" and Other Essays*, ed. Van Wyck Brooks (New York: Harcourt, Brace and Company, 1942).

24. Union Pacific poster at the Nebraska State Historical Society, in *All Aboard!* by Phil Ault (New York: Dodd, Mead & Company, 1976) p. 55.

25. Slotkin, *Fatal Environment*, p. 435.

1 Reemergence: 1870–1872

1. *Across the Continent; or, Scenes from New York Life and the Pacific Railroad* is in *Dramas from the American Theatre 1762–1909*, ed. Richard Moody (Cleveland, Ohio, and New York: World Publishing Company, 1966) and *America's Lost Plays*, ed. Barrett Clark (Princeton: Princeton University Press, 1940; reissued Bloomington, Ind.: Indiana University Press, 1965), vol. IV.

2. A color print of the poster is available in *The Modern Poster* by Arsene Alexandre, M. H. Spielman, H. C. Bunner, and August Joccaci (New York: Charles Scribner's Sons, 1895), p. 72. Alexandre cites the poster as a lurid example of "primitive and confused" nineteenth-century poster art, but the print shows clearly the attempt to highlight this climactic moment of the play.

3. Don B. Wilmeth, "Tentative Checklist of Indian Plays," *Journal of American Drama and Theatre*, vol. 1, no. 2, Fall 1989, pp. 34–54.

4. *Ponteach* is in *Representative Plays by American Dramatists*, vol. 1, ed. Montrose J. Moses (New York: Benjamin Blom, 1964).

5. *The Indian Princess* is in Moses, ed., *Representative Plays by American Dramatists*, vol. 1.

6. *Pocahontas* is in *Representative American Plays*, ed. Arthur Hobson Quinn (New York: D. Appleton-Century Company, 1938).

7. *She Would Be a Soldier* is in Moody, ed., *Dramas from the American Theatre 1762–1909*.

8. *Metamora; or, The Last of the Wampanoags* is in *Staging the Nation: Plays from the American Theatre, 1787–1909*, ed. Don B. Wilmeth (Boston: Bedford Books, 1998).

9. James Kirke Paulding, *The Lion of the West*, ed. James N. Tidwell (Stanford: Stanford University Press, 1954).

10. For additional information on Medina, see Rosemarie K. Bank, "Theatre and Narrative Fiction in the Work of the Nineteenth-Century American Playwright Louisa Medina," *Theatre History Studies*, vol. 3, 1983, pp. 54–67.

11. Louisa H. Medina, *Nick of the Woods* (New York: Samuel French, n.d. [1856]) and Robert Montgomery Bird, *Nick of the Woods* (New York: American Book Co., 1939).

12. See *Early American Theatrical Posters* (Hollywood, Calif.: Cherokee Books, n.d.), p. 28, cut number 377.

13. Priscilla Sears, *A Pillar of Fire to Follow: American Indian Dramas, 1808–1859* (Bowling Green, Ohio: Bowling Green University Popular Press, 1982), indicates thirty-five Indian plays from the 1820s and 1830s and only about five more by 1860 (p. 35). Walter J. Meserve, *An Outline History of American Drama* (Totowa, N.J.: Littlefield, Adams & Co., 1965), indicates fifty Indian plays from 1825 to 1860 (p. 16). Wilmeth, "Checklist of Indian Plays" (pp. 37–40), lists well over a hundred between 1820 and 1840, but that includes plays from America and England, produced and unproduced, set in North or South America, and in some cases likely variations of the same work.

14. *Po-ca-hon-tas; or, The Gentle Savage* is in Moody, ed., *Dramas from the American Theatre 1762–1909; Metamora; or, The Last of the Pollywogs* is in Wilmeth, ed., *Staging the Nation*.

15. A biographical summary appears in the *Pittsburgh Leader*, November 3, 1907. His obituary is in the *New York Times*, October 23, 1920.

16. When a printer accidentally dropped the "C" from her last name, she decided to keep it that way. See the *Toledo Blade*, December 15, 1904, and the *New York Dramatic Mirror*, March 19, 1892.

17. The plot is related in the *New York Herald*, April 13, 1875.

18. Constance Rourke, *Troupers of the Gold Coast; or, The Rise of Lotta Crabtree* (New York: Harcourt, Brace and Company, 1928), pp. 213–216.

19. *Horizon* is in *Plays by Augustin Daly*, eds. Don B. Wilmeth and Rosemary Cullen (Cambridge: Cambridge University Press, 1984).

20. Felheim, *The Theater of Augustin Daly*, pp. 68–69.

21. *Horizon*, p. 110.

22. Ibid., p. 116.

23. Ibid., p. 120.

24. Burl Donald Grose, "Here Come the Indians: An Historical Study of the Representations of the Native American upon the North American Stage, 1808–1969," Ph.D. dissertation, University of Missouri, Columbia, 1979, p. 169.

25. Joseph Francis Daly, *The Life of Augustin Daly* (New York: Macmillan Company, 1917), p. 106.

26. These incidents are recounted in the *New York Clipper*, October 11, 1884, and in "The American on the Stage," by T. Allston Brown, in the *New York Clipper*, February 9, 1889, p. 326.

27. Brown in the *New York Clipper*, February 9, 1889.

28. See "Big Mose, New York's Own Paul Bunyan" by Norman Studerin, in *The Compass*, April 1, 1851, p. 11.

29. Comments on the development of the play are from an article written by Clifton W. Tayleure in the *New York World*, February 15, 1885.

30. On rare occasions Arkansas is spelled "Arkansaw," as in an undated Boston Grand Opera House program, in the Billy Rose Theatre Collection (BRTC) at the New York Public Library for the Performing Arts.

31. Material gleaned from programs at the BRTC.

32. The plot is reconstructed from contemporary reviews (see the *New York Clipper*, May 20, 1871) and programs at the BRTC. In some programs, the prologue was listed as 1856 and the first act as 1871, a fifteen-year gap. The mature Alice is called "Netty Ashton" in the premiere performance and "Nettie Hastings" in some subsequent productions.

33. G. Sheridan, "Stage Plans and Settings of Scenery for Plays Performed at Booth's Theatre 1873–1883" at BRTC. These valuable notes even supply the expected running time of every scene.

34. *New York Clipper*, November 11, 1871, and July 29, 1872.

35. *New York Clipper*, June 20, 1871, p. 54; *New York Sun*, May 10, 1871; and "The American on Stage," by T. Allston Brown, in the *New York Clipper*, February 9, 1889, p. 326.

2 Explosion: 1872–1876

1. The single best source of background information on "Buffalo Bill" Cody is *The Lives and Legends of Buffalo Bill* by Don Russell (Norman, Okla.: University of Oklahoma Press, 1969).

2. The Mormon War serves as background for *May Cody; or, Lost and Won*, one of the melodramas in which Cody appeared.

3. William F. Cody, *The Life of Hon. William F. Cody* (Hartford, Conn.: Frank E. Bliss, 1879; reprinted Lincoln, Nebr.: University of Nebraska Press, 1978), pp. 161–162. Russell refers to the contract in his *Lives and Legends*.

4. For a general biography of Ned Buntline, see Jay Monaghan, *The Great Rascal: The Life and Adventures of Ned Buntline* (Boston: Little, Brown and Company, 1952).

5. Production elements are described in a *New York Herald* review, February 21, 1872, and in an unidentified review of the Brooklyn Park Theatre production of the same play (with J. W. Carroll as Buffalo Bill) from the Buffalo Bill clipping file, BRTC. Many of the incidents from *Buffalo Bill, King of the Bordermen* appear in the Fred G. Maeder manuscript, *The Scouts of the Plains*, at the Harvard Theatre Collection, which I believe is a version of *King of the Bordermen* that Maeder revised slightly and retitled for Cody and "Wild Bill" Hickok.

6. For details, see Joseph G. Rosa, *They Called Him Wild Bill: The Life and Adventures of James Butler Hickok* (Norman, Okla.: University of Oklahoma Press, 1974), pp. 34–52.

7. See also the *New York Clipper*, March 30, 1872.

8. *New York Clipper*, April 6, 1872.

9. Cody, *The Life of Cody*, pp. 323–324.

10. The text of the play has not survived. Sources that comment on the plot include a program from the Boston Theatre for March 4, 1873, BRTC; Cody's *Life of Cody*, pp. 326–328; *Chicago Times*, December 18, 1872, *Chicago Evening Journal*, December 17, 1872, and *Chicago Inter Ocean*, December 17, 1872. In addition, two studies of Buffalo Bill's stage career are: "The Stage Career of Buffalo Bill," by James Monaghan, *Journal of the Illinois State Historical Society*, vol. 31, no. 4, December 1938, pp. 411–423; and "Buffalo Bill on Stage," by William S. E. Coleman, *Players*, vol. 47, no. 2, January 1972, pp. 80–91. In his unpublished dissertation, "Six-Guns on the Stage: Buffalo Bill Cody's First Celebration of the Conquest of the American Frontier" (University of California, Berkeley, 1981), Craig Francis Nieuwenhuyse attempts to recreate *The Scouts of the Prairie*.

11. Unidentified review, "Scalps by the Bale," in "Stage Play Notices and Reviews," *Troop C Ledger*, Buffalo Bill Historical Center, Cody, Wyo. Quoted in Nieuwenhuyse, "Six-Guns on the Stage," pp. 196–197.

12. "Buffalo Bill on Stage," p. 83.

13. Cody, *Life of Cody*, pp. 326–327.

14. Louisa Frederici Cody, with Courtney Ryley Cooper, *Memories of Buffalo Bill* (New York: D. Appleton and Company, 1919), pp. 249–250.

15. *Boston Daily Globe*, March 5, 1873, and *Boston Daily Advertiser*, March 4, 1873.

16. *Chicago Times*, December 18, 1872, and *Chicago Daily Tribune*, December 17, 1872.

17. *Boston Daily Globe*, March 5, 1873. Buntline's declamations are described in the *New York Sun*, April 1, 1873.

18. Cody, *Life of Cody*, p. 328. Considering headliners such as Chanfrau might earn about $10,000 in a year, Cody's $6,000 for a season that began in December with two other key performers does not seem out of line.

19. The handwritten manuscript is in the Harvard Theatre Collection. It contains alterations where some lines are crossed out as well as extensive descriptions and diagrams of the placement of actors. Although the manuscript refers to "Hitchcock," I have used the more common spelling.

20. See Rosa, *Wild Bill*, pp. 72–81.

21. *New York Clipper*, January 9, 1886.

22. Cody, *Life of Cody*, p. 330.

23. J. V. Arlington, *Life on the Border*, ed. Paul T. Nolan (Cody, Wyo.: Pioneer Drama Service, 1965). The play was written for Buffalo Bill, but, as Nolan points out, the manuscript has Crawford's name penciled over Buffalo Bill's.

24. The manuscript of "*Fonda; or, The Trapper's Dream*, a Drama in Five Acts with Original Songs by the Poet Scout," copyrighted by John Wallace Crawford in 1888, is in the Rare Book and Manuscript Collection of the Library of Congress. Crawford copyrighted the title "California Through Death Valley" in 1879.

25. *New York Clipper*, March 20, 1880, and *New York Mirror*, March 13, 1880. The *New York Mirror* became the *New York Dramatic Mirror* in April 1880.

26. Charles Foster, *Twenty Days* [Buffalo Bill's side], Buffalo Bill Memorial Museum, Golden, Colo. Some plot incidents come from the *New York Clipper*, September 9, 1882.

27. *Cleveland Leader*, August 14, 1910; *New York Morning Telegraph*, August 10, 1910; *Billboard*, August 20, 1910; and unidentified articles in the Studley clipping file and Locke envelope 2189, BRTC.

28. *Davy Crockett*, by Frank Murdoch, is in Clark, ed., *America's Lost Plays*, vol. IV.

29. See, for example, the *New York Clipper*, March 8, 1873, and the *New York Herald*, March 23, 1875.

30. Duane Joseph Fike makes this case in his dissertation, "Frank Mayo: Actor, Playwright, and Manager," University of Nebraska, 1980, p. 173.

31. *New York Dramatic Mirror*, May 11, 1895.

32. Laurence Hutton, *Curiosities of the American Stage* (New York: Harper & Brothers, 1891), p. 92.

33. Quoted in *Harper's Weekly*, vol. 39 (June 22, 1895), p. 594.

34. W. A. Lewis, "Frank Mayo – Man and Artist," *Theatre Magazine*, June 1906, p. 149.

35. *Ibid.*, p. 150.

36. Biographical information is taken from Herring's obituary in the *New York Dramatic Mirror*, May 26, 1906, and a retrospective on her in the *New York Clipper*, February 24, 1912.

37. *New York Dramatic Mirror*, May 26, 1906, and *New York Clipper*, September 24, 1881.

38. *Brooklyn Daily Times*, May 21, 1906, and *New York Clipper*, February 24, 1912.

39. Quoted in the *New York Sunday Telegraph*, October 25, 1903.

40. See the program from *The Boy Scout* at Bowdoin Square Theatre, Boston, for February 6, 1899, in *The Boy Scout* file, BRTC, and the *Cincinnati Commercial Tribune*, March 8, 1910.

41. "The Old Time Actor in Moving Picturedom," *Motion Picture Magazine*, June 1915, p. 84.

42. Emmett tells his own story in a *New York Dramatic Mirror* interview, October 7, 1882.
43. The program is in the Alice Placide file, BRTC.
44. *New York Sun*, February 20, 1873.
45. *New York Clipper*, January 1 and 15, 1876. Elsewhere, Cody stated the author of *Life on the Border* was J. V. Arlington; see Arlington, *Life on the Border*, ed. Paul T. Nolan, p. iv.
46. *New York Morning Telegraph*, August 16, 1903.
47. *New York Clipper*, January 31, 1874.
48. Otis Skinner, *Footlights and Spotlights: Recollections of My Life on Stage* (Indianapolis: Bobbs-Merrill Company, 1923), pp. 52–54.
49. *New York Herald* (New York), August 15, 1875.
50. The chain mail skullcap is illustrated in an unidentified advertisement in the Lawrence and Lee Theatre Collection at Ohio State University. Other information about the events of November 30, 1882, comes from the *Cincinnati Enquirer*, December 1 and 2, 1882, the *Cincinnati Commercial Tribune*, December 1, 1882, and the *Cincinnati Daily Gazette*, December 1 and 2, 1882.
51. For details of this conflict see Richard Dillon, *Burnt-Out Fires* (Englewood Cliffs, N.J.: Prentice-Hall, 1973).
52. There are numerous books about Custer. Two thorough standards are *Custer's Luck*, by Edgar L. Stewart (Norman, Okla.: University of Oklahoma Press, 1955), and *The Custer Myth*, a compilation of basic Custer source material by W. A. Graham (Harrisburg, Pa: Stackpole Company, 1953).
53. *New York Dramatic Mirror*, August 8, 1891.

3 Prominence: 1877–1883

1. Daly, *The Life of Augustin Daly*, pp. 170–176, 234. The quotation is from a letter from Boucicault to Daly, quoted on pp. 173–174.
2. *New York Clipper*, July 29, 1876. Bordman, *American Theatre* (p. 98), claims Robson paid $3,000 up front plus another $50 per performance ($25 for matinees) up to $6,000.
3. Unidentified clipping dated August 26, 1900, from the Locke Collection, vol. 405, p. 93, BRTC.
4. The play is in *California Gold Rush Plays*, ed. Glenn Loney (New York: Performing Arts Journal Publications, 1983).
5. Quoted in an unidentified clipping dated August 26, 1900, in Locke Collection, vol. 405, p. 93, BRTC.
6. Margaret Duckett, *Mark Twain and Bret Harte* (Norman, Okla.: University of Oklahoma Press, 1964), pp. 19, 38–39.
7. Albert Bigelow Paine, "Mark Twain," *Harper's Monthly Magazine*, vol. 125, no. 746, July 1912, p. 258.
8. Smith, *American Drama*, p. 1.
9. For more on Miller, see M. M. Marberry, *Splendid Poseur: Joaquin Miller – American Poet* (New York: Thomas Y. Crowell Company, 1953); O. W. Frost, *Joaquin Miller* (New York: Twayne Publishers, 1967); and Harr Wagner, *Joaquin*

Miller and His Other Self (San Francisco: Harr Wagner Publishing Company, 1929). Also the *Chicago Record-Herald*, June 5, 1907.

10. The stories are related in an undated advertising paper in the file for *The Danites*, BRTC.

11. Joaquin Miller's published version of the play, *The Danites in the Sierras*, differs from the version acted by McKee Rankin as described by reviews of the production. Miller's play has no first act with the wagon train; rather, the printed version begins at the Howlin' Wilderness Saloon, where Sandy simply relates the story of the young Nancy Williams pursued and killed by the Danites. In Miller's version, the widow is not just a teacher, but a missionary. Act II of the printed script (at the widow's cabin) is equivalent to Act III of the production. Act III of the printed script (at Sandy's cabin) is equivalent to Act IV of the production. And Act IV of the printed script (at Billie Piper's cabin) is equivalent to Act V of the production. In Miller's printed version, Hickman and Carter think the widow is the escaped Nancy Williams and kill her and her baby at Sandy's cabin. Realizing their mistake, they try to frame Billie Piper for the death and incite the miners to kill Billie. As in the production, however, the truth about Hickman and Carter emerges, they are hanged, and Nancy emerges from her disguise. In the printed script, she is then paired with Sandy. The printed version includes a lapse of three years before the final act. Joaquin Miller's *The Danites in the Sierras* is in *American Plays*, ed. Allan Gates Halline (New York: American Book Company, 1935; reprinted New York: AMS Press 1976).

12. Route information is from Levi Damon Phillips, "Arthur McKee Rankin's Touring Production of Joaquin Miller's *The Danites*," unpublished Ph.D. dissertation, University of California, Davis, 1981.

13. *New York Clipper*, September 1, 1877, and an undated *New York Mirror* item in the *Danites* file, BRTC.

14. For example, the *New York Mirror*, February 1, 1879.

15. *New York Mirror*, May 10, 1879; also *New York Mirror*, September 20, 1879.

16. Phillips, "Rankin's Touring Production," p. 140.

17. *The Danites*, pp. 384, 396 *et passim*.

18. *Louisville Courier-Journal*, March 27, 1879, and *St. Louis Evening Post*, October 28, 1878; Phillips, "Rankin's Touring Production," p. 26.

19. Comments from the London papers are included in advertising copy for *The Danites*, which appeared in the *New York Clipper*, January 1, 1881.

20. *New York Dramatic Mirror*, April 23 and April 30, 1881.

21. Quoted in the *New York Dramatic Mirror*, October 22, 1881.

22. The charges and countercharges are chronicled in the *New York Times*, October 9, October 12, October 14, October 20, and December 3, 1881, and the *New York Dramatic Mirror*, October 22, 1881.

23. Accounts varied as to how much Rankin paid Miller for these rights. Rankin at one time said he paid Miller $3,800 for the use of the author's name, plus a royalty of $40 per night in cities and $20 per night in towns. Elsewhere, Rankin claimed that he was to pay Miller the extraordinary sum of $7,000, but that he deducted $1,800 for expenses, leaving an actual fee of $5,200. See the *New York Times*, October 14, 1881, the *New York Dramatic Mirror*, October 15, 1881, and an unidentified clipping in the *Danites* file, BRTC.

24. Miller also acknowledged that Fitzgerald put *The Danites* into dramatic form in *Joaquin Miller's Poems*, vol. vi, "Poetic Plays" (San Francisco: Whitaker & Ray Company, 1910), p. v.

25. Marberry, *Splendid Poseur*, pp. 119–120. The autobiography was published in London by Richard Bentley and Son, 1873.

26. Rankin's account is in the *New York Dramatic Mirror*, October 8 and October 15, 1881.

27. *New York Mirror*, October 4, 1879.

28. Quoted in the *New York Dramatic Mirror*, November 19, 1881.

29. Joaquin Miller's published version of the play in *Joaquin Miller's Poems*, vol. vi, differs from Rankin's performed play as described in reviews. While the characters and story are essentially identical, the names of many of the characters are different. Furthermore, the published version does not dramatize the prologue, but begins with the lawyer (Colonel Snowe) giving his clerk (Charley Devine) instructions to find the heiress while the wily Lucky Tom Gully looks on. The plot as detailed is from an extensive summary of the production in the *New York Clipper*, October 8, 1881.

30. From an advertising card for *'49* in BRTC.

31. The play is contained in *Joaquin Miller's Poems*, vol. vi, as *An Oregon Idyl*.

32. *Tally-Ho!* is in *Joaquin Miller's Poems*, vol. vi.

33. The difficulties noted in this paragraph come from the *New York Clipper*, March 27, 1888; the *New York Dramatic Mirror*, April 11, 1891; and the *New York Dramatic Mirror*, February 21, 1891. Also, Isaac F. Marcosson and Daniel Frohman, *Charles Frohman: Manager and Man* (New York: Harper & Brothers, 1916), pp. 104–106.

34. *Chicago Daily News*, May 2, 1914.

35. See the *New York Dramatic Mirror*, November 11, 1895, and November 13, 1897; the *New York Clipper*, November 25, 1895; the *New York Morning Telegraph*, September 22, 1890; and an unidentified clipping dated October 15, 1904, from the Rankin file, BRTC.

36. *The Green Book Magazine*, July 1914, p. 39, notes that at one point the family performed *The Rivals* with Louisa Drew as Mrs. Malaprop, Sidney Drew as Bob Acres, Gladys as Lydia, McKee as Sir Lucius Trigger, Kitty Blanchard as Lucy, Maurice Barrymore as Captain Absolute, Lionel Barrymore as Fag, and Ethel Barrymore as Julia.

37. At one point the short story states, "then [M'liss] was nearly 11." Although the chronology is not explicit, that statement seems to occur just a few months into the story.

38. The dispute over the novel is outlined in "Bancroftiana," a newsletter published by friends of the Bancroft Library, University of California, Berkeley, no. 72, May 1979, p. 1. Harte's quotation is from *The Letters of Bret Harte*, ed. Geoffrey Bret Harte (Boston: Houghton Mifflin Co., 1926), p. 23. DeWitt's book was titled *M'liss. An Idyll of Red Mountain. A Story of California in 1863. By Bret Harte.* It ran to 148 pages, with Harte's material ending on p. 31. For an examination of the various versions of the story, see Lucinda R. Ligget's "Bret Harte's 'M'liss,'" unpublished master's thesis, Indiana State University, 1991.

39. Biographical information is from the *Indianapolis News*, October 1, 1932; the *Portland Standard*, July 2, 1877; the *Chicago Daily Tribune*, October 20, 1878; and an obituary in the *New York Times*, June 18, 1944.

40. Mayhew's account of the origin of *M'liss* and the contract with Greene is in the *New York Times*, September 11, 1878.

41. Greene copyrighted "*M'liss, a Romance of Red Mountain*, a drama in five acts by C. M. Greene, based upon the novel of the same title, by F. Bret Harte and G. B. [sic] Densmore" in May 1873. As was routine practice at that time, Greene copyrighted only the title and did not submit a copy of the script.

42. This script is in the Library of Congress Rare Book and Manuscript Collection. A second copyright stamp on the title page giving the date 1877 hardly seems plausible, as the printer's date is May 1878 and the stamp on the cover indicates June 8, 1878. The actress used her married name in legal documents and proceedings, and she switched to "Kate" as her professional name as she began to play more mature roles.

43. The plot, recounted from the Library of Congress script, is also described in numerous reviews of the Mayhew production, such as the *Portland Morning Oregonian*, July 14, 1877. In Chicago the following year the villain was called Manuel Torres, according to the *Chicago Daily Tribune* of October 2, 1878.

44. *New York Times*, September 15, 1878.

45. *New York Clipper*, December 7, 1878, and *New York Mirror*, June 14, 1879.

46. This manuscript, copyrighted by McDonough, is in the Library of Congress Rare Book and Manuscript Collection.

47. See advertising cards from the Bret Harte Collection at the Bancroft Library, University of California, Berkeley.

48. Yuba Bill, Harte's gallant, cynical stagecoach driver, played a central role in "Mrs. Skagg's Husbands" and appeared in several other stories including "Brown of Calaveras," "Miggles," and "An Ingenue of the Sierras."

49. George C. D. Odell, *Annals of the New York Stage*, vol. x (New York: Columbia University Press, 1938), pp. 585–586.

50. *New York Clipper*, November 16, 1878.

51. *New York Times*, November 17, 1878.

52. *New York Clipper*, December 7, 1878.

53. *New York Mirror*, January 18, 1878; *Illustrated American*, April 15, 1893.

54. Biographical information comes from the *New York Dramatic Mirror*, June 4, 1881, and November 18, 1893. Although her birth date was usually listed as 1858, her mausoleum indicates 1855, according to the *London (Ontario) Free Press*, October 1, 1966.

55. *New York Mirror*, February 21, 1880 and *New York Dramatic Mirror*, April 17, 1880.

56. Both comments are from the *New York Mirror*, February 21, 1880.

57. For example, the *New York Dramatic Mirror* April 30, 1880, and the *New York Clipper*, April 3, 1880.

58. See the Chicago correspondent for the *New York Mirror*, June 14, 1879; the *New York Dramatic Mirror*, June 6, 1881; and the *New York Dramatic Mirror*, April 30, 1881.

59. The financial figures come from the *New York Clipper*, October 20, 1880, and the *New York Dramatic Mirror*, May 29, 1880; the description is from the *New York Dramatic Mirror*, February 19, 1881.

60. A *M'liss* program from the Haymarket Theatre, Chicago, for May 14, 1893, boasts "as acted by Annie Pixley over 2,000 times." BRTC.

61. *New York Clipper*, February 25, 1882.

62. November 18, 1893. Information on her place of burial is in the *London (Ontario) Free Press*, October 1, 1966.

63. *New York Times*, June 18, 1944.

64. Biographical information in the *New York Dramatic Mirror*, June 19, 1894.

65. September 20, 1879; see also the Chicago correspondent for the *New York Mirror*, May 10, 1879.

66. *New York Mirror*, October 11, 1879.

67. Bartley Campbell, *My Partner*, in Clark, ed., *America's Lost Plays*, vol. XIX.

68. The Chinese immigrant character remained prominent, notably in the television program *Bonanza*, eighty years later, where the cook was another Hop Sing. With his Asian costume, long, braided hair, and strong accent, Hop Sing represented a stereotypical wise but subservient domestic.

69. Comments come from the *New York Dramatic Mirror*, October 1, 1881; *The Boston Herald*, October 28, 1879; and the *New York Dramatic Mirror*, April 17, 1880.

70. *New York Dramatic Mirror*, August 19, 1882. Although there is no evidence of the exact split, Aldrich probably received a larger share because he handled all business arrangements for the show.

71. *New York Dramatic Mirror*, July 8, 1882.

72. Income estimates were published in the *New York Mirror*, June 14, 1879.

73. Parsloe's comment and reports of his financial difficulties are from the *New York Dramatic Mirror*, July 1, 1882; the *New York Dramatic Mirror*, January 29, 1898; and the *New York Dramatic Mirror*, October 1, 1892.

74. See the *New York Dramatic Mirror*, September 20, 1890; November 22, 1890; and June 29, 1901.

75. A full story of the Actors' Fund and Aldrich's contribution to it is in *A History of the Actors' Fund of America*, by Louis Simon (New York: Theatre Arts Books, 1972). This information comes from pp. 66–67 and from an unidentified clipping in the Aldrich file, BRTC.

76. The figure comes from an interview with Campbell's son, Robert, in the *New York Sun*, July 30, 1942.

77. Edwards' role in the myth-making process is referred to frequently in *Jesse James Was His Name* by William A. Settle Jr. (Columbia, Mo.: University of Missouri Press, 1966).

78. Ibid., p. 180. These included Edwards' *The Guerrillas of the West; or, The Life, Character, and Daring Exploits of the Younger Brothers* (St. Louis: Eureka Publishing Company, 1876).

79. These James gang marketing schemes are noted in the *New York Times*, September 17, 1882; the *New York Clipper*, December 9, 1882; and Settle, *Jesse James Was His Name*, p. 166.

80. See the letter from Lavernie accompanying his copyright application, Copyright Office, Washington, D.C. Lavernie copyrighted his play as "*The James Boys, Missouri Outlaws, Jesse and Frank; or, Run to Death* in five acts and sixteen tableauxs [sic]." In litigation, it was referred to by the *New York Times* (January 27, 1883) as *James Boys, Frank and Jesse; or, Falsely Accused*. Advertisements simply called it *The James Boys*. In February 1883, France copyrighted "*Frank James, the Missouri Avenger*. An Entirely New and Original Drama founded on the History of the Celebrated James Boys." However, when a company headed only by France returned to New York in 1886, they presented a production that bore Lavernie's title, *The James Boys; or, The Missouri Outlaws*.

81. *New York Times*, January 27, 1883. James H. Wallick was not a member of the Wallack theatrical family, famous in nineteenth-century American theatre.

82. *New York Clipper*, February 3 and February 10, 1883; and the *New York Dramatic Mirror*, February 10, 1883.

83. *New York Times*, February 2, 1883.

84. Although the play was not copyrighted at the time, in 1901 Elizabeth Belmer deposited two typed copies of Henry Belmer's "*Jesse James, the American Outlaw; or, The Life and Death of Jesse James*, a sensational western melodrama in four acts."

85. Unidentified review of November 22 in BRTC.

86. Their claims are in the *New York Times*, January 27, 1883, and November 16, 1884.

87. Settle, *Jesse James Was His Name*, pp. 26–27, 76–77.

88. Examples from the Belmer script come from I, iii and III, i.

89. See the copyrighted title page in the Copyright Office, Washington, D.C. The leap through the window was featured in advertisements, as depicted in a small handbill negative and a large poster, BRTC. Other tricks and specialties are mentioned in the *New York Herald*, February 4 and August 21, 1883; the *New York Times*, February 9, 1886; the *Dramatic News and Society Journal*, August 14, 1883; and an unidentified review of November 22, 1902 in the play file, BRTC.

90. *New York Clipper*, March 25, 1881.

91. Don Russell, *The Wild West; or, A History of the Wild West Shows* (Ft. Worth: Amon Carter Museum of Western Art, 1970), pp. 67, 127.

92. *New York Herald*, February 4, 1883.

93. *New York Clipper*, October 14, 1882, and *New York Dramatic Mirror*, October 21 and November 11, 1882.

94. *New York Times*, May 28, 1892, and May 2, 1908; *New York Dramatic Mirror*, May 16, 1908.

95. Harry Meredith, *Ranch 10; or, Annie from Massachusetts* (Chicago: Howard and Doyle, 1882).

96. Bordman, *American Theatre*, p. 137.

4 Phenomenon: 1883–1892

1. See Brooks McNamara, *Step Right Up* (Jackson, Miss.: University Press of Mississippi, 1995).

2. P. T. Barnum, *Struggles and Triumphs; or, Forty Years' Recollections* (Buffalo, N.Y.: Warren, Johnson & Co., 1872), p. 543.

3. Nellie Snyder Yost, *Buffalo Bill: His Family, Friends, Fame, Failures, and Fortunes* (Chicago: Swallow Press, 1979), pp. 116–122.

4. The most thorough accounts of the Wild West shows are Don Russell's *Wild West* and *Lives and Legends*.

5. For more on Carver, see Raymond W. Thorpe, *Spirit Gun of the West: The Story of Doc W. F. Carver* (Glendale, Calif.: A. H. Clark, 1957).

6. For more on Bogardus, see Roger Hall, "Captain Adam Bogardus: Shooting and the Stage in Nineteenth-Century America," *Journal of American Culture*, vol. 5, no. 3, Fall 1982, pp. 46–49.

7. For more on Salsbury, see Roger Hall, "Nate Salsbury: Actor, Manager, Playwright," *Theatre Studies*, nos. 24/25, 1977–78/1978–79, pp. 149–154.

8. Richard J. Walsh with Milton S. Salsbury, *The Making of Buffalo Bill* (Indianapolis: Bobbs-Merrill Company, 1928), pp. 248–249. For more on Annie Oakley, see Glenda Riley, *The Life and Legacy of Annie Oakley* (Norman, Okla.: University of Oklahoma Press, 1994).

9. Walsh and Salsbury, *The Making of Buffalo Bill*, p. 254.

10. Russell, *Wild West*, p. 25.

11. Sarah J. Blackstone, *Buckskins, Bullets, and Business: A History of Buffalo Bill's Wild West* (Westport, Conn.: Greenwood Press, 1986), pp. 18–21, provides details of the Madison Square Garden engagement.

12 Nate Salsbury, "Reminiscences," ed. Roger Hall, *Journal of American Drama and Theatre*, vol. 5, Winter 1993, relates stories about their engagements in France, Spain, Italy, Germany, and England in "Un Mauvais Quart d'Heure," "Nate Salsbury and the Shah," "Advance Agent," "At the Vatican," "Our Chesterfield," and "Visit of the Wild West to Windsor," pp. 58–70.

13. Walsh and Salsbury, *The Making of Buffalo Bill*, p. 304; Russell, *Lives and Legends*, p. 375.

14. Russell, *Lives and Legends*, p. 379. Also, Salsbury, "Reminiscences," "Contract with Bailey," pp. 71–72.

15. Andrea I. Paul, "Buffalo Bill and Wounded Knee: The Movie," *Nebraska History*, vol. 71, no. 4, Fall 1990, pp. 182–190, describes *The Indian Wars*. Only about two minutes of the film is known to exist, and that is at the Buffalo Bill Historical Center.

16. Russell, *Wild West*, p. 88.

17. R. L. Wilson estimated the collective audience for Cody's shows to have been 50 million (*Buffalo Bill's Wild West: An American Legend*, by R. L. Wilson with Greg Martin, New York: Random House, 1998, p. vii.) Although some sports heroes with lengthy careers, long seasons, and large stadia have surely eclipsed Cody, it is unlikely, given the modern dominance of electronic media, that any entertainer will ever appear live to more people than Buffalo Bill.

18. See, for instance, Ralph E. Friar and Natasha A. Friar, *The Only Good Indian: The Hollywood Gospel* (New York: Drama Book Specialists, 1972), John Tuska, *The American West in Film: Critical Approaches to the Westerns* (Westport, Conn.: Greenwood Press, 1985), and Gretchen M. Bataille and Charles L. P. Silet, eds., *The Pretend Indians: Images of Native Americans in the Movies* (Ames, Iowa: Iowa State University Press, 1980). The quotation is from p. xxii.

19. L. G. Moses, *Wild West Shows and the Images of American Indians, 1883–1933* (Albuquerque, N. Mex.: University of New Mexico Press, 1996) and "Interpreting the Wild West," in *Between Indian and White Worlds: The Cultural Broker*, ed. Margaret Connell Szasz (Norman, Okla.: University of Oklahoma Press, 1994) pp.158–178; see also Szasz's "Introduction" for her comments on "cultural brokers," pp. 3–20.

20. Don Russell, "Buffalo Bill – In Action," *Westerners Brand Book*, vol. 19, no. 5, July 1962, pp. 33–35 and 40, details the available motion pictures of Cody and his Wild West. Much of the footage is accessible at the Buffalo Bill Historical Center, Cody, Wyo., and numerous documentaries feature film segments.

21. Quotations from "Reminiscences," "Long Hair and a Plug Hat," p. 50, and "Cody, Manager," p. 73.

22. Origins of the Ghost Dance movement are cloudy, but apparently stem from 1869–71 when a Nevada prophet taught that whites would be annihilated and that dead native ancestors would return to earth. Game would also once again be plentiful. The Ghost Dance was required to prepare for that day of atonement. The movement foundered, but it was revived in 1888–89 under the prophet Wovoka and spread rapidly. When the Sioux adopted the Ghost Dance, partly as a substitute for the banned Sun Dance, some white observers perceived the dance as belligerent, especially the belief that the shirts worn by the dancers were bullet-proof. See James Mooney, *The Ghost-Dance Religion and the Sioux Outbreak of 1890* (Lincoln, Nebr.: University of Nebraska Press, 1991).

23. Russell, *Wild West*, pp. 121–127.

24. See Glenn Shirley, *Pawnee Bill: A Biography of Major Gordon W. Lillie* (Albuquerque, N. Mex.: University of New Mexico Press, 1958).

25. For a full account of the 101 Ranch show, see Michael Wallis, *The Real Wild West: The 101 Ranch and the Creation of the American West* (New York: St. Martin's Press, 1999).

26. Will Rogers, *The Autobiography of Will Rogers* (Boston: Houghton Mifflin Company, 1949), pp. 13–15, 27–30. See also Ben Yagoda, *Will Rogers, a Biography* (New York: Alfred A. Knopf, 1993).

27. A typed manuscript of *Nobody's Claim* by Edwin A. Locke, copyrighted in 1884, is in the Rare Book and Manuscript Collection of the Library of Congress.

28. Various accounts of the story may be found in the clipping files for *On the Frontier* and Hardie and Von Leer, BRTC.

29. *The New York Morning Telegraph*, July 1, 1919, and *New York Dramatic Mirror*, July 18, 1916, and February 25, 1905.

30. A manuscript for *The Gentleman from Nevada* by George H. Jessop and J. B. Polk, copyrighted as "A Comedy in Four Acts" in 1880, is in the Rare Book and Manuscript Collection of the Library of Congress.

31. A manuscript of *The Westerner* by Edward E. Rose, a comedy drama in four acts copyrighted in 1899, is in the Rare Book and Manuscript Collection of the Library of Congress.

32. A typed manuscript of *Wep-ton-no-mah, the Indian Mail Carrier* by Gowongo Mohawk and Charlie Charles, copyrighted in 1892, is in the Rare Book and Manuscript Collection of the Library of Congress.

33. Biographical information is from the *Era* (London), May 20, 1893, and "From Wigwam to Stage" by Alice W. Eyre, an unidentified article in envelope 1495, Locke Collection, BRTC.

34. "An Indian Actress in England," the *Era* (London), May 20, 1893, and the *Des Moines Register and Leader*, March 28, 1910.

35. Quotations in this paragraph are from "An Indian Actress in England," and the *Des Moines Register and Leader*, March 31, 1910.

36. *Vanity Fair*, February 1, 1901, and "From Wigwam to Stage," by Alice W. Eyre.

37. "An Indian Actress in England."

38. *Des Moines Register and Leader*, March 31, 1910.

39. *Des Moines Register and Leader*, March 31, 1910; *Vanity Fair*, February 1, 1901; *Era* (London), April 15, 1893; and "From Wigwam to Stage."

40. Margaret Williams, *Australia on the Popular Stage, 1829–1929* (Melbourne: Oxford University Press, 1983) pp. 169–171.

41. *New York Dramatic Mirror*, August 15, 1891. Virtually every review of the show mentions this feat.

42. *Melbourne Argus*, May 11, 1891, and *Melbourne Age*, May 12, 1891.

43. *Melbourne Argus*, June 22, 1891, and *Melbourne Age*, June 22, 1891.

44. Carver's daughter revived her father's act in 1953, training a horse to dive from a forty-foot tower on the Atlantic City boardwalk into a twelve-foot-deep tank, and she continued the act for several years at fairs and amusement parks according to "Speaking of Pictures," photographs by Peter Stackpole, *Life*, October 12, 1953, pp. 26–28.

5 Respect: 1893–1899

1. Frederick Jackson Turner, "The Significance of the Frontier in American History," *Annual Report of the American Historical Association for the Year 1893* (Washington, D.C.: Government Printing Office, 1894), pp. 199–227. Richard White draws attention to the juxtaposition of the two stories of the frontier represented by Cody and Turner in his essay "Frederick Jackson Turner and Buffalo Bill," in *The Frontier in American Culture*, ed. James R. Grossman (Berkeley: University of California Press, 1994).

2. For a study of the impact of the upper class on the perception of the art of the frontier, see G. Edward White, *The Eastern Establishment and the Western Experience: The West of Frederic Remington, Theodore Roosevelt, and Owen Wister* (New Haven and London: Yale University Press, 1968).

3. Brian Dippie, "The Moving Finger Writes: Western Art and the Dynamics of Change," in Jules David Prown *et al.*, *Discovered Lands, Invented Pasts: Transforming Visions of the American West* (New Haven: Yale University Press, 1992), p. 104.

4. *The Girl I Left Behind Me* is in Clark, ed., *America's Lost Plays*, vol. XVIII.

5. *New York Times*, January 17, 1893.

6. The play was also performed briefly at Sadler's Wells Theatre in early January 1893, for the purpose of securing the authors' copyright. *Era Almanack*, 1894, p. 41.

7. *Saturday Review*, April 20, 1895; reprinted in *Our Theatres in the Nineties*, vol. 1 (London: Constable and Company, 1932), pp. 92–97.

8. *The Girl I Left Behind Me*, p. 147.

9. See, for instance, the *New York Times*, January 26, 1893, and the Shaw critique noted above.

10. "Courts of Indian Offenses," Henry M. Teller, and "Rules for Indian Courts," Thomas J. Morgan, in *Americanizing the American Indians: Writings by the "Friends of the Indian" 1880–1900*, ed. Francis Paul Prucha (Cambridge, Mass.: Harvard University Press, 1973), pp. 295–305.

11. Lisa Marie Strong in her dissertation "Images of Indian–White Contact in the Watercolors of Alfred Jacob Miller, 1837–1860" (Columbia University, 1998) documents this revulsion to Indian dancing as she examines the way that attitude influenced artists' subjects (p. 104).

12. Biographical information is from Thomas' autobiography, *The Print of My Remembrance* (New York: Charles Scribner's Sons, 1922).

13. Amy Leslie, *Some Players* (Chicago and New York: H. S. Stone and Company, 1899), pp. 256–257.

14. See the various unidentified reviews in the *In Mizzoura* clipping file, BRTC.

15. The play is in Moses, ed., *Representative Plays by American Dramatists*, vol. III.

16. See Thomas' "Preface" to the play, in Moses, ed., *Representative Plays by American Dramatists*, vol. III, p. 461.

17. See Ronald J. Davis, *Augustus Thomas* (Boston: Twayne Publishers, 1984), p. 7, and Thomas, *The Print of My Remembrance*, pp. 213–214, 311.

18. For more about Goodwin, through his own eyes, see *Nat Goodwin's Book* by Goodwin and Richard G. Badger (Boston: Gorham Press, 1914).

19. Company lists are from April 2, 1892, March 25, 1893, January 13, 1894, and April 24, 1894. The quotation and estimate are in the issue for January 13, 1894.

20. *New York Dramatic Mirror*, May 19, 26, and June 2, 1894.

21. See the *New York Dramatic Mirror*, September 5, 1896. The plot summary and quotation come from unidentified reviews in the *Northern Lights* clipping file, BRTC. One of the many recent works on the attempts to assimilate Native Americans is David Wallace Adams' *Education for Extinction: American Indians and the Boarding School Experience, 1875–1928* (Lawrence, Kans.: University Press of Kansas, 1995).

22. The play is in *Representative American Dramas*, ed. Montrose J. Moses (Boston: Little, Brown and Company, 1933).

23. *Texas Steer*, p. 17.

24. Ibid., p. 22.

25. Ibid., p. 26.

26. The manuscript for *Heart of the Rockies*, copyrighted in 1896 as a romantic melodrama in four acts by Scott Marble, is in the Rare Book and Manuscript Collection of the Library of Congress.

     The theatrical poster collection at the Library of Congress contains posters for *The Heart of the Klondike* and for many of the plays mentioned in this book, including *Madeline of Fort Reno*, *The Limited Mail*, *The Pacific Mail*, *M'liss*, *Si Slocum*, and others. Many of the posters can be accessed on-line at http://lcweb2.loc.gov/pp/pphome.html.

27. A typed manuscript of Vance's *The Limited Mail*, copyrighted in 1889, is in the Rare Book and Manuscript Collection at the Library of Congress.

28. A typed manuscript of *The Great Train Robbery* by Scott Marble, which was entered for copyright in 1896, is in the Rare Book and Manuscript Collection of the Library of Congress.

6 Dominance: 1899–1906

1. Thomas, *The Print of My Remembrance*, p. 362; *Chicago Inter Ocean*, June 1, 1913.
2. Augustus Thomas, *Arizona* (New York: R. H. Russell, 1902).
3. Arthur Hobson Quinn, *A History of the American Drama from the Civil War to the Present Day* (New York: F. S. Crofts & Co., 1937), vol. 1, pp. 248–249.
4. September 11, 1900, and an unidentified review of September 11, 1900, in the *Arizona* clipping file, BRTC.
5. Quinn, *A History of the American Drama*, vol. 1, p. 249.
6. *Arizona*, p. 9.
7. Ibid., p. 12.
8. Ibid., p. 92.
9. Thomas, *The Print of My Remembrance*, pp. 352–353, 356–358.
10. *Arizona*, pp. 37–38.
11. Davis, *Augustus Thomas*, p. 14.
12. A 1940 movie titled *Arizona* and starring William Holden and Jean Arthur bore little resemblance to the play.
13. Owen Wister and Kirke La Shelle, *The Virginian*, ed. N. Orwin Rush (Tallahassee, Fla.: n.p., 1958). Some programs use the spelling "Hewie," but I have retained the spelling from the published text.
14. Unidentified review of May 5, 1904, in the *Virginian* clipping file, BRTC.
15. Unidentified review in the *Virginian* clipping file, BRTC.
16. *The Virginian*, pp. 25, 41–42.
17. Ibid., p. 60.
18. Ibid., p. 55.
19. Ibid., p. 12.
20. Ibid., p. 47.
21. Lee Clark Mitchell, *Westerns: Making the Man in Fiction and Film* (Chicago: University of Chicago Press, 1996), pp. 169–171.
22. The Leslie quotation is from an unidentified review of May 4, 1904, and the other is from an unidentified and undated review, both in the *Virginian* clipping file, BRTC.
23. Riley, *The Life and Legacy of Annie Oakley*, includes summaries of the plays, pp. 166–171.
24. William C. deMille, *Strongheart* (New York: Samuel French, 1909).
25. *Strongheart*, pp. 82–83.
26. *New York Times*, January 31, 1905.
27. The play is included in a somewhat condensed version in *The Best Plays of 1899–1909*, eds. Burns Mantle and Garrison P. Sherwood (New York: Dodd, Mead & Company, 1944).
28. All three reviews October 24, 1905.
29. Unidentified clipping in the *Squaw Man* clipping file BRTC.
30. *New York Times*, October 29, 1905; *New York World*, October 24, 1905.

31. Unidentified review in the *Squaw Man* clipping file, BRTC.

32. Biographical information on Faversham comes from extensive recollections contained in the Faversham clipping file in BRTC.

33. See, for example, the *New York Evening Mail*, October 24, 1905.

34. *The Girl of the Golden West* is in Moses, ed., *Representative American Dramas*.

35. *Boston Daily Globe*, November 15, 1905, and an undated *New York Tribune* review in the Blanche Bates clipping file, BRTC.

36. *The Girl of the Golden West*, p. 85.

37. Ibid., p. 79.

38. Ibid., p. 96.

39. Ibid., p. 76.

40. Ibid., p. 97.

41. Biographical information is taken from various sources in the Bates clipping file, BRTC.

42. An undated *New York Tribune* review in the Bates clipping file, BRTC.

43. David Belasco and Richard Walton Tully, *The Rose of the Rancho* (New York = n.p., 1906).

44. Biographical information is from *Current Literature*, December 1906, pp. 662–668; "William Vaughn Moody – Dramatist" by Charles Wood, in *The Green Book Album*, December 1910, pp. 1241–1244; *New York Evening Post*, October 18, 1910; an article by Archie Bell in the *Cleveland Plain Dealer*, May 24, 1911; and the *Philadelphia Evening Telegraph*, December 7, 1907. See also Maurice F. Brown, *Estranging Dawn: The Life and Works of William Vaughn Moody* (Carbondale, Ill.: Southern Illinois University Press, 1973).

45. In his introduction to the play in *Dramas from the American Theatre 1762–1909* Richard Moody states that the title was suggested by Mrs. Percy MacKaye, a friend of the author. See also letters to numerous Chicago papers in late December 1907, including the *Chicago Inter Ocean*, December 25, 1907; the *Chicago Record-Herald*, December 29, 1907; and the *Chicago Examiner*, December 29, 1907. Bell asserts in the *Cleveland Plain Dealer*, May 24, 1911, that Miller rewrote the script, as does Brown, *Estranging Dawn*, p. 212.

46. Biographical information is from the Miller clipping file, including a typed reminiscence, "Henry Miller As I Knew Him," by playwright Albert E. Thomas, BRTC; also Frank Morse, *Backstage with Henry Miller* (New York: E. P. Dutton & Co., 1938).

47. Biographical sources include obituaries in the *New York Times*, January 8, 1958, and the *Herald Tribune*, January 8, 1958, as well as other items in the Anglin clipping file, BRTC, and John LeVay, *Margaret Anglin, a Stage Life* (Toronto: Simon & Pierre, 1989).

48. Herbert Whittaker, "The Canadian Who Became America's Top Leading Lady," *Globe Magazine* (*Toronto Globe*), September 7, 1957, pp. 6–7.

49. *The Great Divide* is in Moody, ed., *Dramas from the American Theatre 1762–1909*.

50. See the undated *Chicago Daily Tribune* article in the Moody clipping file, BRTC.

51. Defoe, "Some Dramas of the Day," *The Red Book* (undated), pp. 425–426; see also *Current Literature*, December 1906, p. 662.

52. Undated reviews in the *Great Divide* clipping file, BRTC.

53. See, for instance, Charles W. Collins' unidentified clipping in the Moody clipping file, BRTC, regarding Ruth's "constant moping."

54. *Town and Country*, October 27, 1906.

55. *The Great Divide*, pp. 729, 730.

56. *New York Times*, November 16, 1906.

57. Quoted in Moody's introduction to the play in *Dramas from the American Theatre, 1762–1909* p. 726.

58. *Billy the Kid* by Walter Woods is in Clark, ed., *America's Lost Plays*, vol. VIII.

59. Milton Epstein, "The Shuberts and the New York Hippodrome," *Passing Show* (*Newsletter of the Shubert Archive*), vol. 17, nos. 1/2, Spring/Fall 1994, pp. 2–27.

60. Rachel Crothers, *The Three of Us* (New York: Samuel French, [1916]).

61. *The Three of Us*, p. 81.

62. Richardson, *American Dramas*, pp. 251, 249.

63. Reviews are from the clipping file for *The Three of Us*, BRTC, and from the *Illustrated Sporting and Dramatic News* (London), June 27, 1908.

Summary

1. See above, p. 4.

2. David Radavich, "Western Drama and the New Frontier," *American Drama*, vol. VII, no. 1, Fall 1997, p. 111

3. See above, pp. 8, 9 and 10.

4. See above, p. 10.

5. See above, p. 9.

6. Bank, "Frontier Melodrama," in Ogden, ed., *Theatre West: Image and Impact*, p. 156.

7. See above, p. 8.

8. See above, p. 13.

9. See above, p. 14.

10. See above, p. 14.

Bibliography

Plays and anthologies

Arlington, J. V. *Life on the Border*. Ed. Paul T. Nolan. Cody, Wyo.: Pioneer Drama Service, 1965.

Belasco, David and Tully, Richard Walton. *The Rose of the Rancho*. New York = n.p., 1906.

Belmer, Henry. *Jesse James, the American Outlaw; or, The Life and Death of Jesse James*. Manuscript, Library of Congress.

Clark, Barrett, ed. *America's Lost Plays*, vols. IV, VIII, XVIII, XIX. Princeton: Princeton University Press, 1940; reissued Bloomington, Ind.: Indiana University Press, 1965.

Cox, Richard H. *M'liss, Child of the Sierras*. Manuscript, Library of Congress.

[Cox, Richard H., Greene, Clay M., and Thompson, A. Sisson.] *[M'liss] The Waif of Smith's Pocket*. San Francisco: Francis & Valentine, 1878.

Crawford, John Wallace. *Fonda; or, The Trapper's Dream*. Manuscript, Library of Congress.

Crothers, Rachel. *The Three of Us*. New York: Samuel French, [1916].

deMille, William C. *Strongheart*. New York: Samuel French, 1909.

Dillaye, Ina. *Ramona, a Play in Five Acts, Adapted from Helen Hunt Jackson's Indian Novel*. Syracuse, N.Y.: F. LeC. Dillaye, 1887.

Fitch, Clyde. *The Cowboy and the Lady*. New York: Samuel French, 1908.

Foster, Charles. *Twenty Days* [Buffalo Bill's side]. Manuscript, Buffalo Bill Memorial Museum, Golden, Colo.

Halline, Allan Gates, ed. *American Plays*. New York: American Book Company, 1935; reprinted New York: AMS Press, 1976.

Jessop, George H., and Polk, J. B. *The Gentleman from Nevada*. Manuscript, Library of Congress.

Locke, Edwin A. *Nobody's Claim*. Manuscript, Library of Congress.

Loney, Glenn, ed. *California Gold Rush Plays*. New York: Performing Arts Journal Publications, 1983.

Maeder, Fred G. *The Scouts of the Plains*. Manuscript, Harvard Theatre Collection.

Mantle, Burns, and Sherwood, Garrison P., eds. *The Best Plays of 1899–1909*. New York: Dodd, Mead & Company, 1944.

Marble, Scott. *Heart of the Rockies*. Manuscript, Library of Congress.

Marble, Scott. *The Great Train Robbery*. Manuscript, Library of Congress.

Medina, Louisa H. *Nick of the Woods*. New York: Samuel French, n.d. [1856].

Meredith, Harry. *Ranch 10; or, Annie from Massachusetts*. Chicago: Howard and Doyle, 1882.

Miller, Joaquin. *Joaquin Miller's Poems*, vol. vi, "Poetic Plays." San Francisco: Whitaker & Ray Company, 1910.

Mohawk, Gowongo, and Charles, Charlie. *Wep-ton-no-mah, the Indian Mail Carrier*. Manuscript, Library of Congress.

Moody, Richard, ed. *Dramas from the American Theatre 1762–1909*. Cleveland, Ohio, and New York: World Publishing Company, 1966.

Moses, Montrose J., ed. *Representative American Dramas*. Boston: Little, Brown and Company, 1933.

Moses, Montrose J., ed. *Representative Plays by American Dramatists*, vols. i and iii. New York: Benjamin Blom, 1964.

Nelson, Richard, ed. *"Strictly Dishonorable" and Other Lost American Plays*. New York: Theatre Communications Group, 1986.

Paulding, James Kirke. *The Lion of the West*. Ed. James N. Tidwell. Stanford: Stanford University Press, 1954.

Quinn, Arthur Hobson, ed. *Representative American Plays*. New York: D. Appleton-Century Company, 1938.

Rose, Edward E. *The Westerner*. Manuscript, Library of Congress.

Thomas, Augustus. *Arizona*. New York: R. H. Russell, 1902.

Vance, Elmer E. *The Limited Mail*. Manuscript, Library of Congress.

Wilmeth, Don B., ed. *Staging the Nation: Plays from the American Theatre, 1787–1909*. Boston: Bedford Books, 1998.

Wilmeth, Don B., and Cullen, Rosemary, eds. *Plays by Augustin Daly*. Cambridge: Cambridge University Press, 1984.

Wister, Owen, and La Shelle, Kirke. *The Virginian*. Ed. N. Orwin Rush. Tallahassee, Fla.: n.p., 1958.

Books

Adams, David Wallace. *Education for Extinction: American Indians and the Boarding School Experience, 1875–1928*. Lawrence, Kans.: University Press of Kansas, 1995.

Alexandre, Arsene, Spielman, M. H., Bunner, H. C., and Joccaci, August. *The Modern Poster*. New York: Charles Scribner's Sons, 1895.

Ault, Phil. *All Aboard!* New York: Dodd, Mead & Company, 1976.

Bank, Rosemarie K. *Theatre Culture in America, 1825–1860*. Cambridge: Cambridge University Press, 1997.

Barnum, P. T. *Struggles and Triumphs; or, Forty Years' Recollections*. Buffalo, N.Y.: Warren, Johnson & Co., 1872.

Bataille, Gretchen M., and Silet, Charles L. P., eds. *The Pretend Indians: Images of Native Americans in the Movies*. Ames, Iowa: Iowa State University Press, 1980.

Betts, John Rickards. *America's Sporting Heritage, 1850–1950*. Reading, Mass.: Addison Wesley Publishing Company, 1974.

Bird, Robert Montgomery. *Nick of the Woods*. New York: American Book Co., 1939.

Blackstone, Sarah J. *Buckskins, Bullets, and Business: A History of Buffalo Bill's Wild West*. Westport, Conn.: Greenwood Press, 1986.

Bordman, Gerald. *American Theatre: A Chronicle of Comedy and Drama, 1869–1914.* New York: Oxford University Press, 1994.

Brauer, Ralph, with Brauer, Donna. *The Horse, the Gun, and the Piece of Property: Changing Images of the TV Western.* Bowling Green, Ohio: Bowling Green University Popular Press, 1975.

Brown, Maurice F. *Estranging Dawn: The Life and Works of William Vaughn Moody.* Carbondale, Ill.: Southern Illinois University Press, 1973.

Cawelti, John. *The Six-Gun Mystique.* Bowling Green, Ohio: Bowling Green University Popular Press, 1971.

Cody, Louisa Frederici, with Cooper, Courtney Ryley. *Memories of Buffalo Bill.* New York: D. Appleton and Company, 1919.

Cody, William F. *The Life of Hon. William F. Cody.* Hartford, Conn.: Frank E. Bliss, 1879; reprinted Lincoln, Nebr.: University of Nebraska Press, 1978.

Cody, William F. *Story of the Wild West and Camp-Fire Chats.* Philadelphia: Historical Publishing Co., 1890.

Cooper, Courtney Ryley. *Annie Oakley: Woman at Arms.* New York: Duffield and Company, 1927.

Croft-Cooke, Rupert, and Meadmore, W. S. *Buffalo Bill.* London: Sidgwick and Jackson, 1952.

Daly, Joseph Francis. *The Life of Augustin Daly.* New York: Macmillan Company, 1917.

Davis, Ronald J. *Augustus Thomas.* Boston: Twayne Publishers, 1984.

Dillon, Richard. *Burnt-Out Fires.* Englewood Cliffs, N.J.: Prentice-Hall, 1973.

Dippie, Brian W. *The Vanishing American: White Attitudes and US Indian Policy.* Middletown, Conn.: Wesleyan University Press, 1982.

Drinnon, Richard. *Facing West: The Metaphysics of Indian-Hating and Empire-Building.* Minneapolis: University of Minnesota Press, 1980.

Duckett, Margaret. *Mark Twain and Bret Harte.* Norman, Okla.: University of Oklahoma Press, 1964.

Dulles, Foster Rhea. *America Learns to Play: A History of Popular Recreation, 1607–1940.* New York: D. Appleton-Century Company, 1940.

Early American Theatrical Posters. Hollywood, Calif.: Cherokee Books, n.d.

Edwards, John Newman. *The Guerrillas of the West; or, The Life, Character, and Daring Exploits of the Younger Brothers.* St. Louis: Eureka Publishing Company, 1876.

Emery, Edwin. *The Press and America: An Interpretative History of Journalism.* Englewood Cliffs, N.J.: Prentice-Hall, 1962.

Enkvist, Nils Erik. *Caricatures of Americans on the English Stage Prior to 1870.* Port Washington, N.Y.: Kennikat Press, 1968.

Felheim, Marvin. *The Theater of Augustin Daly.* Cambridge, Mass.: Harvard University Press, 1956.

Friar, Ralph E., and Friar, Natasha A. *The Only Good Indian: The Hollywood Gospel.* New York: Drama Book Specialists, 1972.

Frost, O. W. *Joaquin Miller.* New York: Twayne Publishers, 1967.

Goodwin, Nat, with Badger, Richard G. *Nat Goodwin's Book.* Boston: Gorham Press, 1914.

Graham, W. A. *The Custer Myth.* Harrisburg, Pa.: Stackpole Company, 1953.

Grossman, James R., ed. *The Frontier in American Culture.* Berkeley: University of California Press, 1994.

Harte, Bret [and Densmore, G. S.]. *M'liss. An Idyll of Red Mountain. A Story of California in 1863.* New York: Robert M. DeWitt, [1873].

Harte, Geoffrey Bret, ed. *The Letters of Bret Harte.* Boston: Houghton Mifflin Co., 1926.

Havighurst, Walter. *Annie Oakley of the Wild West.* New York: Macmillan, 1954.

Hazard, Lucy Lockwood. *The Frontier in American Literature.* New York: Barnes & Noble, 1941.

Hornblow, Arthur A. *A History of the Theatre in America.* Philadelphia & London: J. B. Lippincott Company, 1919.

Hoxie, Frederick E. *A Final Promise: The Campaign to Assimilate the Indians, 1880–1920.* Lincoln, Nebr.: University of Nebraska Press, 1984.

Hutton, Laurence. *Curiosities of the American Stage.* New York: Harper & Brothers, 1891.

Jones, Daryl. *The Dime Novel Western.* Bowling Green, Ohio: Bowling Green University Popular Press, 1978.

Jones, Eugene H. *Native Americans As Shown on the Stage, 1753–1916.* Metuchen, N.J.: The Scarecrow Press, 1988.

Kasson, Joy S. *Buffalo Bill's Wild West: Celebrity, Memory, and Popular History.* New York: Hill and Wang, 2000.

Kimmel, Michael. *Manhood in America: A Cultural History.* New York: Free Press, 1996.

Kowalewski, Michael, ed. *Reading the West: New Essays on the Literature of the American West.* Cambridge: Cambridge University Press, 1996.

Leavitt, M. B. *Fifty Years in Theatrical Management 1859–1909.* New York: Broadway Publishing Co., 1912.

Leslie, Amy, *Some Players.* Chicago and New York: H. S. Stone and Company, 1899.

LeVay, John. *Margaret Anglin, a Stage Life.* Toronto: Simon & Pierre, 1989.

Levine, Lawrence W. *Highbrow/Lowbrow: The Emergence of Cultural Hierarchy in America.* Cambridge, Mass.: Harvard University Press, 1988.

Lomax, John A., and Lomax, Alan. *Cowboy Songs and Other Frontier Ballads.* New York: Macmillan Company, 1938.

Marberry, M. M. *Splendid Poseur: Joaquin Miller – American Poet.* New York: Thomas Y. Crowell Company, 1953.

Marcosson, Isaac F., and Frohman, Daniel. *Charles Frohman: Manager and Man.* New York: Harper & Brothers, 1916.

Mason, Jeffrey D. *Melodrama and the Myth of America.* Bloomington, Ind.: Indiana University Press, 1993.

McConachie, Bruce. *Melodramatic Formations: American Theatre and Society, 1820–1870.* Iowa City, Iowa: University of Iowa Press, 1992.

McNamara, Brooks. *Step Right Up.* Jackson, Miss.: University Press of Mississippi, 1995.

Meserve, Walter J. *Heralds of Promise: The Drama of the American People During the Age of Jackson, 1829–1849.* Westport, Conn.: Greenwood Press, 1986.

Meserve, Walter J. *An Outline History of American Drama.* Totowa, N.J.: Littlefield, Adams & Co., 1965.

Mitchell, Lee Clark. *Westerns: Making the Man in Fiction and Film.* Chicago: University of Chicago Press, 1996.

Monaghan, Jay. *The Great Rascal: The Life and Adventures of Ned Buntline.* Boston: Little, Brown and Company, 1952.

Mooney, James. *The Ghost-Dance Religion and the Sioux Outbreak of 1890*. Lincoln, Nebr.: University of Nebraska Press, 1991.

Morse, Frank. *Backstage with Henry Miller*. New York: E. P. Dutton & Co., 1938.

Moses, L. G. *Wild West Shows and the Images of the American Indians, 1883–1933*. Albuquerque, N. Mex.: University of New Mexico Press, 1996.

Myth of the West. New York: Rizzoli, 1990.

Nevins, Alan. *The Emergence of Modern America, 1865–1878*. Vol. VIII of *A History of American Life*, eds. Arthur M. Schlesinger and Dixon Ryan Fox. New York: Macmillan Company, 1944.

Nye, Russel. *The Unembarrassed Muse: The Popular Arts in America*. New York: Dial Press, 1970.

Odell, George C. D. *Annals of the New York Stage*, vols. VII–XV. New York: Columbia University Press, 1931–1949.

Ogden, Dunbar H., with McDermott, Douglas, and Sarlos, Robert K., eds. *Theatre West: Image and Impact*. DQR Studies in Literature. Amsterdam: Rodopi, 1990.

Poggi, Jack. *Theatre in America: The Impact of Economic Forces, 1870–1967*. Ithaca, N.Y.: Cornell University Press, 1968.

Prown, Jules David, *et al*. *Discovered Lands, Invented Pasts: Transforming Visions of the American West*. New Haven: Yale University Press, 1992.

Prucha, Francis Paul, ed. *Americanizing the American Indians: Writings by the "Friends of the Indian" 1880–1900*. Cambridge, Mass.: Harvard University Press, 1973.

Quinn, Arthur Hobson. *A History of the American Drama from the Civil War to the Present Day*. New York: F. S. Crofts & Co., 1937.

Reddin, Paul. *Wild West Shows*. Urbana: University of Illinois Press, 1999.

Rennert, Jack. *100 Posters of Buffalo Bill's Wild West*. New York: Darien House, 1976.

Richardson, Gary A. *American Dramas from the Colonial Period through World War I: A Critical History*. New York: Twayne Publishers, 1993.

Riley, Glenda. *The Life and Legacy of Annie Oakley*. Norman, Okla.: University of Oklahoma Press, 1994.

Robinson, Forrest G. *Having It Both Ways: Self-Subversion in Western Popular Classics*. Albuquerque, N. Mex.: University of New Mexico Press, 1993.

Rogers, Will. *The Autobiography of Will Rogers*. Boston: Houghton Mifflin Company, 1949.

Rosa, Joseph G. *They Called Him Wild Bill: The Life and Adventures of James Butler Hickok*. Norman, Okla.: University of Oklahoma Press, 1974.

Rosa, Joseph G., and May, Robin. *Buffalo Bill and His Wild West: A Pictorial Biography*. Lawrence, Kans.: University Press of Kansas, 1989.

Rotundo, E. Anthony. *American Manhood: Transformations in Masculinity from the Revolution to the Modern Era*. New York: Basic Books, 1993.

Rourke, Constance. *"The Roots of American Culture" and Other Essays*, ed. Van Wyck Brooks. New York: Harcourt, Brace and Company, 1942.

Rourke, Constance. *Troupers of the Gold Coast; or, The Rise of Lotta Crabtree*. New York: Harcourt, Brace and Company, 1928.

Russell, Don. *The Lives and Legends of Buffalo Bill*. Norman, Okla.: University of Oklahoma Press, 1969.

Russell, Don. *The Wild West; or, A History of the Wild West Shows*. Ft. Worth: Amon Carter Museum of Western Art, 1970.

Saum, Lewis O. *The Popular Mood of America, 1860–1890.* Lincoln, Nebr., and London: University of Nebraska Press, 1990.

Scharnhorst, Gary. *Bret Harte.* New York: Twayne Publishers, 1992.

Schlesinger, Arthur M. *Politics and Social Growth of the American People, 1865–1940.* New York: Macmillan Company, 1941.

Sears, Priscilla. *A Pillar of Fire to Follow: American Indian Dramas, 1808–1859,* Bowling Green, Ohio: Bowling Green University Popular Press, 1982.

Sell, Henry Blackman, and Weybright, Victor. *Buffalo Bill and the Wild West,* New York: Oxford University Press, 1955.

Settle, William A., Jr. *Jesse James Was His Name.* Columbia, Mo.: University of Missouri Press, 1966.

Shaw, George Bernard. *Our Theatres in the Nineties,* vol. 1. London: Constable and Company, 1932.

Shirley, Glenn. *Pawnee Bill: A Biography of Major Gordon W. Lillie.* Albuquerque, N. Mex.: University of New Mexico Press, 1958.

Simon, Louis. *A History of the Actors' Fund of America.* New York: Theatre Arts Books, 1972.

Skinner, Otis. *Footlights and Spotlights: Recollections of My Life on Stage.* Indianapolis: Bobbs-Merrill Company, 1923.

Slotkin, Richard. *The Fatal Environment: The Myth of the Frontier in the Age of Industrialization 1800–1890.* New York: Atheneum, 1985.

Slotkin, Richard. *Regeneration through Violence: The Mythology of the American Frontier, 1600–1860.* Middletown, Conn.: Wesleyan University Press, 1973.

Smith, Henry Nash. *Virgin Land: The American West As Symbol and Myth.* Cambridge, Mass.: Harvard University Press, 1970.

Smith, Susan Harris. *American Drama: The Bastard Art.* Cambridge: Cambridge University Press, 1997.

Stewart, Edgar L. *Custer's Luck.* Norman, Okla.: University of Oklahoma Press, 1955.

Swartout, Annie Fern. *Missie: An Historical Biography of Annie Oakley.* Blanchester, Ohio: Brown Publishing Company, 1947.

Szasz, Margaret Connell, ed. *Between Indian and White Worlds: The Cultural Broker.* Norman, Okla.: University of Oklahoma Press, 1994.

Thomas, Augustus. *The Print of My Remembrance.* New York: Charles Scribner's Sons, 1922.

Thorpe, Raymond W. *Spirit Gun of the West: The Story of Doc W. F. Carver.* Glendale, Calif.: A. H. Clark, 1957.

Truettner, William H. *The West As America.* Washington, D.C.: Smithsonian Institution Press, 1991.

Turner, Frederick. *Beyond Geography: The Western Spirit Against the Wilderness.* New Brunswick, N.J.: Rutgers University Press, 1983.

Tuska, John. *The American West in Film: Critical Approaches to the Westerns.* Westport, Conn.: Greenwood Press, 1985.

Wagner, Harr. *Joaquin Miller and His Other Self.* San Francisco: Harr Wagner Publishing Company, 1929.

Wallis, Michael. *The Real Wild West: The 101 Ranch and the Creation of the American West.* New York: St. Martin's Press, 1999.

Walsh, Richard, with Salsbury, Milton S. *The Making of Buffalo Bill*. Indianapolis: Bobbs-Merrill Company, 1928.

Wetmore, Helen Cody, and Grey, Zane. *Last of the Great Scouts*. New York: Grosset & Dunlop, 1899.

White, G. Edward. *The Eastern Establishment and the Western Experience: The West of Frederic Remington, Theodore Roosevelt, and Owen Wister*. New Haven and London: Yale University Press, 1968.

Williams, Margaret. *Australia on the Popular Stage, 1829–1929*. Melbourne: Oxford University Press, 1983.

Wilson, Garff. *A History of American Acting*. Bloomington: Indiana University Press, 1966.

Wilson, R. L., with Martin, Greg. *Buffalo Bill's Wild West: An American Legend*. New York: Random House, 1998.

Yagoda, Ben. *Will Rogers, a Biography*. New York: Alfred A. Knopf, 1993.

Yost, Nellie Snyder. *Buffalo Bill: His Family, Friends, Fame, Failures, and Fortunes*. Chicago: Swallow Press, 1979.

Articles

Bank, Rosemarie K. "Frontier Melodrama." In *Theatre West: Image and Impact*, ed. Dunbar H. Ogden with Douglas McDermott and Robert K. Sarlos. Amsterdam: Rodopi, 1990.

Bank, Rosemarie K. "Theatre and Narrative Fiction in the Work of the Nineteenth-Century American Playwright Louis Medina." *Theatre History Studies*, vol III, 1983, pp. 54–67.

Betts, John Rickards "The Technological Revolution and the Rise of Sport, 1850–1900." *Mississippi Valley Historical Review*, vol. 40, 1953, pp. 231–238.

Coleman, William S. E. "Buffalo Bill on Stage." *Players*, vol. 47, no. 2, January 1972, pp. 80–91.

Dippie, Brian. "The Moving Finger Writes: Western Art and the Dynamics of Change." In Jules David Prown *et al.*, *Discovered Lands, Invented Pasts: Transforming Visions of the American West*. New Haven: Yale University Press, 1992.

Epstein, Milton. "The Shuberts and the New York Hippodrome." *Passing Show (Newsletter of the Shubert Archive)*, vol. 17, nos. 1/2, Spring/Fall 1994, pp. 2–27.

Hall, Roger. "Captain Adam Bogardus: Shooting and the Stage in Nineteenth-Century America." *Journal of American Culture*, vol. 5, no. 3, Fall 1982, pp. 46–49.

Hall, Roger. "Nate Salsbury: Actor, Manager, Playwright." *Theatre Studies*, nos. 24/25, 1977–78/1978–79, pp. 149–154.

Jones, Daryl E. "The Earliest Western Films." *Journal of Popular Film and Television*, vol. 8, no. 2, pp. 42–46.

Lewis, W. A. "Frank Mayo – Man and Artist." *Theatre Magazine*, June 1906.

Matthews, Brander. "The American on the Stage." *Scribner's Monthly*, vol. 18, no. 3, July 10, 1879, pp. 321–333.

McArthur, Colin. "The Roots of the Western." *Cinema*, October, 1969, pp. 11–13.

Meserve, Walter J. "The American West of the 1870s and 1880s As Viewed from the Stage." *Journal of American Drama and Theatre*, vol. 3, no. 1, Winter 1991, pp. 48–63.

Monaghan, James. "The Stage Career of Buffalo Bill." *Journal of the Illinois State Historical Society*, vol. 31, no. 4, December 1938, pp. 411–423.

Morgan, Thomas J. "Rules for Indian Courts." In *Americanizing the American Indians: Writings by the "Friends of the Indian" 1880–1900*, ed. Francis Paul Prucha. Cambridge, Mass.: Harvard University Press, 1973.

Moses, L. G. "Interpreting the Wild West." In *Between Indian and White Worlds: The Cultural Broker*, ed. Margaret Connell Szasz. Norman, Okla.: University of Oklahoma Press, 1994.

"The Old Time Actor in Moving Picturedom." *Motion Picture Magazine*, June 1915.

Paine, Albert Bigelow. "Mark Twain." *Harper's Monthly Magazine*, vol. 125, no. 746, July 1912.

Paul, Andrea I. "Buffalo Bill and Wounded Knee: The Movie." *Nebraska History*, vol. 71, no. 4, Fall 1990, pp. 182–190.

Radavich, David. "Western Drama and the New Frontier." *American Drama*, vol. 7, no. 1, Fall 1997, pp. 99–120.

Russell, Don. "Buffalo Bill – In Action." *Westerners Brand Book*, vol. 19, no. 5, July 1962, pp. 33–35, 40.

Salsbury, Nate. "Reminiscences." Ed. Roger Hall. *Journal of American Drama and Theatre*, vol. 5, Winter 1993.

Teller, Henry M. "Courts of Indian Offenses." In *Americanizing the American Indians: Writings by the "Friends of the Indian" 1880–1900*, ed. Francis Paul Prucha. Cambridge, Mass.: Harvard University Press, 1973.

Turner, Frederick Jackson. "The Significance of the Frontier in American History." *Annual Report of the American Historical Association for the Year 1893*. Washington, D.C.: Government Printing Office, 1894, pp. 199–227.

White, Richard. "Frederick Jackson Turner and Buffalo Bill." In *The Frontier in American Culture*, ed. James R. Grossman. Berkeley: University of California Press, 1994.

Whittaker, Herbert. "The Canadian Who Became America's Top Leading Lady." *Globe Magazine* (*Toronto Globe*), September 7, 1957, pp. 6–7.

Wilmeth, Don B. "Tentative Checklist of Indian Plays." *Journal of American Drama and Theatre*, vol. 1, no. 2, Fall 1989, pp. 34–54.

Theses and dissertations

Bank, Rosemarie K. "Rhetorical, Dramatic, Theatrical and Social Contexts of Selected American Frontier Plays, 1871 to 1906." University of Iowa, 1972.

Deahl, William. "A History of Buffalo Bill's Wild West Shows." University of Southern Illinois, 1974.

Fike, Duane Joseph. "Frank Mayo: Actor, Playwright, and Manager." University of Nebraska, 1980.

Grose, Burl Donald. "Here Come the Indians: An Historical Study of the Representations of the Native American upon the North American Stage, 1808–1969." University of Missouri, Columbia, 1979.

Gustafson, Antoinette McCloskey. "The Image of the West in American Popular Performance." New York University, 1988.

Hyde, Stuart Wallace. "The Representation of the West in American Drama from 1849 to 1917." Stanford University, 1953.

Jones, Eugene H. "Native Americans As Shown on the Stage, 1753–1916." City University of New York, 1984.

Ligget, Lucinda R. "Bret Harte's 'M'liss.'" Indiana State University, 1991.

Nieuwenhuyse, Craig Francis. "Six-Guns on the Stage: Buffalo Bill Cody's First Celebration of the Conquest of the American Frontier." University of California, Berkeley, 1981.

Phillips, Levi Damon. "Arthur McKee Rankin's Touring Production of Joaquin Miller's *The Danites*." University of California, Davis, 1981.

Robinson, Kay Marcella. "The Depiction of the Cowboy in Selected Nineteenth-Century American Popular Dramas." Michigan State University, 1983.

Sitton, Fred. "The Indian Dramas in America, 1750–1900." Northwestern University, 1962.

Strong, Lisa M. "Images of Indian–White Contact in the Watercolors of Alfred Jacob Miller, 1837–1860." Columbia University, 1998.

Tillson, Merl William. "The Frontiersman in American Drama: An Analytical Study of Characters and Plays Reflecting the Phenomenon of Westward Expansion." University of Denver, 1951.

Official papers and other sources

Compendium of the Tenth Census (June 1, 1880). Washington: Government Printing Office, 1883.

The Eleventh Census of the United States, vol. 1, pt. 1. Washington: Government Printing Office, 1894.

Preliminary Report of the Eighth Census, 1860. Washington: Government Printing Office, 1862.

Sheridan, G. "Stage Plans and Settings of Scenery for Plays Performed at Booth's Theatre 1873–1883." Manuscript, Billy Rose Theatre Collection, New York Public Library for the Performing Arts.

Index